God of Daniel S.

God of Daniel S.

In Search of the American Jew

By ALAN W. MILLER

THE MACMILLAN COMPANY

COLLIER-MACMILLAN LTD., *LONDON*

The Hebrew quotation on the front jacket is from the
Ethics of the Fathers, a classical collection of Rabbinic aphorisms:
*Hoo hayah omer: im eyn anee lee mee lee, uchshe-anee le-atzmee
mah ahnee, ve-im lo achshav eymahtay.* He (Hillel, Pharisaic leader
of the first pre-Christian century) used to say: If I am not for myself,
who will be for me? But if I am only for myself, what am I?
And if not now, when?

Library of Congress Catalog Card Number: 69-12652

FIRST PRINTING

The Macmillan Company
Collier-Macmillan Canada Ltd., Toronto, Ontario

Printed in the United States of America

For Naomi

and our children

ACKNOWLEDGMENTS

My spiritual and intellectual debt to Mordecai M. Kaplan, the founder of Reconstructionism, is beyond measure. Without the seminal insights of his thought I would have little desire to be a Jew—and less to be a Rabbi—in the twentieth century. It is because of this debt that I have felt obliged to share some of these insights with Daniel S. Grateful thanks are also due to the Society for the Advancement of Judaism, its Executive Secretary, Miss Judith N. Alper, Mrs. Ralph Stark and Alan Rinzler of The Macmillan Company.

A. W. M.

One

Jews have long occupied the particular attention of the human race. Both Christianity and Islam adopted the history of the Jewish people up to their own respective points of origin. Christians and Mohammedans considered themselves the "true descendants" of Abraham, Isaac and Jacob. Yet the continued existence of the Jews imposed limits on the content of Christian and Mohammedan self-consciousness.

In the modern world, precisely at a time when the bonds of traditional religion have been universally loosened, Jews are again in the forefront of mankind's attention. They were not the only ones to suffer at the hands of the Nazis. The Russian people lost more than treble the six million Jews who died at the hands of Hitler's henchmen. Yet the bizarre mythology invested in Hitler's attack on the Jews and its demonic technology raises the Jewish tragedy to an unparalleled height. By a strange and cruel irony, the very "Chosen People" concept, so deeply admired and emulated by the two daughter religions, was turned against its original propounders by a diabolical inversion. And the fact that the "Final Solution" originated in a Western Christian country will haunt the conscience of Western civilization unto eternity.

The remarkable success of the Zionist venture, nurtured in large part by these sufferings, also helps to keep the Jews squarely before the contemporary imagination. A rare combination of collective determination, an unusual will to live in the face of unprecedented persecution and political happenstance threw the Jewish people, after a hiatus of almost two thousand years, into the mainstream of world history as the sovereign State of Israel. The Jew thereby, with an amalgam of guilt and identification, becomes the prototype of success in failure for twentieth-century man.

When a former Pope remarked that we are all Semites he was referring to a common religious ancestry shared by Jew and Gentile. Today, in the Western World at least, the same could be affirmed in a cultural and psychological sense. We are all Jews, whether Jew or Gentile, because the Jew, in acute measure, represents the human predicament of the second half of the twentieth century. The Negro, understandably, with an envy often turned to hatred, looks at the ethnic solidarity of the Jewish people in the manner of a burgeoning Christianity and Islam of a bygone age. But myths of origin cannot be borrowed in the full blaze of the light of contemporary historical awareness.

This sense of a common "Jewishness" is visible in many areas. It is manifest in the ever-growing number of Hebrew and Yiddish words infiltrating the English language. What began as Hollywood small talk in an industry heavily populated by Jews has become a widespread phenomenon. It is manifest in the ecumenical movement, in the increasing awareness of historic and contemporary Jewish realities in the theory and practice of the Church. It is manifest on the campus, where there are more chairs in Judaica and more opportunities for Gentiles to study authentic Jewish tradition than ever before in the history of the university. It is manifest in the pro-Zionist sentiments of millions of Gentiles who, in an act of mistaken identification, find in the submachine-gun-carrying Israeli soldier a reflection of their own traditional martial ideal. The guilty memory of the passive Jew of the concentration camp selection unit abandoned to his fate by an indifferent world no doubt provides some of the energy which feeds this admiration.

It is manifest in the incredible and unprecedented popularity of Jewish personalities and themes in literature, art, music and, especially, in the world of the mass media. Countless Gentiles in the capital cities of the world identify with the storm-tossed fortunes of a denizen of the European *shtetl*, or small town, by the name of Tevye. A novel dealing with the theme of a friendship between two Orthodox Jewish boys from Brooklyn surprisingly remains on the best-selling list for several months. Innumerable middle-class alienated Gentile intellectuals anguish with Yakov Bok and Moses Elkanah Herzog.

Ironically and paradoxically, precisely at a time when Western Gentiles admire and increasingly identify with Jewish prototypes, the Jewish world itself is divided to a greater extent than ever before. The problem may perhaps best be presented by the following vignettes, which describe but a few of the prevailing disparate types in Jewish life. They are not real people. They are presented as composites of the median within some of the major groups. The intensity of authentic orthodoxy obviously places the traditional Jew higher on the scale of Jewish involvement and commitment than most other types. To be sure, there are more deeply committed Reform and Conservative Jews than those here depicted. Our examples, however, are presented as the average. Here, if anything, the error may have been made on the side of charity.

There can be no gainsaying the enormous vitality which may be experienced at any point of the spectrum in Jewish life in America today. The exuberance and single-mindedness of the devoutly pious *Chasidim* is clearly a case in point. The Lubavitcher movement, an evangelical Chasidic sect, has registered remarkable successes in the postwar period. In these circles of pietistic enthusiasm and evangelism the Jew is transported back into another era.

But the *Chasidim* are not the only Jews who manifest enthusiasm. Commitment and piety, of a markedly different nature to be sure, may be witnessed and experienced in Reform and Conservative circles. Nor is this only visible at conventions and conferences. Second- and third-generation Reform and Conservative families in America have developed their own standards and, admittedly within the framework of their own theological system and ritual outlook, an intense quality of Jewish life.

Secularist, Zionist and Yiddishist Jews also have their conventicles of the dedicated. The alienated Jewish intellectual almost has a religion of his own by indirection. In the absence of any generally recognized norm there is an absence of any particular norm. And here is the paradox. Precisely at a time when traditional standards are being discarded, there is still considerable, separate and often unrelated vitality in Jewish life. The Jew born within such a circle of vitality at least has something to reject, accept, modify or mold. The alienated Jew—often through no fault of his own—looks on bewildered at the many different brands available. Even when he wants to choose, his choice is made almost impossible.

If we have concentrated on the needs of the outsider rather than of the insider it is precisely because his need is greatest. For in an age when the middle-class Gentile intellectual begins to understand a little more of what it means to be a Jew, the Jews themselves, especially the middle-class intellectual outsiders, are more confused than ever.

ABRAHAM Z. is a *Chasid*, a pious one, who lives in a suburb of New York. Chasidism is a religious revivalist movement which began in the early eighteenth century in Eastern Europe and influenced many Jews. Its founder was a charismatic figure called Israel Baal Shem Tov, Master of the Good Name, a miracle worker. The Chmielnicki massacres of the seventeenth century had isolated vast segments of Polish Jewry from the direct influence of the Rabbinic Academies. Chasidism emerged as a warm and emotional reaction to the cold and rigorous intellectualism of the Rabbis. Jewish scholars had found spiritual solace for their suffering through studying the complicated folios of the Talmud and its commentaries. The common people turned to the Baal Shem Tov and his spiritual successors, the various "Rebbes," for religious sustenance, for a sense of joy and love and self-respect. In time, some of them, too, developed an intellectual tradition. With their opponents, who became known as the *Mitnagdim* (from *mitnaged*, to be against), *Chasidim* share an unqualified devotion to the God of Israel, the Torah—or Divine Teaching —of Israel and the People of Israel. But they have their own highly unique way of expressing that devotion.

Abraham Z. lives *in* the twentieth century but is not *of* the twentieth century. He wears a distinctive black homburg, on top of a black skullcap which never leaves his head, and a *kapote*, or long black coat. On the Sabbath he will wear a *streiml*, a fur hat. Both *kapote* and *streiml* are sartorial anachronisms assimilated from a Gentile Polish aristocracy of a bygone age. He wears a white shirt without a tie. He has a beard and sidelocks in strict conformity with the traditional injunction against shaving the corners of the head. His large brown eyes blaze with intensity from a pale face. His fingers are long, delicate and white. He might have come from a different world.

During the week Abraham Z. works in the diamond exchange in the heart of the city. Early in the morning he leaves his home, which is situated in an almost exact replica of an Eastern European *shtetl* transferred bodily from the Old World to the New. He travels to work in a bus in the company of other *Chasidim* of his particular sect. There had been many thousands of them before the war in Eastern Europe. They had their own Rebbe who, by his spiritual succession, shared in their eyes some of the charisma of Israel Baal Shem Tov. But Eastern European Jewry had been virtually obliterated by the Nazis and most of the sect had perished in Auschwitz. Abraham Z. and his parents were among the lucky ones to escape. Gentiles had hidden them in a cellar for over two years. Only a few hundred of the sect had made their way to America. The Rebbe, too, focal point of their lives, had miraculously escaped and was still their spiritual leader. Abraham Z. had been offered a construction engineering job with excellent prospects in the city by a distant relative. He had asked the Rebbe's advice. The Rebbe said "no" and instead, after consultation with the elders of the community, selected the diamond exchange. For Abraham Z. what the Rebbe says is sacrosanct. He is "but a little finger on the body of the Rebbe."

In the bus, on the way to work, the *Chasidim* chant their morning devotions with great feeling, and don their *tefillin*, or phylacteries, in accordance with tradition. When God revealed Himself on Mount Sinai to the Children of Israel thousands of years ago, He gave them a Written Torah (the Pentateuch) and also an Oral Torah, which together contain the six hundred and thirteen *mitzvot*, or commandments, which all Jews must observe. Abraham Z. has no idea of the mechanics of that Divine Revelation. He is convinced only of its reality. Nor has he any clear idea of God. He is convinced only of His existence. At times he agonizes over the loss in Europe of thousands of his fellow *Chasidim* and millions of his fellow Jews. His faith in God's goodness, however, is triumphant. These martyrs were swept away from this world to enjoy a life of unmitigated bliss in the next. The alternative possibility, that they were punished because they were wicked, is unthinkable. They were caught in the web of the sins of others. Their righteousness and God's loving-kindness and tender mercy are thus in no way impugned. Throughout his waking day Abraham Z. will constantly be aware of the ritual and ethical demands God makes on him. His body now sways ecstatically in response to the traditional litany. Later he will recite afternoon prayers in the synagogue. The advantage of his trade is that it leaves him time for God, time for prayer, time for studying the Word.

All the week is a prelude to the Sabbath. On Friday night after Evening Service in the synagogue, Abraham Z. welcomes the Sabbath Queen in his home, together with his wife and children. Mrs. Z. wears a *sheitel*, or wig. She faithfully follows the tradition that after marriage a woman should be attractive only to her husband. The wearing of the *sheitel* is expressly meant to make Mrs. Z. look a trifle dowdy. After marriage she shaved off all her hair, just as her mother had done and her grandmother before. Hers is the onerous and awesome responsibility of supervising the manifold ritual requirements of the traditional Jewish home. The children, with their father's big brown eyes, the boys with skull-caps on their heads and sidelocks curled behind their ears, lustily sing the *Zemirot*, or Sabbath melodies. They will wear skullcaps even when they sleep, as a symbol of God's Omnipresence. The authoritative commentary on the opening sentence of the blue-print of their lives, the definitive and famous legal code drawn up by Rabbi Joseph Caro (1488–1575) known as the *Shulchan Aruch*, the Prepared Table, contains a quotation from the Book of Psalms: "I have set the Lord before me continually." That quotation sums up the family's life. Abraham Z. and his family have time only for God. The children will probably never go to a secular college. Nor are they likely to read novels, histories, bio-

graphies, magazines or newspapers or watch television. All that
the Jew requires for the good life is found in the traditional texts.
These the children will study assiduously at their *Yeshivah*, or
Talmudical College. In the context of the transplanted European
shtetl, they will not be exposed to the blandishments of mo-
dernity.

After the traditional Sabbath eve service at home, Abraham Z.
will go to the Rebbe's *tisch*, or table, a time-honored Chasidic
tradition. Hundreds of *Chasidim* pack into a hall in the Rebbe's
house which also serves as the synagogue, seated thigh pressed
against thigh around long tables as they sway and sing ancient
texts to traditional melodies. Many are *niggunim*, or songs without words. From time to time the Rebbe at the head, surrounded
by the elders, will take a piece of herring or chicken or bread
from a plate and pass the *shirayim*, or remains, to the *Chasidim*
seated at the tables in close proximity. The food has been sanctified by the holiness of the original partaker. The *Chasidim* pick it
up with their fingers and eat in reverence. Then they burst into
wild, ecstatic song again. They drink wine, vodka or cider and
again burst into more frenzied singing. "All my bones shall say, O
Lord, who is like unto Thee." This scriptural injunction the
Chasidim render literally. They worship God exclusively, neither
with heart nor head, but with every fiber of their being. The
Rebbe will usually speak three times. He will discourse on the
traditional Torah reading for the week. He will speak of God and
the meaning of Jewish life. He will offer a *mussar*, or an ethical
homily. Each time he opens his mouth the *Chasidim* will listen in
rapt attention. Each time he concludes, they will burst spontaneously into singing praises to God who has given them the Sabbath
and who, through the Rebbe, sustains them with His Word. And
at the end of evening, men and boys will push the wooden
benches and tables against the wall, take each other around in a
continuing train of warm, bearish bodies and dance together with
stamping feet, joyful noises and a rapturous heart.

On these occasions Abraham Z. is no longer a separate individual. He is fused in ecstatic longing with his fellow *Chasidim*, with the whole house of Israel, with God Himself. This, truly, is a foretaste of the world to come, where all who have served God dutifully in life will be bound up in the bond of Eternal Bliss.

ISAAC Y. is an Orthodox Jew, second-generation American-born, whose grandparents emigrated from Germany at the turn of the century. There is nothing visible to distinguish Isaac from any other young married man of his social and economic group. If Abraham Z. is an archetypical Jew, then Isaac Y. does not "look Jewish." He attended a fine private school and studied law at a leading college. Clean-shaven, impeccably dressed, he commutes daily to the downtown real estate office which he runs with his brother.

Before leaving for the office, even before breakfasting, Isaac Y. worships in the Orthodox synagogue which is within walking distance of his home. He uses neither public nor private transport on Sabbaths and Festivals. Proximity to an Orthodox synagogue is an absolute prerequisite for any home he will ever rent or purchase. Three times a day, morning, afternoon and evening, at precisely designated times, Isaac Y. will pray, in accordance with tradition, in the presence of a *minyan*, or quorum of ten Jewish males over the age of thirteen, which is the age of Jewish religious majority in the male. In the case of girls, the legal coming of age is twelve. After reaching religious majority, all those rules which govern the life of the adult Jew and Jewess must also, equally rigorously, govern the life of the boy and girl.

Isaac Y.'s wife, a charming and attractive woman, visibly differs from Abraham Z.'s wife the way Isaac differs from Abraham. She, too, is impeccably dressed in modern style. Unlike Mrs. Z., who wears a *sheitel* as a matter of Jewish religious principle all the time, she will only don a wig for cosmetic purposes. However, both Mrs. Z. and Mrs. Y. scrupulously obey the rules of ritual purity. Monthly, after each menses, there is a visit to the traditional *mikveh*, or ritual bath. Jewish law prohibits absolutely all sexual relations between husband and wife from the onset of menstruation until a stipulated period of time after its cessation. Because of this, single beds are *de rigueur* for husband and wife and, during her monthly period, Mrs. Y. will not use make-up.

The Y.'s home is strictly kosher, that is, all food is prepared in accordance with traditional Jewish practice. Meat and milk are kept separate. Indeed, milk products are not eaten after meat until three hours have elapsed. All meat must have been ritually slaughtered, soaked and salted for as much blood as possible to have drained away. Should any query arise, Mrs. Y. will consult the Rabbi. Should any accidental mix-up of milk and meat dishes occur, crockery must be thrown away. Metal pots and pans, however, may be repurified and ritually cleansed by heating, and cutlery by leaving it in the earth for a prescribed period of time. Neither Mr. and Mrs. Y. nor the children will eat anything at any time without reciting the requisite traditional benedictions, before and after having eaten. Because of the very modern life the family leads this can create, if not complications, then at least the need for great ingenuity. Isaac Y. and his family welcome the challenge. Jewish law has been Divinely revealed and may conveniently be found itemized within the pages of the legal codes. But beyond this, a Jew can follow almost any pursuit which the law does not explicitly rule out.

Because Isaac Y., unlike Abraham Z., mixes with many different people, Jews and Gentiles, and because his children are also, unavoidably, in the mainstream of modern cultural life, it is not possible for the family to avoid all challenges to faith. Nevertheless they have no real problems. First, there is the axiomatic belief in God. There is a Supreme, Omnipotent, Omniscient, Omnipresent, Omnibenevolent Being who created the world and everything in it, who chose the Jewish people and gave them His Torah. This belief is the fulcrum of Isaac Y.'s universe. His obedience to this God, to whom he thrice daily prays and whose laws and commandments he scrupulously and meticulously follows, is absolute. The Holocaust was traumatic, but not destructive of faith. God knows the answers and, hopefully, one day, in the Great Beyond, Isaac will also. His ideas on the afterlife are not as clearly formulated as Abraham Z.'s. However, that there is an afterlife is for him, also, axiomatic.

Second, Isaac has great and implicit faith in the Rabbis, not just in the Rabbis of old but in those Rabbis whom he regards as their authoritative and accredited successors, the present day guardians of God's law. These men, saintly, devout and learned, are equally versed in secular and sacred matters. Any enterprise which has lasted as long as the Jews must be grounded on the Divine Truth. Isaac Y. listens with concentration to the Rabbi's sermons and lectures and is especially attentive at the Study Group which he regularly attends on Sabbath afternoons in the synagogue between the Afternoon and Evening services. Occasionally the Rabbi himself will admit that there is a difficulty here and a problem there for the believer, but then he will immediately reconcile and harmonize the conflicting notions. The Talmud knew of the problem. Or Maimonides, or some later learned prodigy provided the solution. In the theological world of Isaac Y., all things are reconciled, if not in the mind of the Rabbi, then in the mind of God.

To say that Isaac Y. is an ethical man is to state the obvious. Isaac Y. takes for granted that all men must be ethical. Judaism, the special Divinely revealed duties of the Jew, begins where ethics leaves off. Isaac Y. serves on several philanthropic committees, Jewish and secular, and is generous in his own private disbursement to charity. These tend to be exclusively for the promulgation of those views he himself endorses. His interest in Zionism is limited to the support of the Orthodox element in the State of Israel.

For Isaac Y. there are really only two kinds of Jew, religious and irreligious (by which he means observant and nonobservant). If pressured, he would probably agree that irreligious Jews are lazy Jews. He knows what it costs him in terms of time, money and effort to be a devout Jew. What reason could a Jew have for not being "Jewish," in the only connotation Isaac can give that word, other than laziness? At times the mass exodus from observant Jewish life, which he cannot avoid noticing, unnerves him.

At times he condescends, patronizes, becomes a little smug and self-satisfied, feels a little superior. But these emotions are rare and not typical. He knows God frowns on them. Those non-Jewish Jews will have to answer to God, not to Isaac. Until God Himself decides once again to intervene in the affairs of men, as He once did, and will assuredly do again, Isaac will continue to walk in the paths of his forefathers. A Jew obeys Jewish law. That is the beginning and the end of the matter.

JACOB X. is a Conservative Jew associated with a large and active congregation on Long Island. He used to be involved with the synagogue; he even served on several committees. But that was before his son became Bar Mitzvah, that is, achieved his religious majority at a ceremony in the synagogue on the occasion of his thirteenth birthday. After the boy's Bar Mitzvah, Jacob lost all interest in the synagogue for reasons he cannot quite fathom. His child lost all interest too. When the boy was working toward some goal it had all seemed so much more meaningful.

There was a temporary regression when his father died. His father had been an Orthodox Jew and Jacob X. had never completely emancipated himself from the idea that, for Jews, orthodoxy was the "real thing." His father had always spoken disparagingly of the Conservative synagogue as better than nothing but far from ideal. He used to make jokes about the "million dollar edifice," packed on the Day of Atonement, but virtually empty for the rest of the year. For the Bar Mitzvah, his father had insisted on walking the three miles to the synagogue and back (Jacob X. always used the car as did everybody else in the congregation except the Rabbi), and indicated his displeasure at the fact that men and women sat together. He had been one of the founders of an Orthodox synagogue in the city and felt that his son, by moving out to the suburbs, had somehow betrayed him. He also was unhappy about the relaxed way in which Jacob X.'s wife ran a "kosher" home. Meat was bought from a kosher butcher but separation of meat and milk was far from stringent. Mrs. X., at the insistence of her parents, had gone to the *mikveh* in accordance with tradition before her marriage, but that was the only time. Jacob X.'s father had been heard muttering that nowadays parents have to be satisfied whoever their children marry—as long as they're Jewish!

Jacob X. was stunned by his father's death. He had never realized how much he was emotionally involved with him. There was too much left unspoken between father and son for the father's death not to appear to the son as a veiled reproach. Jacob X. assuaged some of his feelings of guilt by spending far more on the funeral than he had intended, knowing his father would have wished for the simplicity of tradition and not the ostentation of affluence. The highly polished mahogany of the expensive casket seemed to put a gloss on a relationship which had been anything but smooth. He realized he was doing all this for himself, not for his father. He sat *shivah*, or observed the traditional seven days of mourning, during which Morning and Evening services were conducted in his home. It was difficult to obtain a quorum of ten, especially in the morning, and not a little inconvenient for some of his friends, but Jacob X.'s need transcended any other consideration.

After the week of mourning, interrupted only by the Sabbath (on which mourning is prohibited by Jewish tradition), Jacob X. recited *Kaddish*, the prayer in honor of the dead, for the prescribed eleven-month period, attending synagogue morning and evening. The other worshipers were also mourners. During that period Jacob X. found himself growing angry with the Rabbi, who was not always present for these devotions and whose absence caused unnecessary complications when a tenth man was needed. Without the requisite quorum, *Kaddish* could not be recited. During all this period Jacob X. thought only sporadically about God and the meaning of the words he was reciting. He had forgotten most of the Hebrew he had learned as a child and theology had never been one of his strong points. There was, however, a soothing balm in the very motion of running through well-worn grooves of tradition. The act, not the meaning, seemed important. Sometimes he thought of his father but any feelings of guilt had long since been expiated by the considerable inconvenience these early and late ministrations had caused him.

All that was several years ago, however. Jacob X. has now reverted to his original pattern of living. He plays golf regularly on Saturday mornings and occasionally attends the Men's Club on Sundays, for social rather than for cultural reasons. Apart from the High Holy Days and the occasions when he and Mrs. X. are invited to a Bar Mitzvah, he never attends synagogue. He finds the repetition of the prayers boring. The sermons are occasionally interesting but rarely convincing. Life is hard to stomach, thinks Jacob X., and religion is sugar-coating on the pill, a middle-class luxury. He understands the United Jewish Appeal and Israel Bonds and gives to them generously. An Israeli soldier with a gun, a *kibbutznik* with a tractor, a child rescued from behind the Iron Curtain, make good sense. You can actually see them. Jacob X. signs his annual checks with a flourish, acknowledging magnanimously with the firm sweep of his hand a mosaic of images glimpsed in his wife's *Hadassah Magazine*. He can almost hear the bearded Jew at the Wailing Wall muttering his thanks in a voice that resembles his father's. He can see Jewish orphanages, hospitals, homes for the blind, old-age homes. He therefore gives. But Jewish education is a different story. He had no alternative but to contribute his assessment to the Building Fund. After all, he would need the catering facilities himself one day. But he gives to the synagogue reluctantly. Apart from teaching the children about the Festivals and arranging a few lectures which, as far as Jacob X. is concerned, are out of mind even before the car has been garaged for the night, what is it all about?

Some years ago he joined a local B'nai B'rith lodge and even attended some educational conferences which were fairly stimulating. But his interest waned. All that remains of this solitary attempt at taking his own Jewish education seriously is a subscription to a magazine which he is too apathetic to cancel. Occasionally he reads an article which attracts him. From time to time the Rabbi preaches a sermon on civil rights or other current issues.

The Social Action Committee then calls a meeting and sends out literature. In his heart Jacob X. knows that much of this involvement is vicarious. None of his friends would welcome Open Housing in their own immediate vicinity. The concern is genuine, he knows, but the way people behave when the chips are down, that, thinks Jacob X., is a different matter. He makes a generous contribution annually to N.A.A.C.P. That is the least he can do.

Jacob X. is a successful businessman but over the years he has learned to cultivate two compartments in his mind, one for Judaism and one "for real." He would not tolerate in his business the practices he has observed in the management of Jewish organizations. (Indeed, he would probably long since have gone bankrupt.) If his accountant presented his annual audit the way the Rabbi presented the eternal truths of the Jewish religion, Jacob X. would fire him on the spot. But Mrs. X. likes the Rabbi. (Indeed, all the women in the Sisterhood like the Rabbi.) She is kept busy with the Fund Raising Campaign for a new Nursery Wing, now that the children will shortly be off to college. She is also quite active in her Hadassah group. After Mrs. X. has lit the candles on Friday evening Jacob X. recites *Kiddush* and *Motzi*, sanctification over the wine and the bread. They follow that tradition, together with the Passover Seder Service and the kindling of the lights of *Chanukkah*, the Feast of Dedication. Otherwise, there is little to distinguish between their lives and behavior patterns, eating, drinking and recreating, and those of the Gentiles who live in split-level suburbia. Jacob X. looks at his son. He hopes his daughter-in-law will be Jewish. That is about the only real hope he has in this area. The Jewish future is vague.

DAVID W. is a Reform Jew who belongs to a distinguished Reform Temple somewhere on the West Coast. About sixty percent of the Jews in his town are affiliated with one of the two synagogues, Conservative and Reform, which are situated at opposite ends of the new housing developments. Most of the unaffiliated Jews, and even some of the Gentiles, responded to the communal drive for the United Jewish Appeal during the period of the Six-Day War. This surprised David W. He had thought that their assimilation had pushed them beyond even the gravitational pull of that kind of experience. Many of the Jewishly unaffiliated belong to a Unitarian Church, chiefly on account of its Sunday School where their children are taught ethics. On reflection David W. has to admit to himself that part of his intense admiration for the Israeli soldiers was that they were not at all like Jews.

The architecture of both synagogues is strikingly modern and both congregations have heavy mortgages. David W. is not always too clear in his own mind why there is a need for the two different buildings. Both memberships combined run to less than a thousand families. It would have made good fiscal sense to have one building. It is true they use different prayerbooks at the late Friday night services and on Sabbaths and Festivals, but apart from Bar Mitzvah celebrations even the Conservative synagogue is virtually empty at morning services. Even when a visiting Rabbi preaches on Friday, attendance never reaches anything like High Holy Day peak.

Liturgical and theological differences seem to David W. to be of degree and not of kind. There is more Hebrew in the Conservative service and the children study for more hours per week

than at the Reform. David W., who is married to a former Protestant who became converted to Judaism in New York after a
brief series of lessons, does not approve of overdoing the Jewish
element in life. As he sees it, an hour a week at Sunday School is
quite sufficient for a child to absorb the basic ethical teachings of
Judaism. Anything more is bound to weigh too heavily upon the
program of the child and may interfere with other activities. In
addition to an intensely ambitious private school program, his
three daughters study piano and ballet dancing. After all, thinks
David W., there have to be certain priorities in life.

The fact that the Conservative synagogue observes two days of
Festivals and his own Reform Temple only one does not upset
him either. His downtown business, which his great-grandfather
started, precludes his attending services on either day. He also
prefers the custom of worshiping with heads uncovered. The
other place is a little too Jewish for his liking. Under questioning,
David W. might admit that by "Jewish" in this context he means
"exotic," "alien," even a little "foreign." David W. is very proud
that he is fourth-generation American. Dignity and decorum
stand high on his scale of values. He is also proud that his house is
situated in a very non-Jewish district. He regards as a great
cachet the fact that his Gentile neighbors treat him almost as one
of them.

He has always wanted the children to have a Christmas tree.
He could never understand what harm there was in celebrating a
festival of peace on earth and goodwill to all men. His wife has
refused, out of a sense of loyalty to the devout and intense young
Rabbi who taught her about the importance of Jewish symbols in
the home. So, by way of compensation, the family celebrates
Chanukkah, more joyously when Jewish and Christian holiday
coincide chronologically. Otherwise, apart from the candles
which Mrs. W. lights scrupulously every Friday evening, nothing significant distinguishes the W.'s home from that of any Gentile home in the neighborhood. Mr. W. probably feels more at
home in the Reform Temple because so many members of that

congregation, like himself, are either married to converts to Judaism or are the children of converts to Judaism.

David W. is active in civic affairs. He has been Chairman of the
Rotary Club. He began to appreciate his Rabbi for the first time
when several of his Gentile friends commented favorably on a
talk the Rabbi had given them on Jewish-Christian relations. Up
to that time he had found the Rabbi rather insipid. He noted with
pleasure that the Rabbi appeared "genuinely American" to his
friends. He didn't "look Jewish." He could not say the same of
the Conservative Rabbi whom he had occasionally seen at the
joint cultural programs of the two synagogues. The Conservative
Rabbi always wore a skullcap and was always fussing over kosher
food. Doesn't he know, thinks David W., that there is very little
to choose in this sphere between his congregants and the others
outside of the synagogue? Nobody really cares that much. At
times he thinks the only strictly observant Jew in the whole town
is the Conservative Rabbi. A sweet and gentle person, the Conservative Rabbi was trained at an Orthodox seminary and lapsed.
The Conservative Rabbi constantly feels he should be more Orthodox than he really is and tends to let this purely personal
problem get mixed up with the problem of running the congregation.

David W. has heard both Rabbis speak on the subject of God
and the Jewish mission. He remains unconvinced. He has no clear
idea of the Divinity and has no real use for any Jewish mission.
He likes the Temple for its architecture and the music. It helps
him relax. Judaism for him is ethical behavior. He has no time
for the trappings. He has heard some lurid stories about Jews
who perform all the rituals but are dishonest. He has one of the
finest reputations in the business community. He wouldn't care
to have a Negro living next door but he was among the first to
employ Negroes in more than menial roles and is active in integration programs. He is held in the highest regard by Jew and
Gentile, deservedly so. He even dabbled for a while in local

politics and at one time, briefly, seriously considered running for office.

His daughters, the eldest of whom will shortly be going to college, tend to date non-Jews almost exclusively. David W. is quite neutral about all this. He will be satisfied so long as his children marry decent human beings. Religious affiliation seems of secondary importance. Confirmation, marriage and death are the only real occasions when one needs the services of the Temple, and the Rabbi is, thankfully, extremely flexible. Although not articulate in these matters, David W. deeply believes that religious separatism is positively harmful, responsible for many social ills, and that in an ideal state of affairs, a universal combination of church-synagogue would best satisfy his kind. The image is more a negation of and expression of subtle dissatisfaction with the present than a clear-cut program for the future. David W. would never admit, even in his dreams, that it were better, in an age of Holocaust, not to have been born a Jew. He bears his burden proudly, if lightly.

AARON V. is a Zionist whose parents came to New York from Odessa at the turn of the century. He runs a small business but only as a means to an end. His main motivation in life is the love he bears for the ancient homeland of the Jewish people. He was brought up and nurtured on stories about the gaints Theodor Herzl, Nachum Sokolow, Achad Ha'am, Vladimir Jabotinsky. These heroes, their writings, their latter-day descendants, are the warp and woof of the fabric of his soul. He is an avid Hebraist. He reads every Hebrew periodical he can buy and speaks Hebrew with whomsoever he can.

He attends a weekly advanced Seminar on Modern Hebrew, where a group of businessmen like himself discuss current political, economic and social problems in Israel. To understand perfectly a leading article from such Israeli periodicals as *Davar* or *Ha-Aretz* and to be able to discuss its implications and ramifications is to Aaron V. what listening to Bach and Beethoven is to other men. He is active in the local chapter of his Zionist organization and for the last fifteen years has performed the joint duties of Secretary-Treasurer. He is not a wealthy man. He realizes Israel needs financial support, but his contribution is made with the spirit.

Aaron V. has visited Israel on innumerable occasions but, oddly enough, has never seriously considered settling there and taking up Israeli citizenship. There is a quality about his relationship with his beloved land and beloved people which a full consummation might conceivably disturb. He remembers Palestine long before there was a State of Israel. He remembers Petach Tikvah, Jaffa and Tel Aviv in the "good old days." The exploits of Joseph Trumpeldor are history, not legend. He seems to prefer these regular visits which he and his wife have been making for nearly three decades, an ongoing flirtation, rather than a lasting marriage. He becomes a little piqued when he is told that a true Zionist is one who actually settles in Israel, not one who enables others to settle there. For him, Zionism is unashamedly vicarious. "We did a wonderful job!" he exclaimed proudly to one of his regular customers, a Gentile, the morning of the fourth day of the Six-Day War.

He had been just a trifle nervous that his youngest son might get involved in the fighting. The older boy was a realist. Aaron V. had given his sons the finest Hebrew education a man could give his children. They spoke fluent Hebrew at home before they could even speak English. "Speak Hebrew even if you break your teeth" Aaron used to say to his wife, repeating for the "umpteenth" time the story of Eliezer ben Yehudah, the famous Hebrew lexicographer who had played such a decisive role in the heroic rebirth of the Hebrew language. The older boy was a distinguished physicist who had recently accepted a well-paid teaching job on the West Coast. Wonderful boy! Aaron V. already corresponded with his grandchildren in Hebrew. But the younger son had seriously talked of breaking off his studies, giving up everything and going to live on a *kibbutz*, or collective settlement. Aaron V., to be perfectly frank, was relieved when a new girl friend temporarily distracted his son's attention from the weightier matters of life.

The fact that his son's new girl friend was a Gentile did not disturb Aaron V. too much although he would have preferred a Jewish girl with his son's background. For a man of his sophistication, being a Jew had nothing to do with religion. Were the early Zionists religious? A handful of Biluim (the earliest settlers in Israel of the modern period) perhaps, but the *real* men were atheists, pragmatists like himself. Aaron V. had no time for synagogues. In fact he had only consented to the children becoming Bar Mitzvah under pressure from his wife. She, in turn, had been under pressure from her parents. When his elder son had mar-

ried, the girl's family had picked a catering establishment in the
Bronx where the Rabbi and the service merely confirmed in
Aaron V. a deep-seated antagonism to the venality of the clergy
and the vulgarity of organized Jewish religious life in general.
Gentile or not Gentile, his son would raise his children as Jews,
his kind of Jews. His wife was not so sanguine. How will she
break the news to her old mother? How will she answer the first
question her mother will put to her when she announces the
forthcoming marriage of her grandson? Aaron V. pooh-poohs
her fears. There is just an element of bravado in the tone in
which he announces his emancipation from traditional scruples.

Aaron V. has no use for God, little use for Torah as a complex
of traditional Jewish behavior patterns and no time at all for Jews
who do not share his cultural-nationalist approach. He regards
traditionalist and Orthodox Jews as benighted and Reform Jews
as *goyim*, or Gentiles. He tends to lump Conservative Jews together with the confused middle class. Anyway, they are not his
type. Not given to theological reflection, Aaron V. would not
know how to articulate a concept of Jewish Chosenness. He has
an innate conviction that Jews—that is, his kind of Jews—tend to
do things better than Gentiles, and are on the whole smarter. If
only Jews took Zionism and Hebrew more seriously, thinks
Aaron V., the Jewish people would be better off. The language is
what makes for survival.

MOSES U. is a Yiddishist whose three children attend a Sholem Aleichem School. In his youth he was active in Socialist circles, a devoted worker on behalf of unionism, an anti-Communist. Many years of loyal service in an electronics firm have brought him to the rank of Manager of the local branch. Now he is in his sixth decade. He is able to indulge in his chief hobby, writing short articles in Yiddish under a pseudonym for a small-circulation Yiddish journal. At times he has tried his hand, not entirely successfully, at a little Yiddish poetry. If only people knew what can be done with Yiddish, thinks Moses U., perhaps the whole world would use Yiddish.

For him it is more than a language, it's a way of life. He reads new editions of a Yiddish dictionary the way horse racers study form. A new shade of meaning here, a new delicate nuance there, all these constitute his pride and joy. It is more than a language. It is music, art and literature combined.

Any and every production in the Yiddish theater finds Moses U. there. He refuses to recognize the disappearance of the great of yesteryear or to make invidious comparisons. To do this would be to concede that Yiddish is losing its hold. He subscribes to every Yiddish magazine and periodical he can lay his hands on. There is an international fraternity of lovers of Yiddish. Tragically the Second World War wrought havoc with the largest living reservoir of Yiddish-speaking Jewry. He corresponds with old-timers in London and Israel in flawless, flowing Yiddish. Those who survived will still keep the flag flying.

His wife is the daughter of one of the original supporters of the Yiddish Scientific Institute (Yivo). She is a teacher in the Public School system of New York City. It is one of the more integrated schools in a middle-class area and the children, hailing from a reasonable cross-section of Negro, Puerto Rican and Jewish families, are a pleasure to teach.

Mrs. U. brings to the teaching experience an exuberant enthusiasm. She would hotly deny there was anything specifically Jewish in her attitude toward her profession. She does not keep a kosher home, her family attends no synagogue—not even on the High Holy Days of the New Year and the Day of Atonement. She and her husband were married at City Hall without benefit of clergy, which was, even in those days, extremely avant-garde. Nevertheless long generations of savants and scholars have left their mark on her personality.

Occasionally, when Mrs. U. meets a Jew with traditional affiliations at a social gathering, which will invariably be a Bar Mitzvah or a wedding, she will try to impress him by recounting the family pedigree, which includes seven Rabbis, beginning with a scholar who wrote a not insignificant commentary on a traditional text. She makes the confession in a spirit of pride but not entirely without guilt, which is somewhat assuaged only when the traditional Jew has not heard of her ancestral scholar. Somewhere in the back of her mind she has a gnawing doubt as to whether the glory of Judaism that was, that she recognizes her own family to have preserved and transmitted, is destined to end in the extreme secularism which her children absorb at school. Is it enough to converse fluently in a dying language about the literary glories of Mendele Mocher Sforim and Isaac Leib Peretz?

She is shrewd enough to realize that the enthusiasm with which her own father threw himself into his work for Yivo was in no small way related to a deep-seated antagonism to his own Orthodox and dogmatically authoritarian background. Her grandfather had been a kindly enough person and yet there was a harshness in the tenacity with which he had insisted on his children observing all the minutiae of Jewish law long after they had lost all delight in it. She senses that the children would like a little more traditional observance. The pendulum can swing too far in the opposite direction. In their home even Passover becomes a May Day and the *Haggadah* a socialist tract. But her husband is adamant and she knows better than to cross him in this area. He has a profound dislike for the trappings of nostalgia. In his youth he delighted in organizing social meetings precisely at times when traditional Jews were at their devotions on the High Holy Days.

The family tends to mix exclusively with Jews of their kind. During the long summer months they leave the city and go to the mountains where for the last fifteen years they have rented a cabin in a Yiddish-speaking colony. Moses U. is in his element here. To this camp come many whose sole acquaintance with the language is the ability to speak it. To them Moses U. is something of a combination of Arthur Miller and Abraham Goldfaden. He is in charge of the cultural program and occasionally tries his hand at writing a play or translating a section of a Broadway success into Yiddish. These are the days when Moses U. feels ten feet tall.

Jewish religion for Moses U. is past tense. He has a vague hypothesis in his mind which draws on elements from Marx, Freud and Darwin fused together by quotations he has picked up from his favorite Socialist writers. Religion is a drug, a fraud once perpetrated by a priestly caste on an unwitting and gullible public. The only ones who benefit from the Jewish religion are the professionals, thinks Moses U. whenever he ponders the subject, which is infrequently. He has no time for Jewish tradition except insofar as it relates to his beloved language. Zionism, he thinks, is chiefly a human-rescue operation. There should be a country where Jews who can't live anywhere else can go. He identifies with what happens in Israel, especially the fighting and the heroic self-defense. He contributes generously according to his means. But he has no intention of leaving his home. Home, for Moses U., is where Jews in large numbers speak Yiddish.

SOLOMON T. comes from a very fine background. His father is a surgeon associated with one of the leading hospitals in a large city on the West Coast. His grandparents on his father's side were members of an Orthodox synagogue. His grandparents on his mother's side were members of a Reform Temple. Solomon's family has long been associated with the local Ethical Culture Society. When he was younger, Solomon T. used to attend the Sunday School, and later, the meetings of the Society with his parents most Sunday mornings.

His father's parents had been deeply hurt that their grandson was not prepared for Bar Mitzvah. Not that they were really Orthodox themselves. They were members of an Orthodox synagogue but were fairly lax in their own observance. Not having Solomon become Bar Mitzvah seemed to them an affront to all that was holy. They could tolerate the Ethical Culture Society because so many important people were associated with it. They were even secretly rather proud of it because, deep down, they felt that Judaism had little relevance to the important things in life anyway.

But the lack of a Bar Mitzvah hurt them. "I'll find you a Rabbi myself," said Grandfather T. after lunch one Sunday. "All the boy has to do is learn a few verses. And we can do it at my synagogue. There'll be no objections. I'm one of their biggest contributors." But Solomon T.'s father had refused, on principle of all things. He didn't approve. And as far as Solomon T. could see, all that having a Bar Mitzvah meant for most of his friends was getting presents. The idea bored him. He didn't need any presents. Whatever he asked for, his parents had always bought him—in good measure. He had just about everything he wanted by the age of thirteen, including a hi-fi and a tape recorder. So grandfather got no support from Solomon T. "Nevertheless," thought Solomon T., "it would be nice just once really to want something."

Solomon T. attended the finest private school money could buy. His grades were average. He mildly enjoyed going to school. He had started college shortly after reaching his eighteenth birthday and concentrated on getting good grades so that he could enter medical school. One night, a Jewish girl he had met at some party invited him to attend a meeting organized by the Student Nonviolent Coordinating Committee. A speaker was appealing for volunteers to go down South and help the Negroes in their fight for civil rights.

Suddenly, like Paul on the road to Damascus, Solomon T. was overwhelmed by a burning sensation. This was what he had been looking for all his life! Here was something he himself could do for others and, in return for which, enjoy an acceptance that was his and his alone. Not that he disliked his parents. It was just that he felt so small when they were around. They had given him so much. They were so flawlessly successful. Here was something they could not give him. He wanted it desperately.

At first it was just a matter of skipping a few classes here and muffing a few assignments there. He became active in SNCC, organizing, writing, appealing, collecting. By the end of his second year, when Solomon T. packed his bags to go South for an orientation course, he knew he was not going back to college. These people needed him. Who could study medicine at such a time?

Solomon T. was deeply involved in the March on Selma. For the first time in his life he felt he had an identity. He began to read poetry, political tracts. His enthusiasm for the Negro and for the civil rights workers was unbounded.

The moment of truth came at Birmingham, Alabama, when a group of policemen cordoned off a milling bunch of Negroes and whites protesting a city ordinance. They were not going to degrade his black brothers this way! As he edged through the crowd his friends moved aside. He hardly felt the swinging night stick on the side of his forehead. The taste of blood mixed with sweat was sweet in his mouth. He had come through. They had seen him. He was really one of them. The long ride in the paddy wagon and the overnight stay in the jail was a small price to pay for such glory.

But there was no one waiting for him when he was released. Nor was he acclaimed a hero. As the months ticked by, Solomon T. realized his whiteness was the crux of the matter. Suddenly, his black friends found that only black people really understood the agony of the Negro. The slogan "Black Power" sounded the death knell for Solomon T.'s hopes for a new life and a new identity.

Slowly and sadly he made his way back West. His parents were so relieved to see him alive that they mercifully refrained from plying him with too many awkward questions. Only in his mother's eyes could he detect a mute yet eloquent anguish at his unkempt, unshaven appearance and long, shaggy hair. Where had they gone wrong? His father behaved as if Solomon T. no longer belonged to him, a foreign body deposited within the family orbit by accident of birth. He threw himself increasingly ferociously into his work, attending his medical society committee meetings until the late hours. For Solomon T., staying at home was clearly impossible. The tensions were unbearable, if disciplined. In any case, he was more ashamed to remain than they would have been to accept him. He went to live in Haight-Ashbury. He began to smoke marijuana, which a friend gave him one night.

He had no desire to pick up the threads of his medical career. Further studying was out of the question. He was now consumed by an ever-growing desire to change the world. Somewhere, somehow, there had to be a creative outlet for his enthusiasm. He returned to the campus to become involved in the Peace Movement. The eternal crusader within him had found yet another cross. At times he was oppressed with a sense of futility at the puny effects of political protest, however close to the revolutionary wind it sailed. The Establishment was seemingly so omnipotent. If only he could join battle in one worthy cause with even a remote chance of making some real contribution to a better society and a better world. The spark within him from the fire of the prophets of old, lovingly preserved against the wind and the rain of the long night of Exile, almost smothered under the blandishments of affluence, now glowed steadily in hopeful anticipation.

DANIEL S. teaches physics at a college in the New York metropolitan area. He is in his early thirties, married, with a boy of three. His wife is pregnant. Until some years ago Daniel S.'s being Jewish was an occasional irritant, perhaps, but no cause for serious reflection. His parents were thoroughly assimilated. His father often waxed eloquent over the dangerous implications of dual loyalties, in which context he did not merely refer to Israel and Zionism, but also meant any ethnic deviation from Americanism. America had done well by the family, according to S. Senior, and the family had a reciprocal obligation to America. He regretted that a common citizenship had not long since acted as a solvent on the variety of ethnic elements in American life. He was determined, as far as was in his power, to dissolve his own Jewish ties. A man must set a good example.

Daniel S.'s grandparents had also been assimilated. His paternal grandfather, who came to America as a young man, had avoided Jewish contacts as one avoids a plague. He resented that his being Jewish had been nothing but an inconvenience to his advancement in the Old Country. He was determined that it should not stand in his way in the New. Only Daniel S.'s grandmother still clung to a vestige of the Jewish religion. She kept a kosher home. Her husband bitterly resented this. He took great delight when they dined out, and his wife ordered dairy food or fish, in eating aggressively in her presence the most exotic nonkosher foods. He need not have driven himself so hard. The old lady had no real attachment to her religion. Kosher food was at once a conversation point and a convenient stick to beat on the heads of the nonobservant—but committed—Jews they occasionally came across. "You mean you don't keep kosher? And you're Jewish? Hmm!"

Daniel S. loved his grandparents as human beings but deeply resented his grandmother's atavistic logic. When he had confided to her, shortly before his marriage, that he wanted to bring up his children as Jews, Grandmother S. had snorted. She only knew of kosher meat and two sets of crockery. Theology was not for her. Daniel S. knew perfectly well that his future wife would never agree to such an arrangement. She was the American-born daughter of a Dutch refugee who had been reminded by Hitler that his family was Jewish. The word "kosher" had not even been in their vocabulary. Her grandparents had died at Auschwitz, unaware to the end of why they were suffering. Being Jewish for them was a little like being black-skinned, only not so obvious. Was Judaism, thought Daniel S., just a matter of food with the possibility of intermittent martyrdom?

His wife had not objected to a Jewish wedding. On Central Park South the traditional Jewish marriage canopy was considered chic, as long as it did not look too traditional and was suitably smothered with expensive flowers. She had even consented to meet with the Rabbi, an earnest young man, slightly overdefensive, who had made a half-hearted attempt to interest them in a synagogue membership. He had even raised the subject of a Jewish home but dropped it as he detected the cold gleam of hostility in the bride's eyes. She wore her grandparents' death in Auschwitz the way a soldier might wear the Purple Heart. The Rabbi had no medals, only arguments. The indifference carried her through the marriage responses. She was doing this for Daniel because she loved him. Her eyes caught his grandmother, at the reception, superior, abstinent, and triumphant, as the guests consumed huge quantities of shrimp cocktail. If that was religion, you could keep it.

But Daniel S. was not so easily put off. An unarticulated aspiration kept bubbling up from the ancestral wells of his mind, disappearing as it surfaced into consciousness. He was a good enough scientist to recognize the miraculous complexity of life. He was a sensitive enough human being to realize that a man had to live by more than a regular job and a casual affiliation with some *ad hoc* committee for improving the lot of the underprivileged. As he stood by his son's bed in the dimly lit nursery, listening to the rise' and fall of the breathing, he sensed in himself a desperate hunger to pass on to his child an identity that would be truly his. His boy was an American. That part was easy enough. There would have to be explanations and rationalizations for some of the things America was doing. Hopefully that task would be easier when the boy was older. But he was also Jewish. What does a father tell his child about that aspect of his being?

Memories of the Holocaust began to crowd in on him. He remembered from his childhood the stories about the bestial Nazis. The reports of the Eichmann trial had awakened those earlier memories. Recently he had been reading widely on the subject. How do you tell your son that millions of his kind were cremated simply because they were—Jews? There would have to be a context, a history. But what of the meaning and purpose of that history? Suddenly Daniel S. realized that he wanted to give some content to his being Jewish, but didn't know how. If he couldn't run away from it, he had to face up to it. He had to learn to live with it, creatively.

He began to attend Jewish lectures and Jewish exhibitions. The Masada exhibition at the Jewish Museum in New York had a profound effect on him. He had thrilled to the spirit of Jewish self-defense during the Six-Day War. The artifacts, scrolls and reconstructions of ancient battles gave him a sense of historical antiquity as a Jew which nothing he had ever read, heard or seen had afforded. Yet even as he contemplated the narrow chambers where his ancestors had lived their last days and endeavored to imagine what they had looked like, an awareness that Masada showed only one dimension of Jewish life overwhelmed him. It was those who had put their faith in God rather than in man who had survived to tell the tale. He looked around him and saw Jews with minute knitted skullcaps looking at Roman soldiers in battle formation on a hillside. A group of plump Jewish matrons were examining a shred of hair of a far-off ancestress. Earlier, two men with beards had been closely deciphering a faded, dark brown scrap of parchment, reading aloud the Hebrew words which they picked out meticulously.

He began to visit synagogues, methodically, district by district, denomination by denomination. After a few months he became bewildered and confused. Would no one describe to him the common factor, apart from accident of birth, which made all these different people Jews? Was there no explanation which could make sense of all the variegated phenomena that were Jews and also, at the same time, of his own deepest yearnings?

Slowly, it became apparent to Daniel S. that his whole future as a mature human being depended upon his establishing a true sense of identity with his people's past. His parents, for reasons best known to them, had decided to destroy their ties with ancestral tradition. But it was precisely in the potentially health-giving soil of that tradition that Daniel S.'s spiritual yearnings now sought to sink deep roots. He saw all around him the Negro seeking painstakingly to build up precisely that kind of an ethnic tradition which his own loved ones had so improvidently squandered. Seeing his problem as an outright need to reestablish a sense of himself in all his relationships—past, present and future—afforded him a profound feeling of relief. To be sure, diagnosis was not cure. It was, however, the beginning of the search for that which could cure. Daniel S. was certain of two things. He could not possibly be alone in that search and such a deep-seated need must somewhere be fulfilled. If he would only continue to search, he would surely find.

Two

Is there an answer to the dilemma of Daniel S.? There is, if the bewildering diversity of Jewish types today is seen within a historical context.

Wide divergence among Jews about the meaning of being Jewish is a relatively modern phenomenon. Only in the modern world, under democracy, has religious pluralism been found not only acceptable but also desirable. In the past, whenever sharply divergent views arose as to the meaning of being Jewish, a heretical sect developed which soon broke away from the parent body.

The Samaritans constituted such a group. They first emerged in the eighth pre-Christian century. At the end of the tenth pre-Christian century, when King Solomon died, the land of Israel was divided into two kingdoms. Ten of the twelve tribes transferred their allegiance to Israel in the north, and the remaining tribes of Benjamin and Judah constituted the kingdom of Judah in the south. Henceforth the term "Israel" referred either to the people or territory of the joint kingdoms or exclusively to the northern political entity.

Israel, the northern kingdom, was destroyed by the Assyrians in 721 B.C.E. The Assyrians, in accordance with their policy of depopulating conquered territories, sent colonists there to replace the deported intelligentsia, upper classes and skilled workers. These colonists mingled freely with the existing population. The two ethnic groups fused together and became known as the *Shomronim*, or Samaritans, after *Shomron*, or Samaria, the former capital of the kingdom of Israel. In the belief that it was politic to worship the god of the land, whose jurisdiction in those days was believed to extend only to the territorial limits of the country and not beyond, these new inhabitants of the former northern kingdom of Israel embraced a form of Israelitish religion. (Before the sixth pre-Christian century the term "Jewish" may not legitimately be used. "Jewish," comes from Jew, in Hebrew *Yehudi*, or citizen of *Yehudah*, Judah. Only after the destruction of the Solomonic Temple in 586 B.C.E., when the Judeans become the only surviving remnants of ancient Israel, may we properly speak of Jews and Judaism. Before this period we only speak of the religion of Israel.) A deported Israelite priest was sent back from Assyria by the king to instruct them. The Bible suggests that their reason for embracing the Israelite religion was their fear of the marauding lions which prowled the land. Whether or not their conversion, in this respect, was successful, later Jewish tradition contemptuously refers to them as "lion proselytes."

In 586 B.C.E. the southern kingdom of Judah was destroyed by the Babylonians. The inhabitants were exiled to Babylon. When Cyrus the Persian later permitted the Jews to return to Judea in 538 B.C.E., they refused to have any dealings with the hybrid Samaritans. Ezra, one of the outstanding leaders of the fifth pre-Christian century in Judea, in particular, refused to have any truck with them. The Jewish quality of their religion was subsequently strengthened by defectors from the reorganized Judean community. Ezra had introduced some stringent reforms, among them the absolute rejection of all intermarriage with pagans. His views did not go unchallenged even among the Jews. The author of the Book of Ruth clearly objects to such racial extremes. He tells a charming idyll in which a Moabitess, of one of the most abhorred of all pagan tribes, becomes the ancestress of none less than King David. But the restrictions were probably justified in terms of qualitative Jewish survival. Those who refused to send their Gentile wives away were excluded from the nascent Jewish community. (Among the defectors was one Manasseh, son of the High Priest in Jerusalem.) This alone would explain the remarkable similarity between the Samaritan and Jewish religions, which share a common Pentateuch, the former actually retaining the original ancient script.

"Pentateuch" comes from two Greek words, *penta*, five, and *teuchos*, book. It refers to the five books of the Torah, or Law—Genesis, Exodus, Leviticus, Numbers and Deuteronomy —which together form the first and most important section of the Hebrew Bible. The other two sections are the Prophets and the Writings. The first explicit reference to these five books as a unit is found in a second pre-Christian century writer, the author of the preface to the apocryphal Ecclesiasticus. The Apocrypha contains Jewish writings not regarded by the Rabbis as sacred enough to be included in the canon of the Bible. But the unity of the Pentateuch almost certainly goes back several centuries earlier.

In Hebrew the books of the Bible are designated by a word from the opening sentence of each book. The first book, for example, is called *Bereshit* (In the beginning), from its opening words, *Bereshit bara Elohim* (In the beginning God created). The English designations are taken from the Greek translation which sums up the content of each book in a single word, for example, Exodus, or the book which contains a description of the "going out" from Egypt. It is the Greek version of the Bible, known as the Septuagint (because of a tradition that seventy Greek scholars translated it independently yet identically), which is responsible for the rendering of the term "Torah," a Hebrew word meaning, literally, "teaching," as Law or *nomos*. "Way of life" embraces the meaning of the Hebrew more faithfully than "Law."

The Jewish religion continued to develop. The Samaritans merely clung literally to what they had received, primarily the Pentateuch and some associated traditions. They accepted no subsequent Jewish literature as authoritative. Theirs was an arrested form of Judaism, fixated at a primitive stage. They have survived, to this day, but not as Jews, even though many of their practices closely resemble early Jewish practice. Religious pluralism in those days was inconceivable. There could be only one version of the true religion.

The Karaites, founded by Anan ben David in the eighth century, may also be described as a heretical group which, arising within the traditional Jewish people, became schismatic and ultimately split off from the main body. Some of them also remain to this day, but not as Jews. The Karaite movement, from the verb *kara*, to read, unlike the Samaritan, was not a fixation of Jewish religious development at an early stage. It was, on the contrary, a deliberate and conscious return to that early stage. Like the Samaritans and the later Sadducees of the turn of the millennium, the Karaites, as their name indicates, *read* the Torah, that is the Pentateuch, literally and carefully. Theoretically at least, any law, custom or practice not found therein was not regarded by them as binding. (In fact, they adopted many rabbinic traditions.)

But by the eighth century the difference between the literal text of the Torah and actual Jewish religious belief and practice was as great as the difference between the trickle of a mountain stream and a vast river flowing on the plain fed by many tributaries. The Karaites served a useful purpose in goading the mainstream of rabbinic Judaism into putting its own house in order. The Rabbis, now under polemical pressure, studied the Torah anew to defend their own advanced ritual and theological position. The distinguished scholar, philosopher and linguist Saadia ben Joseph (892–942) finally and effectively quenched their claims for the legitimate Jewish succession (though not their literary output) through his brilliant argumentation, precise lexicography and profound biblical exegesis. But, as in all such heretical developments, both sides learned from each other. The Karaites, too, produced some outstanding grammarians and skilled exegetes on the pentateuchal text.

Christianity, likewise, started out as a heresy within the Jewish people with regard to the meaning of being Jewish. The early Christians were all Jews, as were Jesus and the twelve apostles.

They devoutly observed the traditional laws and conducted their lives in all matters as did their fellow Jews. Jesus himself, if the gospel story be accepted as true, was preoccupied exclusively with Jews—"the lost sheep of the House of Israel." In only one respect did the early Christians differ from other Jews. Whereas all other Jews, at the turn of the millennium, believed that the salvation of Israel would come from a Messiah to be sent by God in the end of days, the early Christians believed that this Messiah, anticipated by all Jews, had in fact already arrived, having been sent by God. *Christos*, or the Christ, is simply the Greek equivalent of the Hebrew, *Mashiach*, the Anointed One. With the coming of Paul and the wholesale and indiscriminate conversion of the Gentiles without regard to their observance of the Law, an unbridgeable chasm developed between the two religions. Christianity, like the religion of the Samaritans, was no longer a Jewish religion even though it borrowed largely from the theological universe of discourse of Jewish life at that time.

The wide divergences today among Jews about the meaning of being Jewish are the result of the impact between premodern Judaism and the modern world. Two hundred years ago no such wide denominational divisions existed. All Jews then, with negligible exceptions, shared a relatively common world outlook. They believed in God. He was Omnipotent, Omniscient, Omnibenevolent and Omnipresent. He had created the world from nothing (*creatio ex nihilo*). He had specially chosen the Jewish people to be His own people. Beginning with Abraham, He had solicitously followed the well-being of His favorite children. At Mount Sinai He had given to them, in a unique act of Self-Revelation, His Torah. Owing to their disobedience to the Divine injunctions of that Torah, He had permitted the heathen to destroy His Temple and exile His loved ones to foreign lands. But in the fullness of time, when Israel would again be at one with God, perfectly obedient to Him, He would surely send His Messiah. The scattered of Israel would be gathered up through Di-

vine intervention from the four corners of the earth. The Jews
would return victoriously to the land promised by God to the
Patriarchs. Until that Messianic Age all righteous Jews who died
would go to Heaven. At the beginning of that Messianic era they
would be restored to life to enjoy its terrestrial benefits, especially world peace and Jewish national supremacy. At the end
of that Messianic Age all Jews, and righteous Gentiles, would
enjoy eternal bliss in the world to come after a universal resurrection and Last Judgment. This was the prevailing viewpoint
among Jews before the French Revolution. Their continued
suffering in Exile was, they believed, self-inflicted. If they repented perfectly of their sins, they would hasten the End.

There were, of course, differences of stress within this overall
theological framework, but nothing so radical as that which separated Samaritan, Karaite and Christian from Jew. *Chasidim*
tended to stress the heart, *Mitnagdim* the head. Most of the Rabbis in general tended to a realistic appraisal of Jewish existence.
The Rabbis, or teachers, were the spiritual leaders of the Jewish
people after the destruction of the Herodian Temple in 70 c.e.
They were jurists who interpreted and ruled on Jewish law.
Much of their classical discussion is to be found in the Talmud
(literally "learning"), a kind of Congressional Record of several
centuries. The law they propounded was judge-made law. In the
absence of the Sanhedrin, the legislature of ancient Jewry, they
were unable to innovate. They concentrated their efforts on
studying and teaching the sacred texts and ensuring that their
flocks observed the Torah as faithfully as possible.

But some were caught up in the web of mysticism and cabalis-
tic speculation. Mysticism—the systematic study of esoteric
knowledge concerning God, man and human destiny—has a
hoary antiquity in Jewish tradition. From the earliest days, even
before the Christian era, the representative Jewish scholars
tended to warn against its heady dangers. A scholar who lived in
Jerusalem in the second pre-Christian century, and who conducted one of the earliest academies of Jewish learning on record,

warned his pupils against dabbling in "secret things." That very phrase is used by the earlier author of the Book of Deuteronomy (seventh pre-Christian century) who affirms that "the secret things" belong to God. Only "the revealed things" are for man. From the thirteenth century, preoccupation with mystical speculation received new impetus from the sudden appearance of the *Zohar*, or Light, a complicated mystical commentary on the Pentateuch, purported to have been written by a second-century mystic Simeon bar Yochai but actually emanating from the hand of one Moses de Leon, a thirteenth-century scholar. In this classical work of *cabala*, or traditional lore, two main themes of Jewish mysticism are fused. One is the theoretical metaphysical speculation about the nature of God, the creation of the world and the end of time. The other is the practical application of mysticism to daily life in prayers, incantations and a form of theurgic technique intended in part to force God to bring about the consummation of history.

In the eighteenth century, as in previous centuries, there were those who were impatient with the Messiah's delay in coming. False Messiahs had constantly misled the people into believing that the End was close at hand. Periods of acute suffering made the task of these pseudo-Messiahs all too easy. From the first century onward false Messiahs abound in Jewish history. Josephus describes some who proclaimed the End before Jesus. The most notorious was Sabbatai Zevi (1626–1676), who caused an upheaval which agitated Jewish life for over a century and drew into its vortex some outstanding Jewish personalities as well as masses of the simple Jews. In the aftermath of the Sabbatean movement, one Jacob Frank (1726–1791) who had come under the influence of the Dönmeh, a sect founded by the followers of Sabbatai, formed a group of semi-Christians, the Frankists.

But these very aberrations would have been impossible in the absence of a unified world outlook. The mystic student of *cabala*, who endeavored to storm Heaven by force, ultimately believed that the same God resided there whose Torah and commentaries thereon the more sober rabbinical student assiduously cultivated. Ideas of God may have differed between student of Talmud and student of *Zohar*. The fulcrum of both spiritual worlds was the Torah, revealed by God on Sinai.

Chasid and *Mitnaged*, student of the Talmud and student of the *Zohar*, even the dabblers in pseudo-Messianism (to the extent that they did not, like the Sabbatean movement and the wilder excesses of Frankism, become radically schismatic and break away from the parent religion) operated within the same basic theological framework. The pseudo-Messianists, after all, simply misread the cosmic Divine calendar. The same is true of the Jewish philosopher or rationalist. Reason was, in the premodern period, simply a laborious method of arriving at the truths vouchsafed by Revelation. Philosophy in premodern Judaism is not free speculation. It is speculation in the service of One God. The greatest medieval Jewish philosopher, Moses Maimonides (1135–1204), who, in his famous *Guide to the Perplexed*, all but reconciles the Bible and Jewish religion with the philosophy of Aristotle, is also the author of a comprehensive legal code which treats heretics harshly.

More unifying even than theological framework in the premodern era was overall Jewish ritual practice. Here again minor differences abound. *Minhag*, or custom, differentiates behavior patterns from one country, or region, to the next. *Ashkenazim*, or Eastern European Jews, often differed in ritual stress or liturgical rubric from *Sephardim*, Spanish and Portuguese Jews exiled from their homeland in the fifteenth century. But these minor differences, manifold and widespread as they were, paled into insignificance next to the unifying architectonic of traditional Torah observance. All Jews meticulously observed the cycle of the Jewish calendar. All Jews worshiped in synagogue. All Jews wore the distinctive Jewish *tzitzit*, or fringes, in accordance with traditional injunction. All Jews maintained strictly the rigorous dietary laws governing what a Jew may or may not eat. One community might wait a little longer between eating meat and milk but all waited for the minimum prescribed limit. All Jews married and divorced *ke-dat moshe ve-yisrael*, or according to the law of Moses and Israel, with documents sanctioned by tradition. All Jews conformed with the regulations concerning the purity of family life and strictly governing the relationships between the sexes. All Jews were buried in accordance with standard Jewish practice and mourned in accordance with tradition.

Had the eighteenth-century Jew been asked why he believed and behaved the way he did, he would no doubt have referred to the Torah as the authoritative source for his way of life. The Hebrew term *Torah* can simply mean "teaching," such as the *ad hoc* teaching of a priest, prophet or sage. It can also mean "the Five Books of Moses." Sometimes it means "the whole Bible." In its distinctive theological sense it means the teaching par excellence of God enshrined in the Written Torah (Pentateuch) and also the Oral Torah.

But this conception of Torah itself has a history. If we turn back the clock of Jewish history, not two hundred but two thousand years, we are again in the presence of what look like divergences in the meaning of being Jewish. The ancestor of the eighteenth-century Jew would again point to the Torah as the authoritative source for his way of life. But the Oral Torah was, at this point of time, in the very process of being articulated. At the turn of the millennium the problem of the meaning and purpose of Jewish existence could again be presented in terms of different types of Jews: in the eighteenth-century *Chasid*, *Mitnaged*, mystic, rationalist, pseudo-Messianist; in the first-century Pharisee, Sadducee, Essene, Zealot, devotee of apocalyptic. But these different types also operated within a basic theological framework. Religious pluralism is of the modern world.

In order to discuss Jewish history, the context of Jewish theology, which covers a period of almost four thousand years, without invoking a host of qualifications, it is essential to oversimplify by drawing some relatively sharp demarcation lines between various eras. First there is that period of history when, for the most part, excepting the early wanderings, the Children of Israel lived on their own soil, the biblical era or the period of the First Commonwealth. Second there is that period of history when, for the most part, the Jews, on their own soil, were subservient to alien powers, the period of the Second Commonwealth. Third there is that period of history when the Jews were a Diaspora people, living in Exile, but in hopeful anticipation of a Divine restoration to their Promised Land. Finally there is the modern period.

We may best designate the period in Jewish history beginning with the destruction of the Herodian Temple by the Romans in 70 C.E. and ending with the French Revolution the *rabbinic* period. This is a "shorthand" method of referring to a complicated phenomenon. There were Rabbis interpreting the Torah before the Temple fell and there are some today who claim to represent that identical rabbinic tradition. Periods of history should not be too sharply delineated. Perhaps it would be more accurate to speak of rabbinic *culture* than of the rabbinic *period*. Nevertheless two important considerations point to the need to make 70 C.E. a watershed. The loss of the Temple effectively meant the end of the sacrificial system in Jewish life, and the ultimate demise of the Sadducees, the priestly party in whose hands, together with the Levites, the proper conducting of the Temple ritual was invested. The Rabbis, who were the Pharisees, were now in effective control of Jewish life. Between 70 and 1789 a Jew either adhered to rabbinic Judaism or ceased being a Jew. With the coming of the Emancipation the exclusive jurisdiction of the Rabbis came to an end. Religious pluralism now emerged as a possibility and as a desirability.

With the Jew as a citizen of the modern democratic state, being a Jew became a voluntary matter. This factor alone makes the Emancipation, which may conveniently be linked with the French Revolution, another crucial watershed. Voluntarism in Jewish life is a radical novelty. It provides the necessary context for that unity in diversity characteristic of religious pluralism. It is tempting to see in the Samaritan supporter Manasseh (who, because Ezra refused him permission to keep his Gentile wife, went over to the opposition) an image of a Jew affiliated with an Orthodox synagogue who, because the Rabbi refuses to convert his son's Gentile fiancee, resigns and founds a Reform Temple. But Manasseh did not have the alternative of having City Hall confer a moral status on his marriage.

It is equally desirable to refer to the period from the destruction of the Solomonic Temple by the Babylonians in 586 B.C.E. to the destruction of the Herodian Temple by the Romans in 70 C.E. as the theocratic, or *ecclesiastical*, period in Jewish history. This, too, is a "shorthand" method of referring to a complicated phenomenon. This is no more a monolithic period in Jewish history than is the rabbinic period. In the very middle of this period, in fact, a radical theological innovation was introduced into Jewish life, a twin doctrine of resurrection and immortality.

The Bible knows only of *existence* after death, not of *life* after death. Existence after death is in accordance with the fashion of the Greek Hades, a disembodied and wraithlike existence bereft of all feeling and emotion. The Hebrews called this nether world *Sheol*, or the Pit. Thence the Witch of Endor summoned up the lifeless ghost of Samuel. The anguish of Job (fifth pre-Christian century) would be meaningless had the consolation of belief in life after death, where terrestrial inequities are redressed, been readily available. But commencing in the third century, under the impact of Greek ideas of immortality and Persian ideas of resurrection, a systematic eschatology, or doctrine of that which will happen at the end of days, emerges. By the time of Jesus, the Pharisees had elevated the belief in life after death to the rank of a dogma.

The theocratic, or ecclesiastical, period in Jewish history is distinguished by virtue of the fact that the Jews are led by priests rather than, as in previous centuries, by kings or, as in subsequent centuries, by Rabbis. In the eighth pre-Christian century the ten northern tribes constituting the kingdom of Israel were carried away into captivity by the Assyrians. Only the poor and the unskilled were left behind. The Wild claims have been made as to the subsequent fate of the ten "lost" tribes, ranging from the assertions that everyone from the English to the Falashas, or Abyssinian Jews, are descended from them. In truth these tribes assimilated with their captors, as was common practice in those days. The descendants of Abraham were now limited to the tribes of Judah and Benjamin, who together constituted the kingdom of Judah in the south in the geographical vicinity of Jerusalem.

In 586 B.C.E. the Babylonians sacked Jerusalem and the bulk of the inhabitants of Judah were also carried away into Exile. This time there was no assimilation, partly due to the lessons learned by the spiritual leaders of Judah from the rapid demise in Exile of erstwhile Israel and partly because the people were blessed with leaders of the caliber of Jeremiah and Ezekiel. By far the most important factor to account for their survival was a philosophy of Jewish history propounded by a group of spiritual geniuses and developed from the eighth pre-Christian century onward.

In contemplating the emergence of the classical Hebrew prophets (the biblical major and minor prophets as opposed to the earlier and historically more vague characters such as Elijah and Elisha) onto the stage of history between the eighth and sixth pre-Christian centuries, one is sorely tempted to adopt Karl Jaspers' designation of the period between 800 and 200 B.C.E as the "axial age" in human history. What the prophets accomplished had epoch-making results, not only for the Jewish people but for mankind. Of this axial age, Jaspers writes:

Extraordinary events are crowded into this period. In China lived Confucius and Lao Tse, all the trends in Chinese philosophy arose, it was the era of Mo Tse, Chuang Tse and countless others. In India it was the age of the Upanishads and of Buddha; as in China, all philosophical trends, including skepticism and materialism, sophistry and nihilism, were developed. In Iran Zarathustra put forward his challenging conception of the cosmic process as a struggle between good and evil; in Palestine prophets arose: Elijah, Isaiah, Jeremiah,

Deutero-Isaiah; Greece produced Homer, the philosophers Parmenides, Heraclitus, Plato, the tragic poets, Thucydides, and Archimedes. All the vast development of which these names are a mere intimation took place in these few centuries, independently and almost simultaneously in China, India and the West.

Such a bunching together of unusual genius is visible between the appearance of Amos and Hosea and Zechariah and Malachi, a period of approximately three centuries. But there is no need to posit the miraculous or the mysterious for the emergence of the prophets. Their accomplishments lay in the fact that their genius erupted at a crucial time in association with a unique and unprecedented combination of political and social circumstances. Genius in the absence of such supporting circumstances can often be stillborn. The prophets were responsible for developing a new conception of Israel's destiny and cosmic role and for rewriting the entire previous history of the people in terms of that new conception. As the Assyrians approached Israel and as the Babylonians approached Judah the prophets were led to a new conception of God. "Depend upon it, Sir," observed Samuel Johnson, "when a man knows he is to be hanged in a fortnight, it concentrates his mind wonderfully." One did not have to be a clairvoyant in the Middle East in the eighth pre-Christian century to realize that history was henceforth for the great powers. The age of empires had arrived. The small nations would be annexed or go under. This certain knowledge of impending national catastrophe concentrated the prophetic mind wonderfully.

Gods in the ancient world, in general, were regarded as tutelary deities. In return for protection by the god the subject rendered homage. Judging by archeological evidence from the ancient world, human fealty to such gods was rarely exclusive and single-hearted. The presence of a plethora of divinities in household shrines excavated at ancient Ur would appear to testify that ancient man tended to play it safe, "hedging his bets," as it were, by taking out several insurance policies at the same time. It is true that each policy had its own distinctive strong points. One god did not always carry as much protection as another in a particular sphere of life. One deity was good for love, another for crops and yet another for children. Nevertheless, the theological promiscuity of ancient man leaves the modern mind aghast. It was also common to believe that if one's country was defeated in war by another country, then one's own god or gods had also been defeated. A god who could not physically protect was clearly no god. This belief invariably led in the ancient world either to the complete abandoning of one's former, vanquished gods entirely in favor of the conqueror's gods as worthier gods or to the hyphenation of those former gods with the gods of the conqueror—something in the nature of a theological "take-over" in which the erstwhile proprietor, in becoming the managing director, still retains a modicum of status.

Before the eighth century the Israelites, in common with other peoples of that age, had such a god, Yahweh, or Jehovah, by name. Yahweh had been their God since they left Egypt. They had made a covenant with Him in Horeb, or Sinai, which was His original abode. He would be their God and they would be His people. Symbol of that covenant was the Ark and the tablets of stone, the Decalogue, prime symbol of the Revelation of Yahweh. On entering Israel, Yahweh had had a difficult time with His people. The local Canaanite gods, or Baalim (from "Baal," or master), had a much more seductive form of worship than the austere discipline of the desert God. These Baalim were believed to possess the power to grant corn, wine and oil, staple commodities of ancient life. The Canaanite religion involved orgiastic fertility rites. Sexual excesses in the worshiper, sanctioned by religion, by process of sympathetic magic, were believed to elicit fecundity from the soil and rain from the heavens. Many Hebrews were understandably seduced away from Yahweh. "She did not know," says Hosea in the name of Yahweh, in anguish, of Israel through the painful imagery of his estranged wife, "that it was I who gave her the corn and the wine and the oil."

Through the staunch loyalty of a handful of spiritual leaders

Yahweh fought off the Baalim. But the struggle against syncretistic tendencies was arduous and drawn out. Under Jeroboam (tenth century) gold calf gods were worshiped in the northern kingdom in Dan and Bethel. As late as the ninth century the people were still uncertain as to whether Yahweh or Baal was responsible for giving rain. That is, in the land of Israel, it was still not determined which god deserved the exclusive loyalty of the people. Finally, on Mount Carmel, the people were sufficiently impressed by a miracle staged by Elijah to affirm "Yahweh is God," not Baal. Pure monotheism is clearly a much later development. Only with the classical prophets is the authentic divinity, if not the existence of other gods, categorically denied. Before their preaching it was widely believed that whereas Israel had Yahweh, Ammon had Milkom and Moab had Chemosh. Yahweh, Milkom and Chemosh are proper names like Abraham, Isaac and Jacob. Yahweh, as God of Israel, was deemed to have exclusive jurisdiction only over Israel's territory. Only there could He be worshiped. In Ammon, Milkom was to be worshiped; in Moab, Chemosh. For King David to be exiled from his native country was tantamount to his being asked to worship other gods. Hosea even refers to Palestine, in a most revealing phrase, as "Yahweh's territory." But Amos clearly conceives of Yahweh as punishing other peoples, as well as Israel, for their moral shortcomings. This, if not pure monotheism, insofar as Yahweh still possessed a proper name, was nevertheless an advanced stage on that road. Yahweh now had an international status.

One significant element in Yahweh's make-up prevented Him from following the fate of other gods of the ancient world in being eclipsed. Since the Exodus from Egypt He had been regarded as champion of the underdog. Had He not delivered Israel from the hands of the Egyptian oppressors? Recollections of a "democratic" way of life in the desert, bereft of the decadence of relatively affluent Canaanite civilization, must also have assisted in making Yahweh a God of justice. Suddenly, in the eighth cen-

tury, the prophets reached through to a new conception of Yahweh. He is the God of Israel but, since He is also a God of
justice, He must also be God of all the world. The other gods are
really not gods. They do not measure up to what a real god must
be—just. When Israel and Judah fall, as fall they must, this will
not be due to the superiority of the Assyrian and Babylonian
gods. Yahweh will use these conquerors as sticks to chastise His
sinful people: "Assyria, rod of My anger."

This is a radical innovation in ancient theology. For the next
twenty-five centuries the theme of Jewish existence will be: "Because of our sins we were exiled from our land." Such a position
was, as long as one, in fact, survived, theologically impregnable.

One is tempted to find some rational explanation for this remarkable burst of genius with all its profound implications for
the survival of the Jewish people. Had Winston Churchill died in
1938, or had Hitler capitulated at Munich, the world would not
have witnessed that remarkable phenomenon of Churchill in the
Second World War. A genius may be born out of his time and
"waste his sweetness on the desert air." The prophets were able
to make their remarkable spiritual breakthrough because they
came at the right time. Their unusual talents were elicited in full
measure by events.

We cannot entirely rule out the thought that the more spiritually minded men in Israel had been impressed by the unification
of Israel under David in the face of the Philistines. The formation
of great world empires would also stimulate thought of unification. England once consisted of several principalities, each with
its own king and army. In the process of time a unification
took place leading to one king and one army. Each principality
retained its own dialect and mores. All live together in peace.
England thus, to some extent, becomes a prototype for a world
federation of nationalities and peoples, possessed of ethnic and
civilizational distinctions but bereft of armies and the weapons of
war. These would be in the hands of a single world authority.

By the same token David had united an erstwhile constantly embattled group of loosely knit tribes. Bitter internecine rivalry was wiped out by strong leadership in the face of a common enemy, leading to an era of unparalleled prosperity in Israel. It is no accident that in later days, when national fortunes were at a low ebb, the Davidic era was looked back upon lovingly and nostalgically as the high-water mark in Israel's collective life. Under increasing pressure from the outside world, the idea of a Messiah was born, one who would restore Israel to her terrestrial good fortune and fully extended territorial boundaries as in the time of David.

At first the Messiah was conceived of as a man who would re-store Israel to her former glory. Later, as the pressures increased, the Messiah was transformed into a celestial being supported by God and His heavenly Hosts. In either case the Messiah was a descendant of David. It cannot be ruled out that the unification of the tribes of Israel and the concomitant national well-being that unity fostered, if only briefly, gave rise to the belief that the tribes of all the earth, the various peoples, could also be united under One Divine King of Justice. That, at least, is the idea which emerges in Israel with increasing clarity from the eighth century. Nor is it remarkable that a small country sandwiched between two great power blocs should be the first to develop the concept of terrestrial peace, *shalom.*

The prophets were right for the wrong reasons. Clearly Assyria was not the rod of God's anger against a sinful people any more than Nazi Germany was in our own day. Even had the Israelites been as virtuous as the driven snow the Assyrians, in their drive for an outlet to the Mediterranean, would have over-whelmed them. The clumsy theological idiom in which the prophets expressed their intuition must not be allowed to blind us from seeing its profundity. They had discovered that God *does* righteousness (we would prefer to say God *is* righteousness) and that it is not what happens *to* a people or an individual which matters but how the group or the individual reacts to what happens to them.

History, like the jungle, is neutral. To be able to give a moral interpretation to an inevitable defeat buttressed the inborn will to survive of those who had suffered the double traumas of 721 and 586. Faced with the ultimate limitation of the ethics of power, the prophets discovered the power of ethics. Newton sitting in the proverbial orchard, hit on the head by the falling apple, discovered the law of gravity, intuited a correlation between falling apples and orbiting planets. So the people of Israel, through their spiritual virtuosi, struck on the head, as a small power, by the cruel forces of world history, intuited a correlation between their inner moral reactions and the destiny of mankind.

At first the people did not take the prophets seriously. Not until after 586 did they remember the dire predictions which had been made about the fall of Jerusalem. In Babylon the exiled captives gathered together on Sabbaths and Festivals to study the words of the prophets, hitherto preserved only by a small handful of their immediate disciples. Stunned by their defeat, they now lovingly cherished every word of fulfilled rebuke and every anticipation of future consolation. They must repent to be restored to their former state. How could they learn more about what they should do? Where was the Word of God?

Already in the seventh century, in 621 B.C.E. precisely, we read of the discovery in the Temple of a Book of Law, almost certainly the newly written Book of Deuteronomy. A process was now under way to edit all the ancient myths, memories, traditions and customs of the people, some no doubt in manuscript, most unquestionably transmitted orally. Some of these traditions went back to antiquity. Many bore the impress of a common ancient Middle Eastern mythological idiom. All were now recast to account for the current realities. Traumatic suffering often has the effect in the individual of eliciting a new and more intensive form of self-awareness. So it is with a people. With the traumas of 721 and 586 the people, through the prophets, became self-conscious to a greater degree than heretofore. The first fruits of that self-consciousness were the editing of the Pentateuch in the fifth pre-Christian century.

The Torah, or Pentateuch, may best be described as a mythical hypothesis, propounded by the prophets, to account for the reality of Israel's self-consciousness in its axial age. When we think of a human being, we think in terms of his unique and distinctive personality rather than in terms of the digestive and procreative processes he shares with other men and the animal kingdom. By the same token, when we think of a people, we should think in terms of its most unique and distinctive representatives, its spiritual virtuosi, rather than in terms of its masses. There is an inextricable bond between the two. The Jewish people may be regarded as the People of the Prophets not merely because it produced the prophets. Peoples have been known to kill their prophets, ignore them or attempt to obliterate their memory.

The Jewish people at first riduculed its prophets. Then, under stress, they took them seriously. We who live in an age when dissent, regarded as entirely legitimate by the bulk of intelligent and sensitive people, has been termed unpatriotic in high places, may well marvel at the relative immunity possessed by those in ancient days who did not refrain from pointing an accusing finger at the supreme symbol of the ancient polity, the king. The examples of Nathan before David and Elijah before Ahab may well be regarded as prototypes for a latter-day democracy of how to tolerate, if not necessarily to accept, the sharpest dissent.

The Jewish people is, then, the People of the Prophets by complicity, if nothing else. When the prophets spoke they were ignored but tolerated. At the time the prophets spoke the masses of Israel were probably indistinguishable from the masses of the Canaanite religion in their moral behavior. Some of the prevailing depravity is reflected in the prophetic writings. But after 586 the prophets captured the imagination of all who survived the burning. A spiritually shaken but rejuvenated people sat, pondered and wept by the rivers of Babylon. What had begun as the faith of the few was now the dominant belief of the many. Archeological evidence is witness to a remarkable religious renaissance in Babylon, reflected even in the "Jewish" names given to children.

A myth is the equivalent, in a universe of discourse bereft of the concept of the natural, of a hypothesis in our own scientific universe of discourse. A myth is an attempt to account for a natural phenomenon in the absence of a concept of nature. The biblical authors had no concept, no word, even, for nature. For them all things came from Yahweh. Yahweh caused rain and Yahweh brought the sun and the moon from their places. The sun could stand still for Joshua because the sun did not possess the law of its own being. It is Yahweh who made the sun move. Therefore, if Yahweh willed it, He could also make the sun stop.

Ancient man was puzzled by the phenomenon of fire. It possessed powers transcending his imagination. It cooked, warmed, protected and gave light. He had to have some hypothesis to account for it. In the absence of a natural hypothesis in terms of the principle of combustion, a myth was propounded. Fire originally belonged exclusively to the gods. Prometheus, one of the Titans, stole it from heaven. Man benefits therefrom: Prometheus suffers. The anthropomorphism is taken directly from the nursery. It is in this sense of myth (by which we mean a story involving men and gods which explains for prescientific man some natural phenomenon) that the early chapters of the Bible may be described as consisting of myths.

The existence of the world and the origin of the species are explained in the opening chapters of the Book of Genesis by their having been created by Yahweh. Human guilt is explained by the myth of the Fall. Pain in childbirth, the harsh struggle for existence in a pretechnological era and death are accounted for by human sin in the context of the same myth. Sense of guilt and the divine punishment both derive from the first act of disobedience. The plethora of languages, primitive technology and culture, all are accounted for by myths. The very institution of the human family and, since there are no children in the Garden of Eden, love between man and woman are accounted for by a myth. The very account of the Revelation on Sinai in the Book of Exodus is a myth to account for the phenomenon of law. The image of Yahweh descending on Mount Sinai to give the tablets of the Law to Moses is the exact literary mythical equivalent of the visual myth of Hammurabi receiving his Code from the sun god as depicted on the famous stele in the British Museum.

With the emergence of Abraham, myth gives way to legend, which is the rewriting of history with a substratum of reality. But in a sense, the legendary reconstruction plainly visible in the historical sections of the Bible, including all the other historical sections of the Bible edited under the influence of the prophets, is all part of one synoptic myth. It is a prescientific hypothesis to account for the reality of Israel's existence as it was anticipated in the eighth pre-Christian century and as it was actually experienced in ensuing centuries up to and after the Babylonian Exile.

Yahweh was not only the special God of Israel. He was also the God of all mankind. Israel was His Chosen People. But that did not mean they would enjoy any preferential treatment. On the contrary, precisely because Yahweh had singled them out, they would be punished for their shortcomings more severely than the other peoples. For Yahweh wanted men to be holy and just. In the beginning He had created only Adam and Eve. They were intended to live forever in the bliss of Eden. But they were disobedient. They ate of the fruit of the tree of the knowledge of good and evil in spite of Yahweh's express prohibition. Yahweh therefore banished them from Eden and cursed them with hard work, pain in childbirth and death.

Generations elapsed from Adam until Noah. Having tried to create holy and just human beings individually, Yahweh now experimented on a cosmopolitan and universal scale. All the world would be fit subjects for spiritual perfection. But He no more succeeded with the masses than with Adam and Eve. The masses, too, proved disobedient. The earth was full of violence.

Yahweh decided to bring a flood to destroy all mankind, saving only Noah and his family from whom salvation might ultimately spring. In his generation Noah was a righteous man. Generations then elapsed between Noah and Abraham. In Abraham, Yahweh recognized a man who would not only lead a holy and just life but, more importantly, would transmit these values to his seed. Herein lay the hope of a perfect world. Yahweh therefore selected Abraham to be the father of His people. Adam and Eve had failed Him, so also had mankind as a whole. Now Yahweh would seek to fashion a single people, just and holy. Through that people, embodiment of the Divine ideal, all the other peoples of the world would be blessed.

But, alas, that people also sinned. It failed to follow the Law of holiness and justice which Yahweh had revealed. Yahweh decided to punish Israel severely. He would not utterly destroy them as He destroyed the generation of the Flood. He had made a covenant never to do that again. Nor would he alter his cosmic plans. He had made a covenant with Abraham, too, that could never be broken. Thus He would use Assyria and Babylonia as "rods" to chastise His recalcitrant people. But ultimately, when they repented, He would restore them to the land He had promised to Abraham. This mythical hypothesis, originally propounded by the prophets and embellished in subsequent centuries by the spiritual leaders of the people, is basically how the people of Israel regarded itself in the fifth pre-Christian century. Its ground plan was already laid in the eighth. It is this conception which provides the framework for the Torah.

In 444 B.C.E. Ezra, priest and scribe, read from the Torah to the assembled people on the first day of the seventh month of Tishri, in the forecourt of the Temple. The first day of Tishri is *Rosh Hashanah,* or the Jewish New Year. At that time it is clear that the people as a whole, and even some of the priests, did not observe this day with any particular ceremony or ritual. None of the glory later to be associated with the New Year can be de-

tected in the biblical narrative. *Rosh Hashanah*, at this stage in
the development of the Jewish religion, was a day commemor-
ated strictly within the precincts of the Temple. The priests
performed the traditional sacerdotal, or priestly, rites in accordance with ancient prescription. This seems to have involved offering certain specified sacrifices and the blowing of trumpets.

The whole procedure seems to parallel the traditional ceremonies conducted in the Tower of London, when the keys are
handed over at the end of each day. Everybody knows that it
happens but everybody goes about his business regardless. Ezra's
summoning of the people into the forecourt of the Temple to
hear the words of the newly promulgated Torah was thus no act
of disrespect to the priestly ministrations proceeding inside the
Temple. Religion was primarily priestly at that time. He was,
however, introducing a radical innovation into Jewish life. The
people as a whole were being involved in a collective religious
and educational project. The Bible states quite explicitly that,
when Ezra read, "the ears of all the people were attentive unto
the book of the Law" and that after he had finished reading, his
assistants, the Levites, "caused the people to understand the Law
. . . and they read in the book, in the Law of God, distinctly; and
they gave the sense, and caused them to understand the reading."
A revolution in adult education was under way in Jewish life, the
full import of which must be seen within its wider historical
context.

Cyrus, King of Persia, had reversed the depopulation policies
of the Assyrians and Babylonians. In 538 B.C.E. the Jews were
permitted to return to their ancestral home (many remained behind in Babylonia where they had prospered during the years of
Exile) and in 516 B.C.E. the Temple was rebuilt. The Torah, or
Pentateuch, which Ezra brought with him from Babylon was
probably almost identical with the Torah which now rests in the
Ark of the modern synagogue. In the ninth chapter of the Book
of Nehemiah we read how the people solemnly accepted this
Torah as their constitution. The Book of Genesis was, couched in

the language of myth, the "Declaration of Independence." The "Bill of Rights" and the "Constitution" were incorporated in the other books.

The Persians had granted only religious autonomy to the Jews who had returned to Judea. They had also specifically empowered the religious leaders of the people to enforce religious law. Henceforth the Jews would live under an enforceable theocracy. The head of the government was God. His representatives on earth were the priests. The scribes, a class to whom Ezra the priest belonged, were those who faithfully preserved, transmitted and, above all, explained the meaning of the "Written Constitution."

From the year 444 B.C.E., thanks to the genius of prophet and priest allied with the benign authority of Persian suzerainty, Jewish religion functioned as a book religion. It was generally assumed that God had made known His Will for all time in the Torah which He had revealed. The fact that the editing of the Torah and its reconstruction had taken place within living memory proved no obstacle to the new religious developments. Under the prevailing categories of thinking, the Law revealed to Moses must clearly have included the truth, even the truth which only became evident at a later stage in history. The ancients utterly lacked what we would designate as a sense of historical perspective. This mode of thinking was to facilitate the development of a profoundly important concept which radically changed Jewish life—the concept of an Oral Torah alongside of the Written Torah.

From the moment the Torah was confined to writing it became, like all written law, out of date. Interpretation was necessary to make it relevant. This function was first performed by the scribes. There must always have been an oral tradition in addition to the written, but never before had the spiritual leaders had the right to enforce such law. Moreover, the spiritual need was the greater because the Jews were now a Church (*ecclesia*) rather than a people. They were neither sovereign nor autonomous in their own right. Their preoccupation with religion was, understandably, greater.

The details of the process which produced the Oral Torah are not too clear. Systematic commentary on and interpretation of the Torah began with Ezra. Influences of Greek thought have been detected. By the time of the Maccabees, some two and a half centuries later, zeal for the Torah was widespread. (We may contrast this zeal with the wide prevalence of Jewish intermarriage with Gentile wives, even in the family of the High Priest, in the time of Ezra. Nehemiah describes serious lapses in religious observance.) A group of *Chasidim*, or pious ones (not to be confused with the Chasidic movement of the eighteenth century), would rather die than refrain from observing the Sabbath, even when attacked in battle. They followed rigorous laws of ethical, moral and spiritual discipline. On pain of death, against the express edict of Antiochus Epiphanes, children were circumcized, the Torah studied, the dietary laws observed. (The dietary laws have negligible pentateuchal support. The vast majority of their minutiae are part of the Oral Law.)

By the second pre-Christian century the Pharisees, descendants of the *Chasidim*, emerged as a full-fledged party in opposition to the priestly Sadducees. It is they who brought the concept of Oral Torah to its full stature. By one of the strangest paradoxes of history that incident which more than any other set into motion the chain of events which would lead to those Pharisaic interpretations which were to dominate Jewish life and thought for close on two thousand years: the public promulgation of the Torah by Ezra, took place on the first day of the seventh month, *Rosh Hashanah*. By the time the Pharisees had finished with the New Year it would no longer be a merely sacerdotal occasion celebrated in the confines of the Temple so that the whole people could blissfully pursue an entirely different course of action in the courtyard outside. *Rosh Hashanah* would become a day of Judgment for the whole House of Israel, a day when all Jews

would throng the house of God, proclaiming His sovereignty and
Divine justice.

The process of interpretation of the Torah commenced seriously with the priest-scribes. It ended with lay leaders. In the
time of Ezra, the Jewish religion was largely a sacerdotal matter.
While Ezra was expounding the Torah to the people gathered in
the Temple courtyard the priests were performing the New Year
ritual within, blowing the trumpets as prescribed by tradition,
offering the requisite sacrifices. At that time Jewish education,
for what it was, apparently was exclusively sacerdotal. The
priests had some form of schooling system by which they transmitted the skills required in the correct performance of the
Temple rites to a new generation of priests.

It is an ancient rabbinic tradition that the education of the
Jewish child commence with the Book of Leviticus. This, the
third book of the Torah, consists largely of the detailed laws
governing sacrifices. It specifies the different occasions which call
for sacrifices, the kind of animals which may properly be sacrificed on these occasions, their mode of slaughter and the legal
minutiae governing their subsequent immolation or consumption.
But why should children first be introduced at a tender age to the
details of the sacrificial system especially by the Rabbis whose
life's work, in a sense, was to provide in their legal and liturgical
creations a substitute for the sacrificial system?

The evidence points to the Book of Leviticus as the core curriculum of the earliest schools in ancient Israel. These schools
clustered around the sanctuaries and, later, the Temple. As in the
manner of Samuel's apprenticeship to Eli, the young priests
would there be trained in the techniques of the sacrificial system.
These techniques were to be found detailed in the Book of Leviticus. There was no formal education at this stage for non-
priestly children or, indeed, for adults.

But by the turn of the millennium, when Jewish education
among old and young was widespread, thanks to the religious

revolution started by the scribes and carried to its consummation by the Pharisees, the original reason for the selection of the Book of Leviticus as a core curriculum was no longer relevant or valid. When the Temple fell in 70 C.E. sacrifices ceased. Whether or not the later Rabbis remembered the original reason, they continued to maintain the ancient tradition but with a new rationale. Now that the Torah, as the Word of God, was available to any Jew prepared to study its meaning, priestly prerogatives were given an ethical significance and were extended to the whole people. Since the sacrifices offered in the Temple, the Rabbis argued, atoned for sin and thereby made the Jewish people pure, let those who were pure, that is, the innocent young children, occupy themselves in their first stage of Jewish education with what makes for purity, namely, the detailed laws of the sacrificial system. An old ritual and sacerdotal tradition was thus typically made to embody a new ethical insight. Even after the destruction of the Temple the Rabbis prayed for its rebuilding and the restoration therein of the sacrificial system. The traditional prayer book still includes those prayers.

By the time of the Pharisees a revolution had taken place in Jewish life. The dominant interpretation of what it meant to be a Jew was no longer sacerdotal but lay. When the Pharisees emerged on the stage of Jewish history they were one party among others in Jewish life. They were, however, according to all reports, the party most loved by the masses of the people. The religion they propounded was no longer narrowly sacerdotal but democratic. Not only those who were born priests, descendants of Zadok (hence, probably, *Zadokim* or Sadducees) the High Priest in the days of King Solomon, from whom priestly status descended, could be holy but all the people could be holy. Heredity was not the determining factor in the Jew's status in his religion; it was his ability to interpret the Torah and lead a holy and just life in accordance with its dictates. No single saying of the Pharisees sums up more aptly the nature of the revolution they accomplished in Jewish life than their affirmation that an illegitimate scholar of the Torah, who derives his status solely from his expertise in interpreting the Torah, takes precedence over a High Priest who is an *am ha-aretz* or ignoramus, literally, one of the people of the land. The aristocracy of birth had given way to the aristocracy of learning.

The Hebrew word for the Pharisees may derive from the verb *parash* (plural noun, *perushim*, or Pharisees), which means "to expound," that is, to expound the Torah. This, certainly, was their prime goal in life. "The Torah which Moses commanded us was intended to be the inheritance of the whole congregation of Jacob." This unique rendering of an ancient scriptural verse was the Pharisees' religious byword. The synagogue as an institution for sacred gathering together on Sabbaths and Festivals undoubtedly goes back to the time of the Babylonian Exile. Then, in the absence of the Temple and purifying rites, the survivors discussed sacred texts and listened to moral exhortations from their spiritual leaders. Indeed, the very concept of a nonsacerdotal religion must have first occurred there to the minds of the spiritual leaders. The absence of a Temple, even if only for a short period of time, gave birth to a new idea about the possibilities of a Jewish religion without a Temple. To the Psalmist's anguished question, "How shall we sing the Lord's song on foreign soil?" the spiritual leaders replied, "By studying the Word of the Lord."

By the time the Pharisees emerged on the stage of Jewish history, the synagogue was their unique distinguishing institution. It was more than a house of prayer. They fashioned it in their image. It was primarily a house of study. It was the place where any Jew, be he priest, Levite or Israelite, the three hereditary castes, might come and achieve direct communion with God solely through the study of His Torah within a context of tradition. (The common Hebrew patronyms Cohen, Levi and Israel stem from these original hereditary distinctions.) It was the Pharisees who were responsible for the dissemination of Jewish

learning in the ancient world. They instituted synagogues and
schools in every place where there was a settlement of Jews and
strongly advised against living in places which lacked these fundamental religious facilities.

It is more than likely that the nascent idea of democratic Jewish education of a nonsacerdotal nature, whose origins must be
traced back to the reforms of Ezra, received added impetus and
stimulus from Greek ideas. These began to permeate Palestinian
life as early as the fifth pre-Christian century. The concept of
paideia, or education as practiced in the Greek gymnasia, must
have fascinated those Jews who came into contact with it. But
the difference between *paideia* and the Pharisaic concept of
Talmud Torah, or the study of Torah, is crucial. The Pharisees
were obsessed neither with virtues nor skills but with holiness.
Talmud Torah is *moral* education, not just merely education.

We cannot rely too much on Josephus or the New Testament
for our knowledge of the Pharisees. Josephus was an apologist for
his Roman patrons. The authors of the New Testament, in their
desire to diminish the role of Pontius Pilate in the crucifixion of
Jesus (for obvious propagandistic reasons in the Roman Empire),
quite deliberately vilified the Jews. Because of their rejection by
the Pharisees, or Rabbis, as these leaders are referred to by the
turn of the millennium, the early Christians tendentiously substi-
tuted Pharisees for Sadducees throughout the gospel story.

The Sadducees, as the ruling aristocratic class, had the closest
associations of all Jews at the time of Jesus with the Roman
forces occupying Palestine. The Pharisees tended to shun all political involvement. They wanted to be free to serve God alone.
Their experience at the hands of the Hasmonean dynasty had not
been happy. They had seen how the Maccabeean revolution,
which began with moral and religious idealism ended, in the later
Hasmonean kings, with political corruption and religious oppression. "Try to avoid all contact with the Roman government in
Palestine," cautioned Shemaiah, a leader of the Pharisees in the
first pre-Christian century.

The Sadducees, rather than the Pharisees, would have been most concerned with assisting the government in putting down any sedition on the part of Jews. A pseudo-Messiah claiming to be, or permitting himself to be claimed, King of the Jews, as Jesus is described in the gospel story, would have been a thorn in the side of the Sadducees as well as of the Romans. Such a one would be a prime target for suppression. Sadduceean status quo was intimately bound up with that of the Roman government. The Romans were, above all, anxious for peace on their borders. Pretensions to the throne of Judea, albeit couched in theological idiom, were invariably ruthlessly crushed by them. The Jews were notorious for sedition and constant insurrections flared up in Palestine under Roman rule.

The supreme legislative body of the Jews at the time of Jesus was the Sanhedrin, a Greek word meaning "sitting together." It is believed that there were two of these institutions operating at the time of Jesus. There was a religious high court of justice controlled by the Pharisees, which was the legislative body for their legal reforms. This was grounded on democratic principles. It was open to the most distinguished students of the Torah, regardless of their origin. Indeed, some of its most distinguished members were proselytes. The other Sanhedrin, based on aristocratic principles, was controlled by the Sadducees and was the body which functioned as a political link between the Jews and the Romans.

If Jesus were indeed condemned by the Sanhedrin it would have been the Sadduceean Sanhedrin, or political governing body of the Jews, which handed over Jesus, as a potentially seditious troublemaker, to the secular arm of Pontius Pilate. On any reckoning, crucifixion was an exclusively Roman form of punishment. At that time the Jews no longer possessed the power to try capital offenses. Jewish involvement in the death of Jesus even to this extent is not unequivocal from the sources. Jesus would have been primarily the enemy of Rome, not of a broken and subject people policed by an army of occupation.

When the early Christians realized that the Jews were largely uninterested in Jesus' Messianic pretensions they turned to the Gentiles in the Roman Empire in the hope of making converts. But how could the gospel story be effectively presented to a Roman world in which the chief protagonist, Pontius Pilate, and the Sadduceean supporters of Rome, were presented in an unfavorable light as the prime persecutors of Jesus and ultimately responsible for his death? A deliberate and tendentious rewriting of history took place. The Jewishness of Jesus was minimized (it could hardly have been denied). Pontius Pilate, an unscrupulous rascal according to Roman sources, was translated into a Socratic saint. He was made to appear devoid of all responsibility for the crucifixion, permitting himself to be browbeaten by a handful of Jews in his courtyard on the Eve of Passover into crucifying Jesus, against his better judgment. This portrayal of the representative of Roman power in Judea of the first century is contradicted by unimpeachable historical evidence. The philosophical, mild and gentle Pilate is a figment of the imagination of those who rewrote the gospel story for conversion purposes.

At the time of this rewriting, the early centuries of the Christian era, the Jews and the Pharisees were one and the same. All other sects had declined or disappeared when the Temple was destroyed in 70 c.e. It was the Pharisaic Jews who rejected Jesus. All the more reason for substituting them in the gospel story for the formerly pro-Roman Sadducees as the arch instigators of the death of Jesus. So the Jesus of the rewritten gospel, who has kind words for brigands, thieves, prostitutes and women taken in adultery, has nothing but vicious contempt for the Pharisees, those spiritual and ethical geniuses who translated the precepts of the prophets into the tangible currency of rabbinic custom and ritual.

If the dictionary definition of "Pharisee" is still given as "being strict in doctrine and ritual, without the spirit of piety; laying stress upon the outward show of religion and morality, and assuming superiority on that account; hypocritical, formal; self-

righteous," this is in no small measure due to those who deliberately vilified a most honorable group of spiritual leaders for the
purpose of gaining converts to Christianity in the Roman Empire.

Every religion which stresses form is bound to have its quota
of formalists. The Pharisees themselves were extremely self-
critical in this respect. But to designate the sect as a whole as
"hypocrites . . . blind guides, which strain at a gnat and swallow a
camel . . . whited sepulchres, which indeed appear beautiful outward, but are within full of dead men's bones" is a monstrous
historical inaccuracy and profound religious injustice which has
played no small role in fomenting anti-Jewish feeling in the medieval and modern periods. Indeed the well-deserved and long-
overdue rehabilitation of the Pharisees has only been effected in
our own century through the labors of Jewish scholars of the
caliber of J. Z. Lauterbach and Christian scholars such as George
Foot Moore and R. Travers Herford. The results of their re-
search are now accepted by most Christian scholars.

The other consuming passion of the Pharisees was their desire
for holiness. They did not reject the Temple. They even had a
synagogue in the Temple. But their desire was to transform the
whole of the Jewish people into priests. By a process of extension
they applied many of the laws originally applicable only to the
priests to themselves, especially those laws governing ritual purity. Here we arrive at the second possible significance of their
Hebrew designation, *perushim*, which can also mean "the sepa-
ratists." This name may have been given them by their opponents. Or they may have adopted it voluntarily. In either case
there is much substance to the designation. For in order to maintain the most rigorous discipline in religious matters the Pharisees
grouped themselves together in the cities into *chavurot*, or cells.
Each Pharisee was known also as a *chaver*, or associate. The
chaverim were pledged to maintain scrupulously all the laws
governing their lives as found in the Torah or as interpreted

therefrom by them or their predecessors, and which together constituted the Oral Law.

Clearly such strictness in religious life could not at first be for the masses, any more than the early intuitions of the prophets could be shared by the masses. At the time of Jesus the Pharisees were merely an extremely powerful party within Jewish life. Most importantly they were utterly beloved of the people. Even those Jews who did not follow their strict regimen regarded them as outstanding representatives of the good life. When the secular authorities attempted to interfere with the Pharisees they had the whole people to reckon with.

This brings us to the crucial difference between the Pharisees and the Sadducees. Both groups existed within the framework of what had been accomplished by Ezra. The Torah was their common ground. But the Sadducees claimed that the many laws and interpretations derived from the Written Torah, and not actually found literally therein, were not binding. The Pharisees not only insisted that such inferences from the Torah were binding; they claimed that the Oral Torah, whose development they had done so much to foster, was equal in authority to the Written Torah. Since they were the experts in the interpretation of the Torah such a claim conferred great status on them. They were at the edge of an expanding universe of Torah. Moreover the Pharisees claimed that many traditional practices beloved by the masses of the people, but for which no sanction could be found either in the scriptural text or by interpretation therefrom, were originally revealed by God to Moses on Sinai. The Oral Torah and the authority for its continued expansion through the authoritative and accredited representatives of those to whom the Revelation had originally been given were, they believed, coeval with the original act of Revelation.

Like the Samaritans and the Karaites the Sadducees understood the Torah narrowly. They took literally the injunction, "Ye shall kindle no fire in your habitations on the Sabbath," sitting in the cold and the dark. The Pharisees introduced the custom of lighting candles before the commencement of the Sabbath. They also permitted the consumption of food, cooked before the Sabbath, kept hot by any act of combustion which was not performed on the Sabbath. They transformed the Jewish home into a Temple, as if anticipating the loss of the actual Temple and making spiritual preparations against that day. But the sanctuary of the home which they elevated was warm and familial, not ritualistic and sacerdotal. They transformed Sabbath and Festival into days of joy and happiness. They buttressed valuable rituals, enshrining important moral insights, with protective regulations. They made "a fence round the Law." Rabbinic religion has, not without justification, been described as "applied" prophetism. It purged Jewish religion of many superstitions and primitive conceptions. Above all, the Pharisees were ethical geniuses, refracting their ethical theory into the practice of the Law. They were universalists within the framework of a specific ethnic context. The universalism of the prophets, they believed (although they did not articulate their belief as such), would best be preserved through the agency of a people with a definite identity dedicated to that goal. Although they were responsible for introducing many new laws, they tended to be more flexible and progressive than the Sadducees in their legal interpretations.

When the Temple was destroyed by the Romans in 70 only the Pharisees were able to cope with the spiritual challenge to Jewish religion without a Temple. The synagogue and the home became the focal points of Jewish life. The Rabbi (the word simply means "my teacher") became the spiritual leader in his capacity of interpreter of the Torah, or jurist. The Pharisaic interpretation of what it meant to be a Jew now swept over the whole Jewish people, even as had, in a previous generation, the prophetic interpretation. From being merely one sect, the Pharisees now remained alone in the field. Jewish religion for the next two thousand years would be rabbinic-Pharisaic.

The Torah contains history as well as law. Commentary on the historical and nonlegal sections of the Torah yielded a rich and fertile field of folklore and legend. In their recasting of Jewish religion and Jewish history in terms of their own highest ideals, the Pharisee-Rabbis tended to reconstruct the past in their own image. The prophets had, at an earlier stage of history, reconstructed their past in similar fashion. All records, memories, laws and traditions existing up to the time of the prophets had been turned by them into one vast cosmic plan with the Divine Creator in charge of the cosmic timetable. Since the prophets, through a combination of their own spiritual genius and the environmental conditions prevailing at the time, had arrived at the intuition that only a God who demanded justice deserved to be considered authentically divine, it was natural that they should superimpose upon the earliest recollections of the people their own burning passion for justice and their own conception of authentic Godhood.

Abraham thus, for the prophets, becomes the embodiment of the man of justice. God knows of Abraham that "he will command his children and his household after him to observe the way of the Lord to do righteousness and justice." In a military foray to defend his nephew, Lot, Abraham refuses to accept any booty. In a dialogue with God over the fate of Sodom and Gomorrah, Abraham manifests a sensitivity for divine justice which appears to exceed Yahweh's. Such memories may well have had a historical substratum. Abraham undoubtedly must have been a charismatic figure. E. A. Speiser has observed: "Although there is no proof so far of Abraham's historicity, many biblical historians would probably agree that if some such figure had not been recorded by the ancients, it would have to be conjectured by the moderns." Nevertheless the biblical narrative bears clear evidence of legendary reworking. The desire to see a burgeoning of justice, the embodiment of the divine in the father of the Jewish people is unquestionably the result of the process of editing the

Torah instigated by the classical prophets and concluded by their immediate successors in ensuing centuries.

In the same fashion, the Pharisees and their successors, the Rabbis, reconstructed the past in their own image. Abraham was conceived by them as a rabbinic Jew who observed meticulously the commandments of the Torah even before they had been revealed by Yahweh. The implication of this profound insight is that the Divine *mitzvot* are as much rooted in the cosmos as are the natural laws. Just as Newton could discover gravity without Revelation so also could Abraham discover the *mitzvot* concerning the Sabbath, even their minutiae, without Revelation.

The Rabbis would not have thus been able to articulate their intuition, but analysis of the sources clearly indicates that both the natural law and the moral law were regarded by them as a covenant established by God and not the result of arbitrary *ad hoc* divine decisions. Jeremiah affirms that Yahweh would as lief break His covenant with the day and the night, the heavens and the earth, as break His covenant with Israel. What we mean by natural law, the ancients referred to as covenant, or *brit*. Since the heavens and all their hosts were not believed to possess the law of their own being, a concept of natural law not being available, their apparent regularity could only have arisen because Yahweh had made a *brit* with them. Indeed, such a covenant with the cosmos is recorded after the Flood, when Yahweh placed the rainbow in the sky as a symbol of the covenant which he now was making with "sowing and harvest, cold and heat, summer and winter, day and night" that they would never cease. Such a *brit* He also made with Israel.

So Abraham, according to the Rabbis, in perhaps the most delightful of these theological anachronisms, baked and partook of *matzah*, or unleavened bread, to celebrate the Festival of Passover some six hundred years before the events on which the Festival is grounded are supposed to have taken place. *Pesach*, as it were, existed before its projection into the world the way gravity existed before Newton discovered it or the way neuroses existed before Freud discovered them. Abraham was such a spiritual genius that he could anticipate Yahweh's Revelation. However extravagant such a claim, the rabbinic view of Abraham is probably far closer to the truth than that of Martin Luther who saw Abraham as a hermit, praying and fasting day and night in anxious anticipation of the coming of the Christ.

The commentary on the nonlegal sections of the Torah became known as *Midrash Aggadah*, or narrative exegesis. In it the Rabbis extended and embellished the bare scriptural narrative. The commentary on the legal sections of the Torah became known as *Midrash Halachah*, or legal exegesis. (*Halachah*, plural *halachot*, literally means "walking," "the way which should be followed," hence, "law.") In the early days, when the amount of interpretation and commentary could be handled easily, the *Halachah* and the *Aggadah* were taught in association with the text which usually was their starting point. Sometimes laws were given which did not have scriptural sanction. These were either new laws which could not be deduced from the text or ancient traditions which, while not deducible from the text, were claimed to possess equal authority with the original Revelation.

In the course of time the commentary grew so vast that it had to be separated from the scriptural text and systematized. Hence emerged the various collections of *Mishnayot* (singular *mishnah*, from the verb *shanah*, to repeat, to teach) culminating in the classical *Mishnah* par excellence of Judah the Prince (135–220). Collections of *Aggadah* also developed, extending their scope to the rest of the books of the Bible. The *Mishnah* of Judah proceeded to elicit the selfsame expansion and exegesis to which the Torah itself had originally been subject. This further interpretation at the hands of many generations of scholars ultimately produced the Talmud (from the verb *lamad*, to learn, hence, learning). The Jerusalem Talmud was edited in the fourth century and the Babylonian, which is the Talmud par excellence, in the fifth.

The same process of commentary and interpretation continued, with the Talmud now as its focus. The massive bulk of the legal literature which developed required further systematization. The bare laws were removed from the mass of argumentation and discussion and organized into Codes. Two of the most famous of these Codes are the *Yad Hachazakah,* or the Mighty Hand, by Moses Maimonides (1135–1204) and the *Shulchan Aruch,* or the Prepared Table, by Joseph Caro (1488–1575). These Codes also became subject to further commentary and interpretation. They were amplified by a vast Responsa literature of questions and answers into a comprehensive system of case law providing precedents.

The attitude of the Pharisees and the Rabbis to the Torah is summed up in the story of the psychiatrist who, when greeted by a fellow psychiatrist with "Good morning," immediately asked himself, "I wonder what he meant by that?" Nothing in the Torah could be taken at face value. It was the Word of God, and God does not speak like ordinary men. The psychopathology of everyday life which Freud detected in our repetitions, slips of the tongue, amnesia, is that which the Rabbis found a thousandfold in the Torah. Not only were repetitions, omissions, strange uses of words, seized upon as profound clues to the workings of the Divine Mind but even innocuous grammatical and syntactical formations were regarded as proof of the most incredible revelations.

From our modern standpoint the Pharisees were using the Torah text largely as a peg on which to hang their own advanced ethical and legal sensitivities. We dare not, however, underestimate their profound belief that the Torah represented the quintessence of Divine Teaching. They would have been horrified at the suggestion that they were innovating. How could the Word of God be improved upon? They were merely eliciting what was already there. A rabbinic comment sums up the Pharisaic attitude toward the comprehensive nature of the original revelation. "Whatever any distinguished disciple of the Sages will at any future date innovate was already given to Moses by God on Mount Sinai."

The Sadducees were thoroughly compromised by their role in the assimilationist Hellenizing which took place in Jerusalem shortly before the Maccabeean revolt of 165 B.C.E. They were also involved in the decadence of the Hasmonean Dynasty when for a brief and, for the most part, inglorious episode the Jewish people regained a modicum of autonomy in their own land after having successively been subject to Babylonians, Persians, Greeks and Seleucids. In 63 B.C.E. Pompey entered Jerusalem and Palestine came effectively under the control of Rome. By the turn of the millennium the Pharisees had succeeded in enforcing their interpretations of Jewish law even upon the Sadducees themselves.

In the decades preceding the destruction of the Temple the High Priest, on the holiest day in the Jewish year, *Yom Kippur*, the Day of Atonement, performed the sacred sacrificial rites in the Temple in accordance with the rulings of the Pharisees. Of the many crucial differences of opinion, one may be singled out. The Sadducees refused to give up the old belief that there was neither resurrection nor immortality. The Torah knew nothing of these "newfangled" theological innovations. The Sadducees also tended to hold to the ancient and more primitive conception of Yahweh reflected in the Torah. This primitive conception held that Yahweh had bodily form and actually resided on Mount Zion in the Temple. On *Yom Kippur* He would be found in the Holy of Holies whither the High Priest alone would go to intercede for the people. But if the High Priest saw Yahweh, he would die. Had not Yahweh said, "No man shall see me and live"?

To prevent such an appalling eventuality, tradition had sanctioned an understanding of the scriptural regulations concerning the entry of the High Priest into the Holy of Holies which afforded a safeguard. Before entering, the High Priest would place burning embers on incense and thus enter surrounded by swirling clouds of smoke. He could not see Yahweh and thus would not be harmed. The Pharisees, in their efforts to elevate the conception of God from an angry Yahweh to the God of all mankind "who is the place of the world but the world is not His place" refused to accept the notion that God could be seen. One of their favorite names for God was *Ha-makom*, literally, the place, pointing to God's omnipresence. They accordingly insisted, against the clear traditional practice, that the High Priest enter the Holy of Holies first and only then, when inside, put the glowing embers on the incense. The Sadducees complied.

The Sadducees were the ruling classes who tended to assimilate. The Pharisees were the party of the people who, with their little cells inside the cities, endeavored to raise the spiritual level of Jewish life by their own personal example. The Essenes were one of many groups who met the problem of being Jewish by turning their backs on society altogether. They left the cities and founded monastic units on the shores of the Dead Sea. There they lived austere, often celibate, lives, studying the Torah and meticulously following the laws concerning ritual purity. As opposed to the Pharisees, and in line with the Sadducees, they tended to a strict interpretation of pentateuchal law.

Scripture said, "Let no man leave his *makom*, or place, on the Sabbath day." The Sadducees interpreted this literally and refused to permit any walking on the Sabbath. Some of the Essenes understood the verse so literally they would not physically leave their tents on the Sabbath even to relieve themselves. The Pharisees, in line with their global attempt to make the cycle of the Jewish year joyful and relevant rather than gloomy and morbid, permitted travel up to two thousand cubits outside of the city limits and, in special circumstances, even beyond. This they achieved by extending the original meaning of *makom*. God, they argued, was good. He would not have enjoined upon the people a pattern of behavior which to them appeared unusually harsh. Therefore *makom* must mean more than place of abode. In fact they were wrong. Their concept of God and religion was far in advance of that implicit in the Torah. The Torah to them was the sounding board for their own active consciences.

The Sadducees, as the ruling class, tended to side with the official government. The Pharisees, with notable exceptions, wished only to be left alone to study the Torah and perform the *mitzvot*. The Zealots who died at Masada followed, for the most part, the rulings of the Pharisees. The Essenes were, on the whole, pacifists but some of them joined the fight against the Romans. One of the greatest of all Pharisaic Rabbis, the great Akiba, pronounced one Bar Kochba to be the Messiah who would save the Jews from the Romans. But these were the exceptions rather than the rule.

Nor were these the only groups in existence at the turn of the millennium. Philo describes an Egyptian sect, the *Therapeutae* who, related to the Essenes, performed constant ritual ablutions. Damascus had a sect which was related to the Sadducees. This group, known as the Sons of Zadok, appears to have emerged within the Sadducees the way the Pharisees emerged within the people at large, as a group demanding higher standards of spirituality. They were at loggerheads with the Sadducees from whom they broke in the second pre-Christian century, presumably because of the Sadduceean policy of Hellenizing. But they were also bitterly opposed to the Pharisees who, they claimed, had usurped the rightful supremacy of the Sadducees. In this they were perfectly right. Authority in Jewish life had indeed passed to the Pharisees. The Sons of Zadok went to live in Damascus and waited hopefully for the Teacher of Righteousness. The Dead Sea Scrolls have thrown light, in recent decades, on other sectarian variations.

Another preoccupation, which tended to cut across "party" lines, was a morbid interest in eschatology, or the doctrine concerning the End. A class of literature emerges in the second pre-Christian century which elaborates on the End of Days and attempts to detect, in the triumph of the wicked and the suffering of the righteous, a foreshadowing of a Final Cosmic Judgment.

This literature, called Apocalypse from a Greek word meaning
"uncovering" (because such intimate cosmic knowledge was only
revealed, disclosed or "uncovered" to the elect few and their
disciples by God), was popular in many of the sects. The Sadducees eschewed it as they tended to shun all practices and beliefs
which had no scriptural warrant. The Pharisees, in sympathy
with the masses, embraced a comprehensive angelology, which is
a prime characteristic of much apocalyptic literature. God is too
holy and remote to speak Himself. His revelations come through
angelic messengers. But they, too, tended to frown on the fantastic excesses of most of the writers of Apocalypse.

All these many sects and groupings which characterize Jewish
life in the first century c.e. share in common the great revolution
effected by the prophets and priests of the previous age. The
Torah is the common theological context of Pharisee, Sadducee,
Essene, Zealot, student of Apocalypse, Damascus sectarian, Dead
Sea Scroll writer. What had seemed a reasonable affirmation of
Jewish *raison d'être* in the fifth pre-Christian century was now
splitting under the strain of manifold interpretations, some of
them mutually exclusive. In the fall of the Temple the problem
was resolved. Only that group which had become sufficiently
decentralized to survive in the absence of the Temple and in the
absence of any hope for political autonomy lived on.

The destruction of the Temple in 70 c.e. spelled the demise of
all groups save the Pharisees. The literalness of the Sadducees
would emerge again in the eighth century in the pentateuchal
textbound sect of the Karaites. The asceticism of the Essenes and
the other sectarians of their ilk would reappear in a variety of
forms, from the self-mortifications of some of the medieval mys-
tics to the rigorous harshness, under pressure of the cruel conditions of medieval life, of some rabbinic authorities. The preoccupation of students of the apocalyptic with the End would surface
again in the study of *cabala*. Pseudo-Messianism, manifest in the
heroic affirmation of an Akiba, would continue intermittently to

function as a pathetic will-o'-the-wisp, deceiving and misleading countless Jews anxiously anticipating the End of days and a release from Exile.

The incredible stamina of the Zealots of Masada, culminating in a collective act of suicide in 73 C.E., would be, at least in its final stage, repeated in medieval York and elsewhere. That selfsame martial spirit, overwhelmed with the Maccabees, almost quenched in the Zealots, would go underground until an incredible resurrection in the Jewish self-defense units of pogrom-ridden Russia, the gallant defenders of the Warsaw Ghetto, the Haganah, the Irgun and the armed forces of the modern State of Israel. But it was the Pharisees who would be the bearers of all these spiritual, political, social, cultural and moral genes. For them the years immediately following 70 were the years of their greatest creativity. To them had fallen the succession. This was the age of giants, of Yochanan ben Zaccai and his famous pupils, of Ishmael and Akiba, of Meir and Tarphon. The stage was set for two thousand years of further survival.

The prophetic notion that Yahweh was not only God of Israel but of all the world prevented Israel from succumbing when she was exiled successively by the Assyrians and Babylonians. The belief that God had permitted the Exile, nay, engineered it, was a profoundly important ingredient in Jewish survival. It provided sustaining fuel for the flickering will to live. In the same fashion that it was inevitable in the eighth pre-Christian century for small nations to succumb in the path of Assyria's drive to the Mediterranean, so it was inevitable in later centuries for Israel, despite the short-lived glory of the Maccabeean episode, to be destined to be a Diaspora people. Never again would Israel's people be entirely coterminous with Israel's soil. By the turn of the millennium it is estimated that as many Jews lived outside of Palestine as within.

Although the Pharisees did not consciously plan it thus, their religious reforms gave every Jew a portable homeland and a portable polity. Wherever a quorum of ten Jewish males existed, a full Jewish life could be led. If the Jew survived in a hostile world until the French Revolution, without serious inner deterioration, it is to the religious genius of the Pharisees that he is indebted.

"The distortion of a text," wrote Freud, "is not unlike a murder. The difficulty lies not in the execution of the deed but in the doing away with the traces." We cannot accuse the Rabbis or the prophets of distorting the past deliberately. Distortion of that kind presupposes a degree of sophistication and perspective which neither the Rabbis nor the prophets possessed. Nevertheless, a dispassionate and objective survey of the evidence clearly indicates that both the Rabbis and the prophets projected onto the past ideas and conceptions which their predecessors could not possibly have entertained. In their belief that the Torah of the Lord was perfect, the Pharisees assumed that anything which they themselves deemed perfect must therefore be found somewhere in the Torah of the Lord. They thus claimed scriptural proof for the doctrine of resurrection and immortality. But the biblical period knows nothing of this doctrine, which first emerges in the third pre-Christian century. Moreover "traces" of the original biblical doctrine abound which belie such theological naiveté. The Pharisees were not disturbed. Their faith was great. What to the modern are warts on the face of the Torah were to the Pharisees beauty spots.

The prophets likewise "distorted" the text of their past by projecting onto pre-eighth-century Israelite history their own ideas about God, Israel and human destiny. No more than the Pharisees who "distorted" their text could they do away with the abundant traces which may be found in the Bible of preprophetic Israelite religion and history. Those vestigial traces, together with evidence from comparative religion and archeology, combine to present us with a picture of the origin of Israel somewhat different from that described in those ancient texts and traditions subsequently edited under the influence of the prophetic view of history. The prophets saw in the history of Israel the unfolding of a Divinely planned Cosmic Timetable. Reality, insofar as we can reconstruct it, tells a somewhat different story.

In their origin the Israelites seem to have been no different from other seminomadic Semites who wandered from the Arabian desert into the Fertile Crescent in the beginning of the second pre-Christian millennium. Vast migrations of people occurred in this region at that time. The mass exodus from the desert undoubtedly was related to the drying up of oases and cognate changes in living conditions. Such mass migrations are often the starting point for the birth of a people. The Greeks are a case in point. Of the many clans involved in these migrations one particular Semitic family was later remembered as having passed through Ur of the Chaldees. Ur was destroyed in war in the early part of the second pre-Christian millennium (1960 B.C.E.). If Abraham and his family had departed thence before the destruction, as may reasonably be conjectured, we can imagine with what feelings of relief such an escape must have been interpreted. It was an exodus from Egypt in microcosm. It was given, as was the later Exodus, a personal and divine connotation. Deliverance was for a purpose.

Two ancient insights in the scriptural record give us some idea of the tensions in the days of wandering. The clashes that must have taken place when the seminomadic Semites with their sheep and goats impinged upon the more settled agriculturists of the Fertile Crescent are probably remembered in the story of Cain and Abel and the biblical injunction against wearing clothes made of a mixture of linen and wool. The friction between those who depended for their livelihood on settled patterns of agriculture and those who wandered from place to place with their cattle, a prime source of destruction of growing crops, must have been bitter and intense. Many of the migrating families kept on the move. Some tilled the soil for a while and then, with their herds, continued on their wanderings in the search for more fertile soil and richer pasture. Some of those associated with Abraham's family went as far as Egypt. Others remained in Canaan. The Torah unequivocally remembers that "my father was a wandering Aramean."

A change of ruler in Egypt led to those Hebrews (the word probably means those who have come from the other side of the river), descendants of Abraham who had wandered there, being subjected, in common with other ethnic minorities, to slavery. The later Isaiah was to see in Cyrus the Persian's reversal of the depopulation policy of the Babylonians and Assyrians a personal gesture by Yahweh on behalf of His chosen people. In fact Cyrus did for the Babylonian Jews what he did for all depopulated peoples. Nevertheless, Isaiah calls Cyrus God's "anointed." Even so, in Egypt, a decision to press ethnic minorities into slave labor was interpreted by later generations as a deliberate singling out by Pharaoh of the Children of Israel. Yahweh, indeed, is envisaged as having predicted to Abraham that his seed would be subject to such bondage for four hundred years. The Cosmic Timetable must run in accordance with Yahweh's planning. The original inhabitants of the Promised Land must not be disturbed until their iniquity is full and the time of their destruction has arrived. Only then can God's chosen ones enter.

The Hebrews escaped from Egypt under the leadership of Moses. At the commencement of their wandering through the desert they entered into a covenant with Yahweh and, at Horeb-Sinai, received His Torah. It is this escape from Egypt which was to leave an indelible impression on the minds of generations of Israelites. That experience of being delivered from bondage engendered in them, and especially in the countless generations who rehearsed that experience in every age, a feeling that freedom was not expedient but grounded in the very cosmos. The imperative to freedom was Divine in origin. God had brought them out of Egypt. At the crossing of the Red Sea an ancient poet, describing what he himself had witnessed or, in the manner of poets, identifying with those who had crossed, points to God as the deliverer: "This is my God."

It is in connection with the departure from Egypt that the Torah records a fusing between two ideas of God. "I appeared to Abraham, Isaac and Jacob as *El Shaddai*, or God Almighty" says Yahweh to Moses at the episode of the burning bush at Horeb. "They did not know Me as Yahweh." The God associated with the traumatic experience of release from bondage to freedom is thus linked with the God of past generations. In general the impact by the tensions of the journey made on the Israelites who left Egypt under Moses were so profound that when they finally returned to Canaan even those of their erstwhile blood brothers who had remained in Canaan identified with their experiences. They, too, had been delivered from bondage under Pharaoh. Those who descended from the Egyptian survivors and those who merely identified with them would together affirm in subsequent commemorations of that incredible experience of deliverance: "We were slaves to Pharaoh in Egypt."

Yahweh is a wild and savage God. He is a fighter. He drowned the Egyptians in the Red Sea. "Who is like Thee, Yahweh, among the other gods?" He speaks in the thunder and the earthquake, in the lightning and the storm. Mount Sinai is not volcanic and yet the description of Yahweh's revelation there is unquestionably the description of an earthquake. The pillar of cloud by day and the pillar of fire by night which accompanied the people on their wanderings also seem to relate to a volcanic phenomenon. Yet there are no extinct volcanoes in the desert, either in Sinai or in Midian, in which the Israelites wandered, reportedly for forty years. The volcanic image comes from the Arabian desert as does also the image of the thunderstorm. In Hauran and Arabia both these experiences must have been immediate. The two most awe-inspiring recollections of those who had once endured the hardships of the Arabian desert and the ascent of the Arabian mountains were the wild storms and the volcanic eruptions. These childhood experiences of the group were now projected onto current awareness of the divine. Present experience of God is described by a vocabulary, imagery and idiom one

stage removed from direct experience. The process is well known
to students of religion and culture. It is the clue to religious
development and evolution. The religious present must be approached through the religious past.

In the early centuries of the settlement in Canaan there is little
to choose between the loosely knit clashing tribes with memories
going back to Egypt and Abraham with their protecting God of
Hosts, Yahweh the mighty, and the local inhabitants. The recollection of Yahweh as a God who delivers from oppression is
carried along by a handful of devotees who cluster around the
Ark and the tablets of stone which symbolize the Decalogue and
Divine Revelation.

None of the neat and systematic patterns with which the
Torah describes the wanderings of the Israelites, nor even of
their settlement, can be taken at face value. We have to remember who wrote these records. The disciplined transmission of the
promise made to Abraham through the sons of Jacob, the geo-
metrical patterns of the sanctuary and the lines of march through
the desert are all part of later projections. Raw reality did not
measure up to the ideal dreams of later spiritual minds who saw
the entry into Canaan as a falling off from a former perfection.
The desert trek was a constant tussle between a slave people with
a slave mentality against which the spiritual aspirations of a minority leadership battled almost in vain. Once in Canaan, the spiritual leaders were all but swamped by the prevailing decadence.
The Torah itself conceded that the people were stiff-necked. It
does not mince words in describing the rebellions against Moses
and Aaron, the golden calf, the following of strange gods, the
betraying of Yahweh, the loss of faith in His power to save. Yet
even these concessions are framed within an ideal context. The
spiritual leaders undoubtedly played a lesser role than that as-
signed by Scripture. The affluence of Canaanite civilization and
its seductively immoral religious fertility rites are seen by them as
a deadly peril. They stress the austerity and discipline of the

desert. But these recollections are as much of a remote as of an immediate past.

The Rechabites, otherwise known as the Kenites, descendants of Jethro, the father-in-law of Moses, embodied the ideals of which the spiritual leaders speak. They maintained the simple ways of the desert, living in tents, refusing wine and strong drink. In their adherence to the earlier nomadic ideal in protest against the decadence of Canaanite affluence they kept alive the recollection of Yahweh and His ethical demands on His people. But the biblical record gives the impression that the ideal is constantly in view of the people even though they rejected it. The impression is given that the prophet is in the forefront of life, that the devotee of Yahweh plays a crucial role in historical development. In fact this, too, is a later reworking of reality. There is clear evidence in the Bible that the religion of Yahweh was virtually forgotten during these centuries.

It is difficult for those of us who look at the preprophetic period through the eyes of the prophets to appreciate how low the fortunes of Yahweh sank after the entry into Canaan. It is even more difficult for those of us who look at the biblical God through the eyes of the prophets to appreciate how primitive and savage was the conception of divinity in preprophetic days. In the story of the binding of Isaac we see how closely even the finest representatives of biblical thought came to the notion, commonly believed and widely practiced in those days, that God demanded the sacrifice of the first-born son.

Jephthah's treatment of his daughter is a case in point. Yahweh is displeased with Onan and promptly kills him for an act of *coitus interruptus*. When the Ark of Yahweh is being brought from the house of Abinadab at Gibeah to Jerusalem in the presence of King David the oxen stumble so that the Ark almost falls. Uzza, the son of Abinadab, puts out his hand to steady the Ark, which was in danger of falling. Yahweh kills him on the spot. Nadab and Abihu commit an error in the performance of a ritual associated with a sacrifice in the Tabernacle in the wilderness. Yahweh kills them.

Despite the apparent barbarisms associated with Yahweh, an important insight is nonetheless conveyed in all these ghoulish stories. Yahweh's favor is so vitally important for the well-being of Israel that the way He is approached is literally a matter of life and death. The nearest analogy to the manner in which these ancients conceived of the divine in its relationship to man would be that of electricity. Electricity is a force which, when utilized properly, can provide man with many necessities. When approached without proper precautions, electricity can kill. So also with the Divine. Yahweh can provide all sorts of good things for man if man treats Him respectfully, especially approaching Him through the requisite ritual paraphernalia. But if, by accident, man should come upon Yahweh without such precautions having been taken, Yahweh will kill. It is not that Yahweh wants to kill as much as Yahweh has to kill. It is in the very nature of divinity. Yahweh, as it were, cannot help Himself. The state of mind of the victim is irrelevant.

A later generation would see in the Temple a veritable power-house of Divinity generated constantly through the ministrations of priest and Levite. The central turbine, as it were, the sacrificial altar, constantly fed, with appropriate "fuel," provided a steady ongoing flow of Divine beneficence. But the ritual had to be performed exactly. Ritual purity must reign supreme. Should any dust of ritual impurity be permitted to enter the Holy Place, the generation of divinity would cease. Should anyone who entered the Temple, even unwittingly, do so in a state of ritual impurity dire consequences would follow. The fate of Heliodorus, chancellor of Seleucus IV who, as described in the apochryphal books of Maccabees, entered the Temple to steal its treasures, may be likened to a man who touches an electrical wire without having taken proper precautions. He is carried out unconscious.

Up to the eighth pre-Christian century when the classical prophets first appear the devotees of Yahweh are an unimportant and unnoticed minority. In the biblical period the king rules. The leaders of the people are the priests, the judges, the sages, the warriors. There is no real attention paid to the classical prophets even when they begin to preach. There are a group of false prophets who tell the king what he wants to hear, that Yahweh will protect the people regardless of their behavior. Only in the aftermath of destruction do the survivors of the fall of Jerusalem repent them of their evil ways. Israel and Judah have to fall before the prophets are taken seriously. But for the prophets, ancient Israel would have gone the way of all ancient political flesh. And but for the Pharisees who translated their ethical insights into tangible behavior patterns, the Jewish people would not have survived the destruction of the Temple in 70 C.E.

A people may be compared analogically to a single human being. No analogy is perfect but a good analogy can throw light on a mass of details, highlighting the essentials. In the time of Abraham the Jewish people is conceived. At the time of the Exodus it is born. With the prophets it achieves self-consciousness. In Pharisaic Judaism it arrives at a formulation of maturity. But even maturity has different levels. The impact between modernism and Pharisaic-rabbinic Judaism in the modern world has shattered that first formulation of maturity. As with an individual, so with a people, the shattering of a world outlook due to unprecedented traumas and conditions leads to a "nervous breakdown." In a sense the Jewish people suffered such a "nervous breakdown" in the nineteenth century. This breakdown was compounded in the twentieth century by the Holocaust and the not unrelated resurgence, for the first time in almost two thousand years, of Jewish nationalism. Zionism, of course, originated before the Nazi era. It was, however, profoundly intensified by the rise of Hitler. The fragmentation of contemporary Jewish life is a direct outcome of this situation.

The Jewish people is currently undergoing a stage of radical transition in coming to terms with life in the modern world. One type of therapy used on the individual in connection with a "nervous breakdown" arising from traumatic shocks is psychoanalysis. One of the prime goals of psychoanalysis is the unraveling of early childhood memories which unconsciously tie past subjective emotional reactions to current external and objective realities. Cure is effected when the patient ceases to cope with current realities in terms of reactions built up in the context of childhood memories.

Perhaps it would be more valid to say that the individual cannot but cope with current realities in terms of reactions built up in the context of childhood memories. Our patterns of interpersonal relationships, our very falling in love, are grounded in a matrix of emotional responses built up in relationship to those we first loved and hated. It is when we suffer "nervous breakdowns," when our neurotic behavior seriously interferes with the creative control of our lives, that the origin of our patterns of reaction become important. The man who falls in love and marries a woman who, on some unconscious level, reminds him of the woman whom first he loved, is healthy. The man who falls in love with and marries a woman he consciously identifies as his mother, which leads to profound sexual maladjustment, is sick and in need of help. The difference between "normal" and "abnormal" is the presence of debilitating symptoms.

There is an important sense in which the Jewish people endeavored to provide for itself an "autopsychoanalysis" in the aftermath of the breakdown resulting from the impact between modernism and premodernism. There arose a movement in Germany dedicated to the proposition that every fact about the early childhood of the Jewish people should be discovered and articulated. If only we can demonstrate what the origin of synagogal liturgy really is, if only we can show who the Pharisees really were, then the condition of Jewish life will improve. But fundamental to the psychoanalytical process, even when performed on oneself as in the case of Freud, is a profound feeling of love and concern for the subject. The doctor must deeply care for his patient to within a hairsbreadth of being himself involved in a countertransference. In the absence of an authentic transference relationship between patient and doctor, the magic spell of relating the past inappropriately to the present cannot be broken. In the absence of such therapeutic insight, symptoms remain and multiply.

Many of these learned scholars who busily dissected manuscripts and analyzed texts, bringing to light for the first time unknown facts about the early childhood of the Jewish people, often did so destructively, albeit unwittingly. Some were quite articulate about their belief that the Jewish people was sick unto death. One of the most distinguished even affirmed that, in his phenomenal task of cataloguing all extant Jewish books and manuscripts, he was providing the Jewish people with a decent burial. Let the world know what the Jewish people was.

Even the best of these scientific scholars of the Jewish past had only a partial grasp of the essential nature of the Jewish people. They tended to see the Jews as representatives of a pure monotheistic ideal, a people of metaphysicians. Others saw the Jews as transmitters of a Revealed Religion. It remained for a scholar by name of Mordecai M. Kaplan to approach the sick patient with a love for the total Jewish people, in all its manifestations, to break through to a radically new concept of the nature of Judaism and the Jewish people. Judaism, Kaplan argued, was the evolving religious civilization of the Jewish people. Such a synoptic hypothesis to account for the realities of the Jewish people's past and present also gave hope for a future.

Judaism, according to Reconstructionism (which is the name given to the philosophy of Jewish existence developed by Kaplan), is more than religion. It is a total civilization. In the past Judaism has gone through three distinct stages, the *biblical* (to 586 B.C.E.), the *ecclesiastical* (586 B.C.E. to 70 C.E.) and the *rabbinic* (70 C.E. to 1789). In passing from the biblical to the ecclesiastical and from the ecclesiastical to the rabbinic stages, Judaism

underwent a radical metamorphosis. In fact one might be for-
given for believing that the religion of the biblical stage and that
of the later stages are different religions did he not know that the
same historically continuous people identified with all three
stages. Identity in change was possible because the Jewish people
in all of these different stages cherished the same *sancta* (from
sanctum), or holy things. Three basic sancta, God, Torah and
Israel, were radically reconstructed over these three stages. But
the reconstruction took place within the framework of an ongoing historical people.

In the biblical stage, when the people lived an autonomous life
on their own soil, religion was but one of many preoccupations,
as is the case with all peoples. In addition to religious interests
there were military, political, artistic and general cultural con-
cerns characteristic of a total normal civilization. In the ecclesiastical stage, when the Jews were no longer politically autonomous, they became preoccupied with religion. It was as if those
energies which a normal people would expend in political and
cultural outlets were now sublimated into religion. In the rabbinic stage, when the Jews were not only lacking in political
autonomy but were also exiled from their own soil, religion became their exclusive preoccupation. The plurality and diversity
of definitions of what it means to be a Jew in the twentieth
century arise from a faulty diagnosis of the past. Those religious
or secular groups which see Judaism exclusively in ritual behavior, revealed religion, ethical monotheism, secularism, language or nationalism are mistaking the part for the whole.
Judaism is the total civilization of the Jewish people. Whatever
contributes to the welfare of the Jewish people also contributes
to Judaism.

History has made of that civilization a religious civilization.
But under the impact of modernism a reconstruction of Jewish
life must take place. Religion, while a primary ingredient of
Jewish life, cannot continue to be its exclusive preoccupation
now that Jews live under democracy. This fourth stage in Jewish

life, Kaplan argues, is the *democratic* stage. It is characterized by the Jew living in two civilizations, his own ethnic Judaism and that of the country in which he is domiciled. Because of the conditions of freedom in modern democracies, where being Jewish is a purely voluntary matter, neither theological nor ritual conformity can henceforth be the unifying force in Jewish life. Jews are subject to far too great a variety of influences for this to be possible or even desirable. The central preoccupation of Jewish life must be the Jewish people. When the Jewish people is healthy Jewish religion will look after itself. Jewish religion will continue to be grounded in the sancta. But the sancta will admit of wider interpretation than before, as befits the democratic stage of Jewish existence.

Crucial to the thesis of Reconstructionism is the assertion that the changes which took place in previous historical eras took place unconsciously. By a process which Kaplan describes as *transvaluation*, meanings were read into the past which the past could not possibly bear. The most flagrant example of this, perhaps, is the manner in which other-wordly rabbinic Judaism could be grounded on a this-wordly Bible. The center of gravity of human life in the biblical period is this world. There is only one stage on which the drama of human life is played out. Hence the anguish of a Job. The Bible sees blessing in the goods of this world, a wife, children, possessions, longevity. The prophetic philosophy of history and the prophetic theodicy see a direct relationship between human behavior and the human condition. Good men prosper. Wicked men suffer. Under the impact of new religious insights and the observation of intolerable suffering on the part of good men the stage of human life is extended, in the latter part of the ecclesiastical period, to the next world. The paradox of Job is resolved. Good men who suffer in this world will be rewarded in the next. For the next two thousand years Jewish life would be exclusively other-wordly. The center of gravity of human life was no longer this world but the next. The Jew led a pious and devout life in this world so that he might enjoy unmitigated bliss in the next. A saying of one of the second-century Rabbis sums up the dominant attitude of the rabbinic period: "This world is to be compared to a vestibule to the future world. Prepare yourself in the vestibule so you may be accorded entry into the main hall." By a process of transvaluation the Rabbis found no discrepancy between their own radical other-worldliness and the profound this-wordliness of the Bible. The down to earth paean of praise to human sexuality in the Song of Songs is interpreted by them as a spiritual dialogue between God and the community of Israel. " 'Thy two breasts'—these are Moses and Aaron. Just as the breasts are the beauty and the ornament of a woman so Moses and Aaron were the beauty and ornament of Israel."

The fact that the metamorphosis from one stage of Jewish history to another was arrived at, in the past, through an unconscious process of transvaluation does not mean that ancient insights do not often profoundly foreshadow modern ideas. It means that we must not affirm that the ancients were aware of these modern ideas. Transvaluation is only possible in the absence of any understanding of its dynamics. In the modern world the transition from the rabbinic stage of Judaism to the democratic can only come about through revaluation, which Kaplan defines as "disengaging from the traditional content those elements in it which answer permanent postulates of human nature, and in integrating them into our own ideology." This is the only way in which the sancta may be made relevant for moderns, deliberately and consciously; hence the need to "reconstruct."

A human being is not aware of himself at the time of conception though much of the adult potential is hidden in the genes and chromosomes of the undifferentiated protoplasm in the womb. Nor is the child aware of himself during the crucial years of infantile development. Yet the child is father of the man. Only at the point of self-consciousness do the realities of conception, birth, early development and adolescence become subject to the scrutiny of the inquiring mind. Parents, relatives and friends are looked at in a new light. A change of house, a father's change of job, an emigration, an appendectomy even, none of which was truly "conscious" at the time, suddenly loom before the mind as profoundly critical in the development of self and identity. New meaning is afforded ancient experience, often experience which has been forgotten and of which others have to remind us.

By the same token the burgeoning self-consciousness of the prophets is the crucial point in the history of the Jewish people, when the past is reconstructed to serve the needs of the present. A pedigree must be found for current theology, a genealogy for current ritual practice. Many a man who, as a child, moved from Egypt to Canaan has equally developed the need to see in past and forgotten events crucial determining factors in current attitudes and postures. But if Judaism is truly to be seen as an evolving religious civilization, the context of our perspective must be larger even than the history of the Jewish people. Nothing less than the canvas of the cosmos itself can fix the coordinates of Daniel S.'s place on the map of Jewish and human existence. The modern Bible, no less than the ancient, must begin with a cosmogony.

In the beginning were the gravitationally unstable clouds of hydrogen atoms. Science needs no other postulate than this to account for the existence of the heavens, the earth and all their hosts. There is no point in asking ultimate questions which admit of no answers. All the variegated elements and organic forms of life which exist today are assumed to have developed by natural evolutionary process from those early beginnings. ("In short, it is known how, in principle, all elements could have evolved from an assumed primordial universe of hydrogen alone," says George W. Beadle.) Indeed, many of the steps which must have taken place in this process have been re-created in the laboratory. It is not just Judaism which is an evolving religious civilization. The totality of reality is evolutionary process.

Life itself is believed to have originated in a "making" situation, a rare combination of the right chemical elements in the right atmospheric conditions. This is natural selection and mutation operating on an inorganic level. To say that life is accidental, therefore, is meaningless. Given the amount of time involved in the process of evolution, and the infinity of possible mutations, one would be more correct in affirming that it was inevitable, given the earliest conditions, for sentient life to emerge. We live in a life-producing cosmos.

From the inorganic to the organic, from the inanimate to the animate, from the most primitive forms of life to the most complicated, mutation, natural selection and time are all that were required for the emergence of human beings. Fred Hoyle, the distinguished astronomer, has suggested that if human life were to exist on other planets it would probably resemble our own (". . . I expect that all highly intelligent creatures on planets like our own, and based on a similar chemical system, will be land animals as we are and will possess substantial similarities of construction—eyes, skeletons, heads and so on.") There is an inevitability about the creative process operating in the cosmos.

Evolution does not permit teleology. We cannot speak of the purpose of a particular development. We can only speak retrospectively of the meaning of a certain sequence. It is almost as if, with the history of the Jewish people, only what happens with the prophets and the Pharisees determines the true meaning of Abraham and the Exodus. Only what a man does with his adult understanding of who and what his parents are can retrospectively determine the truth for him of his conception, birth and childhood development. But something more can be said.

Ethologists and biologists are in the habit of asking whether birds fly because they have wings or whether birds have wings because they fly and whether men think because they have brains or whether men have brains because they think. The answer, buttressed by the insights and observations of generations of evolutionists, is that birds have wings because they fly and men have brains because they think.

At some stage in the biological evolution of the animal we now designate as a bird the bird had no wings. A survival situation developed in which all birds, in the absence of wings, were doomed to destruction because of a radical change in environmental factors. Perhaps the ecological situation had changed, or a new predator had emerged. The wingless birds were not conscious of their predicament. They were simply dying off or were being picked off one by one. Then, suddenly, by the process known as mutation, the effect of radiation on the chromosomes and genes, a bird was born with a rudimentary wing. Under normal circumstances such an appendage would have been a distinct impediment. The animal might well have been ostracized by its own species. It might well have perished, under normal conditions, precisely because of its new rudimentary differential. Under the conditions of crisis, however, the appendage, affording a crucial survivalist factor, saved the bird and its descendants. Birds without these rudimentary wings disappeared.

Robert Ardrey, in *African Genesis*, has described a recent recorded example of entomological mutation in the history of the peppered moths which lived near Manchester, England. Before the Industrial Revolution, these moths had thrived against the background of the local trees, protected by their barklike coloring. But the pollution of industry blackened the trees until the moths became visible to their predator enemies and were almost wiped out until, one day, a black mutant emerged. The species survived through the new mutation. The visible moths were picked off by the birds. "The black is today the common moth of the Manchester area, the peppered the collector's item. We may deal casually with such a story, yet in an oversimplified form, it is the story of evolution . . . by such a marginal chance was the human promise saved."

Men have brains because they think. At a crucial point in the development of Homo sapiens a vital evolutionary differential emerged in a rudimentary system, which permitted the extension of intelligence into hitherto unprecedented areas. Subsequent mutation and the survival of those with the most marked cerebral advantage produced man as we know him. By the same token we may ask, by analogy with the biologists' question, whether the Jewish people survived because of the preaching of the prophets or whether the prophets preached because the Jewish people survived.

The answer is that the Jewish people survived because the prophets preached. Under normal circumstances, in a country which was not threatened with imminent destruction at the hands of great powers, the peculiar ethical sensitivity manifested by the prophets might either have gone unnoticed or brought about their destruction. Hypersensitivity to moral problems is not normally a faculty which endears those who possess it to their fellow human beings. Had Israel's affluence been unchallenged by the Assyrians and the Babylonians the prophets might never have left a ripple on the surface of history. The mutant of their thinking, like so many other mutants in the sphere of biological evolution, would not have taken.

But the prophetic mentality emerged as a psychosocial mutant at a crucial point in the history of Israel. The embryonic spiritual wing, the embryonic theological brain, which under other and happier circumstances might have been stillborn now, under dire stress, assumed prodigious survivalist implications. If a way could be found of surviving in the face of political annihilation the inexorable chain of universal national growth and decline could be broken.

The prophets discovered the way. Yahweh, the embodiment of the ideal aspirations of the people, of their collective will to survive as articulated by the prophets, would not be vanquished. Yahweh would permit, nay, encourage the vanquishing of His people—as a punishment for their sins. "Because of our sins we were exiled from our land." Physical defeat is definitive. Moral chastisement is open to redress. There is always the possibility, if one in fact survives, of repentance. Job was chastised, but Job was restored to his original state. By placing the center of gravity of national survival within the collective human conscience rather than in the external vicissitudes of collective national physical survival the prophets provided an escape from impending doom. The Jews who accepted that version of their history as propounded by the prophets survived. The others became the historian's "collector's item." In the face of the imminent danger of being picked off by Assyrian and Babylonian predators and assimilation, a prophetic psychosocial mutant emerged to save the day. "We may deal casually with such a story, yet in an oversimplified form, it is the story of evolution . . . by such a marginal chance was the human (Jewish) promise saved." The same process was repeated in the emergence of the Pharisees. The Reconstructionist conception of Judaism may, perhaps, best be considered a psychosocial mutant in modern Jewish thought.

Biological evolution ceases in man when man becomes self-conscious and able to manipulate his environment through technology. Evolution then continues in man through his ideas. Teilhard de Chardin described the environment in which that conceptual evolution now takes place as the "noösphere," a belt of intellectual atmosphere spanning the earth in which the ideas of men of all ages manifest the same evolutionary development that paleontologists and biologists discover in the more tractable material of fossils, vestigial organs and living animals. Religions may best be regarded, from this point of view, as psychosocial organs developed to enable man in society the better to cope with his environment. They are as much extensions of man as are arms, legs and brains. They have emerged in the same way.

If prophetic religion and Pharisaic religion are mutations within the stream of Jewish history, the Jewish people which results from these mutations is itself a mutant among world peoples. In a nuclear age the survival value of basic Jewish attitudes becomes a prototype for world survival. The Jewish people, threatened with destruction or assimilation by the ethics of power, learned, discovered (the ancients would prefer to say "had revealed to them"), the power of ethics. The fact that Israel was "forced" to discover the basic truth of nonviolence as a means to survival—"not by might, nor by strength, but by My Spirit"—is as irrelevant as the fact that the primordial fishes living in evaporating ponds were "forced" to live on dry land. A cosmos, in which biological and societal mutations are possible, produces a Jewish people. The Jews are thus no more the chosen people than the DNA molecule is the chosen molecule.

Had Newton not been startled by the falling apple, another man would sooner or later have discovered gravity. Had the Israelites failed to respond to the impact on their collective head of the apple of Assyrian and Babylonian history, then some other people would, sooner or later, have become the Jewish people. The ethical use of power must inevitably prevail, else the species will perish. In an age when all men live under the shadow of the hydrogen bomb, the meaning of the prophetic challenge "the peoples shall walk in Thy light" is quite simply that unless peoples with power learn to use that power ethically or dispense with that power altogether, there is no future for mankind. That is an application, on the level of peoplehood, of the lesson of the Mancunian moths.

Nor is the Jewish people the only part of nature which teaches the survival value of cooperation, responsibility, ethical behavior in action. The survivalist value of what humans call ethics within an ethnic framework is foreshadowed in the animal kingdom. Ethology, the study of the innate behavior patterns of animals, has discovered in recent decades a remarkable foreshadowing in the animal kingdom of societal tendencies, even rituals, among the higher animals. Animals in groups which cooperate, which have developed ritual means of sublimating intraspecific aggression, tend to survive. There are protopsychosocial organs visible in animal "societies." The need for the kind of religion first articulated by the prophets, given flesh and blood by the Pharisees, is a natural need foreshadowed in the animal kingdom whence we stem. For thousands of years religion intuited "thou shalt love thy neighbor as thyself." Modern science can now demonstrate the physical and visible corrosive powers of hatred in the laboratory. For thousands of years the spiritual leaders of the Jewish people urged their charges to live up to the highest ideals of responsibility to each other, to the poor, the orphan, the widow, the stranger. Modern science now adds the insight, drawn from observation of nature, that "ethical" behavior and survival are related. Again, the prophets were right for the wrong reasons.

Traditional Jewish religion commences with God. In the beginning God exists alone. He then creates a perfect way of life, a Torah. He then creates a world and a potentially perfect people whom He chooses to follow that perfect Torah. Reconstructionism, in line with its religious humanistic and religious naturalistic assumptions, effects a Copernican revolution on the traditional sequence of God, Torah and Israel. In the beginning was not God but the Jewish people. Out of the evolving in-life striving of the Jewish people there emerged a way of life. This way of life, conceived as grounded in the cosmos, not as merely expedient, became known as the Torah. God is experienced as the Cosmic Guarantor of that way of life, the source of meaning and purpose in Jewish existence. The fact that the prophets conceived of God as a King, who could be seen sitting on a throne, who dispensed justice, should no more be a source of concern to the religious humanist than the fact that the prophets believed that God opened little windows in the heavens when it rained should be a source of concern to the meteorologist. Modern meteorology makes sense of ancient as well as modern rain. So also Reconstructionism accounts for ancient as well as modern experience of divinity. What the prophets believed God to *be* was less important than what they believed Him to *do*. His function transcended His substance. He was believed to perform deeds of loving-kindness, justice and righteousness on earth. His substance

may have been Person, His function indubitably was ethical behavior in terrestrial action.

The center of gravity in traditional Judaism was believed to be
God. The center of gravity of Jewish religion was, in fact,
always the people. The people maintains its identity in change.
And its ideas change radically. In the beginning the people
emerges onto the stage of history. A people does not emerge full
panoplied onto the stage of history like Athena from the head of
Zeus. There is a slow process of development which may be seen
in retrospect. The birth of the Jewish people is the Exodus from
Egypt, even though the full awareness of the significance of that
event is not articulated until the time of the prophets.

A people is no more an aggregate of individuals than a chemical
compound, carbon bisulphide, for example, is a mixture of carbon
and sulphur. It is a special mixture in the right proportions and
subjected to certain "traumatic" conditions. The resultant chemical compound possesses properties not previously possessed by its
chemical constituents. There is profound significance in the fact
that an author who lived at the time of the prophets, the time
when Israel became self-conscious, looked back on the Exodus
from Egypt and used a striking "chemical" analogy: "But you
hath the Lord taken and brought forth *out of the iron furnace,*
out of Egypt, to be unto Him a people of inheritance, as ye are
this day." The traumatic experience of slavery in Egypt and the
sudden shock of freedom welded the erstwhile loosely knit aggregate of seminomadic wanderers into a societal compound.
Henceforth Israel would possess qualities and attributes as a
group which its separate Semitic constituents had not previously
possessed as individuals. A prime attribute of the new people is a
God. The relationship with that God would then be projected
backward. He would be associated with the earliest recollections
of the forebears of the later people.

The biblical authors conceived of God, in common with all of
the ancients, in the analogy of man. Nevertheless, close study of
the Bible reveals that the term "God" is used as a correlative

rather than as a substantive. It is mostly the "God of Israel," the "God of the Hebrews," "our God," "I shall be your God and you shall be My people." A correlative term points to a relationship. It presupposes the existence of its counterpart. A father presupposes a child, a general an army, a king subjects. So also a god presupposes a people of whom that god is god. We do not *see* correlative terms. We *think* them. When the Israelites left Egypt under Moses, the shock of their redemption, the radical change in their condition from the abjectness of bondage to the openness of freedom, like the plunging of a white-hot blade into cold water which tempers, engendered in them a phenomenal sense of group solidarity and faith in their leadership. Reconstructionism would prefer to say they experienced God as the soterical reality of the cosmos, the cosmos from the standpoint of human salvation. There is a power of mutual responsibility in the cosmos which, when men cooperate with it or experience its workings, functions or is experienced as God.

The ancients knew nothing of the inner workings of the human mind. Whenever they experienced an intense awareness of some profound reality they tended to project it onto the cosmos. When they came across great men they assumed automatically that such could not have arisen out of the union of mere mortals. A god must have been at least one of the progenitors. Nor was this merely the belief of the common people. Julius Caesar is said to have believed that he descended from Venus and Anchises. When the ancients came across a great idea or an intense experience they assumed automatically that an external Being, cast anthropomorphically in the image of man, was the source of such an idea or experience. Under animism many external gods are the source of these inner experiences. Under supernaturalistic monotheism, which is the last vestige of animism, one God is responsible.

Had we moderns been at the crossing of the Red Sea we would have identified God as the other part of that relationship between the intense awareness of a people at a moment of release from

bondage into freedom and the cosmos. Freedom would have been
experienced as having roots in the cosmos, not merely as being a
matter of expediency. We would have identified God in the sense
of solidarity felt by the people, in the quality of the leadership
of Moses, in the resolve on the part of the people, at however low
an intensity, that they would strive to embody what they had
learned from being slaves in their relationships with each other.
We would have *thought* God, not *seen* God. We would have
witnessed the operation in the cosmos of a power making for salvation the way we witness that power in the civil rights movement. The God of America is revealed in the slow but sure
emancipation of the Negro even as the God of Israel was revealed in the sharp and sudden emancipation of the Hebrew.
There is a power operating in the cosmos which, when men
cooperate with it, enables them to achieve ever greater fulfillment,
for society as a whole as well as for its constituent members. But
we could not have seen that power. When a landslide occurs
we see rocks falling in conformity with the law of gravity. We
do not see gravity. We experience it, observe its functioning,
or think it.

But the Israelites at the crossing of the Red Sea actually saw
God, experienced God as an external sensate being. In the same
manner children have been known to experience intensely the
presence of an imaginary friend in the nursery. A lack of knowledge of reality makes for a greater emotional intensity. Under
such conditions inner sensations are projected outward. The reality of the functioning of divinity, however, transcends the limitations of its ancient modes of conception. Reconstructionism
affirms, in the spirit of the prophets, that there is a moral system
operating in the cosmos: in the physical world natural law, in the
human world "Torah," or moral law. Polarity, the principle of
independence and interdependence, the idea that everything
which exists is itself but at the same time is inextricably related to
everything else, which operates in the sphere of physical objects

as gravity, operates in the sphere of human society as Divinity when it is consciously recognized as such.

A steak cannot be injected directly into the bloodstream. By a complicated process of metabolism it has to be reduced by several stages until it can be a source of sustenance and growth. By the same token, values in the abstract cannot be assimilated directly by the individual. There is a spiritual metabolism whereby God, as the Value of all values, the Cosmos from the standpoint of human salvation or fulfillment, is first experienced by the people. That experience, through the metabolism of ethnicity operating through sancta, permeates through the family to the individual. Kaplan writes: "The idea of God is a map of the Cosmos. It selects those features of the Cosmos that enable man to become fully human. It is no more subjective than a map which locates only the mountains, rivers and cities."

The basic unit of the religious life is the people. The basic unit of the people is the family. The people is a molecular construction, to use a physical rather than a chemical analogy. The atoms of which it is formed are meshed together in the energizing bonds of historical ethnicity. Molecular existence, like chemical compound existence, commences with trauma. The Exodus from Egypt is the first nuclear fusion in the history of Israel. The calamities of 721 and 586 B.C.E. are also fusively creative. The atom of the family, intimately bound up with the whole, consists of the nucleus of the proton-neutron, father-mother, conceived as one energy unit, bound as one flesh, with the electron children whirling around the nucleus. Marriage is a splitting off of an electron to form a new atomic unit. The Torah conceives of the People of Israel as a family of families and the human race as a family of families of families. The creative yet potentially explosive symmetrical tensions of human interpersonal relationships marvelously mirror the symmetrical tensions of nature. To exist, matter itself must be bound in the bonds of reciprocal energy. But then human society and its needs are also part of nature.

Once a people has emerged onto the stage of history and has satisfied its basic physical needs there arises a need which transcends the physical. Certain men arise, heroes, who embody for the people something of that sense of transnatural longing in which a people seeks for meaning and purpose in life. These men are seen larger than life. Regardless of who or what they actually were in reality, occasionally regardless of whether or not they actually existed in reality, they become the embodiment of the ideal aspirations of the people. Their physical existence becomes a spiritual magnifying glass which brings the vague and inchoate yearnings of the masses into creative focus. They are catalysts which set huge societal transformations into process merely because of their presence. On the canvas of their original personalities the people lavish all the vivid hues of their own incipient spiritual imagination.

The words which these heroes leave behind them become, in the process of time, sacred texts which are believed, by virtue of the divine origins or associations of the heroes, to be revealed texts. Places associated with the heroes in their lifetime, either where they lived or where they were believed to have received revelations from God, are regarded as sacred. Objects or institutions which they cherished or founded become sacred. Either their anniversaries of birth or the anniversaries of important occasions, critical episodes in the life of the people in which they were directly involved, become holy days. All these heroes, objects, texts, events and days are technically referred to by Reconstructionism as sancta.

Sancta are the bare bones of religion. Historical ethnicity clothes them with flesh. A people maintains its identity in change by reconstructing them constantly in the face of new conditions. They function in the ongoing life of a people the way early and crucial childhood experiences function in the ongoing life of the individual. They set a pattern of spiritual and emotional parameters in terms of which all of later life will be experienced. Sancta are to religion what syntax is to language. They are the

structure which all religions share in common. They are the alge-
braic variables to which historical ethnicity assigns specific values.
Religions may be compared with languages. They are the means
whereby a people communicates with the living, the dead and the
unborn about the meaning and purpose of collective and, hence,
familial and individual life. There is no single religion any more
than there is a single language. Religions grow out of the in-
history, ongoing life of a people. To ask whether one religion is
better than another is as meaningless as asking whether one language is better than another. French is better than English for
certain kinds of poetry. German is better than Italian for certain
kinds of philosophy.

"... the same things uttered in Hebrew," observed the Greek
translator of the apocryphal Ecclesiasticus in his Prologue to
that work, "and translated into another tongue, have not the same
force in them: and not only these things, but the law itself, and
the prophets, and the rest of the books, have no small difference,
when they are spoken in their own language." He was right.
There is always an area in one language, abstract and noncon-
crete, which cannot be translated exactly into another language.
How does one go about translating into German:

> *The same that oft-times hath*
> *Charm'd magic casements, opening on the foam*
> *Of perilous seas, in faery lands forlorn.*

Or translating Rilke into English? Some languages are stronger
than others in certain respects.

So it is with religions. It was profoundly significant that John
F. Kennedy was buried by a *Catholic* priest. Christianity has, as
its central myth, the notion of a great man crucified for the sins
of others. Jewish religion is largely expressed in the collective.
The first-person plural dominates traditional Jewish liturgy. Even
the Isaianic Suffering Servant is conceived collectively as Israel.
A Rabbi would not have been able to render so meaningful so
meaningless a tragedy. Jewish religion finds it hard to regard

suffering on this profoundly individualistic level as redemptive. Its consolations to the mourners are couched in a collective idiom: "May the all-Present comfort you among those who mourn for Zion and Jerusalem." In the moment of supreme personal grief the Jewish mourner is consoled by being reminded of his existential coordinates on the eternal map of his historic ethnic collectivity.

We may compare the sancta embodiments of one religion with another to illustrate their centrality in religion. The American people was born in the traumatic experiences of the War of Independence (Exodus?) and the Civil War (the uniting of the tribes under David?). A former agglomeration of Anglo-Saxon settlers was fused, in the crucible of tension, into a new societal unit. That unit now possessed attributes not previously possessed by its individual constituents. The God of America ("in God we trust," "one nation under God") is the Cosmos from a salvational standpoint vis-à-vis the American people. It is a dimension of divinity experienced by American citizens over and above their awareness of God as members of their historic ethnic groups. Those Americans who, like the Jews, have their own ethnic tradition, live in two civilizations. They have two religions and experience divinity as Americans and as Jews. The American religion is the common faith of Americans regardless of whether they are Catholic, Protestant or Jew. American heroes such as Washington, Jefferson, and Lincoln function in the American religion the way Abraham, Moses and Yochanan ben Zaccai function in the Jewish religion. The American flag, the Statue of Liberty, and the Liberty Bell function in the American religion the way the *Sefer Torah*, or the scroll of the Law, the *mezzuzah*, or the box containing extracts from the Torah affixed to the right doorpost of the Jewish home, and the *tallit*, or the prayer shawl, function in the Jewish religion. Plymouth Rock, Independence Hall, Gettysburg and the Lincoln Memorial function in the American religion the way Mount Zion, the Wailing Wall, the

Tomb of Rachel, Jerusalem and *Eretz Yisrael,* or the land of Israel, function in the Jewish religion.

The discovery of America by Columbus, the ratification of the Constitution, the Civil War and the Emancipation Proclamation function in the American religion the way the wanderings of Abraham, the Exodus from Egypt, the Revelation on Sinai, the fall of the Temple, function in the Jewish religion. Without the birth of America in the eighteenth century the discovery of America by Columbus would probably have been as of little religious significance as the "discovery" of Canaan by Abraham without the ensuing Exodus with its prophetic interpretation. The Declaration of Independence, the Constitution and the Bill of Rights function in the American religion the way the Torah, Talmud and *Midrash* function in the Jewish religion. Independence Day, Lincoln's Birthday, Washington's Birthday, Veterans Day, Thanksgiving Day and Election Day function in the American religion the way Passover, Pentecost, Tabernacles and the Day of Atonement function in the Jewish religion.

A case could even be made out for comparative cuisine sancta. Roast turkey, pumpkin pie, ice cream, hot dogs and apple pie share a common "religious" function with *gefilte* fish, chicken soup, potato *latkes, kneidlach, blintzes* and *tzimmes.* In the case of these Jewish comestible delights their unique association is originally with religious celebration. Just as the liturgy and the ritual changed from Sabbath to Festival and from Festival to Festival, so did the type of food served change. The fact that *Sephardim* developed different food sancta from *Ashkenazim,* Spanish and Portuguese Jew and Eastern European Jew assimilating to the delicacies of the local environment, is irrelevant to the issue. Food sancta existed. Different Jewish traditions had different delicacies. All were regarded as sancta. Madison Avenue notwithstanding, one does have to be a Jew to enjoy Real Jewish Rye!

Sancta emerge within a civilization which grows out of the total life of a people. By themselves they do not guarantee the

ethical quality of religion. Sancta may be used against, rather
than in support of, maximum human fulfillment for the group
and its constituent members. Communist Russia and Nazi Germany both had religions which, insofar as they militated against
fulfillment for vast numbers of their citizens, were distinctly unethical. Yet both peoples developed sancta through their respective civilizations. They had their "sacred" heroes, objects, texts,
events and days. *Das Kapital* and *Mein Kampf*, Lenin and Hitler,
the Red Square and Nuremberg, the Red Flag and the Swastika,
all functioned as sancta. It is not sufficient for a civilization to
have sancta to have an authentic religion. The sancta must serve
as a means of ethical fulfillment. In each age the mode of em-
bodying the sancta must be made compatible with the most advanced ethical insights available. These may have to be borrowed
from another civilization.

Judaism is unique in that it became, under the pressures of
history, a religious civilization. Americanism can hardly be described as the evolving religious civilization of the American people. Americanism is, perhaps, the evolving technological civilization of the American people. The American religion is as yet
embryonic. "In God we trust" may appear on dollar bills but
there is no lively awareness of the nature of the American God as
a power making for American salvation. He is not consciously
identified as such. That is why when *denominational* prayer is
rightly abolished in American public schools, no alternate possibility of an *American* act of worship is considered. The task,
however, of all religions, historic and those more recently developed in the full blaze of the light of history, is to utilize their
sancta as means of maximizing the ethical content of the lives of
their adherents. Jewish values are universal values refracted
through the prism of Jewish ethnicity. Where our sancta fall
short of the ethical level of other civilizations it is our duty to
elevate them accordingly. In two specific areas, the equality of
the sexes and the separation of Church and State, Judaism, at least
in the State of Israel, falls sadly behind the ethical insights of
Western democracy.

Through the past three stages of Jewish history Jewish sancta have been radically reconstructed, albeit unconsciously. We need only compare the rigid Sabbath of the biblical period with the warmth of the Sabbath of the rabbinic period or the Bible as it was understood by its original authors and the Bible as it was understood by the Pharisees. Today that reconstruction can only be conscious and deliberate. There will be, for example, one Sabbath, but many different patterns of Sabbath observance. The time of a monolithic theology and ritual is past. Judaism under the freedom of a democracy, which is the precondition of modern Jewish life, will mean unity in diversity. The common factor uniting all Jews as Jews will be the love of the Jewish people.

The crucial question to be put to the modern Jew is not, "How much Hebrew do you know?" "How long do you wait between eating meat and milk?" or "What kind of God, if any, do you believe in?" but, "Do you want the Jewish people to survive meaningfully?" "Do you want to belong?" Once the act of belonging is achieved, then the quality of that belonging becomes important. A pyramid of values can be erected. One Jew will decide to become a *chalutz*, or pioneer, on a *kibbutz*, another will opt for orthodoxy, another may seek a life of Jewish scholarship, yet another may be satisfied in running a local charity appeal or studying Yiddish. Each Jew will, hopefully, responsibly, in the light of as much information and evidence available, choose that particular contribution to Jewish life which to him is most fulfilling and meaningful.

But the choice must be made within the context of a total Jewish people. The value of the parts will depend on the whole and the quality of the whole will determine the parts. If the fragmented Jews of the twentieth century cannot see their place on the ongoing map of evolving Jewish civilization the chasms will prove unbridgeable. The Jewish people will die. Some sects may survive, but as fossils, as repetitions of a past era, not as authentic, living responses to the challenge of living in the modern world. ". . . I have never yet met a healthy person who worried very much about his health, or a really good person who worried much about his own soul," observed J. B. S. Haldane, a distinguished modern scientist. Jewish religion will become healthy when Jews stop being preoccupied with theology and ritual and start being concerned with the quality of collective Jewish life. Look after Jewish civilization and the religion will look after itself.

Daniel S. is confused because he is unaware that Judaism is once again in the throes of a radical metamorphosis. The sancta are again being reconstructed. He sees the fragments which spell the breakdown of a past stage without the binding possibilities of the emergence of a future. Judaism is again becoming this-worldly after over two thousand years of other-worldliness. The modern Jew must live in two civilizations. The richer his Judaism the profounder his Americanism.

In the struggles of the contemporary Negro to create sancta, heroes, objects, texts, events and days, the Jew can see reflected the need for modern man to draw the richness from the ethnic as well as the political civilization to achieve a full identity. Daniel S. may have to make a choice. Within the broad context of Jewish peoplehood he may choose one or another denominational, philanthropic, cultural or political approach. In suggesting to him some options from the Reconstructionist standpoint, we simply offer an approach which cuts across the visible fragments in placing the decision to be a Jew today within the context of a total historical people. It is a synoptic approach: how to be a Jew in the modern world within the context of Judaism conceived as an evolving religious civilization.

Three

Daniel S. is a Jew because he was born a Jew. He is not a Jew because being Jewish is better than being anything else. He had no choice in the matter. By the same token he is an American because he was born an American. The biblical insight that the family rather than the individual is the basic unit of society, and that the family achieves its identity through its relationship with the people to which it belongs, closely approximates reality. The individual achieves an identity from the ethnic or political group mediated through the family. Unless Daniel S. is to achieve only a partial identity, he has to come to terms with both civilizations in which he lives.

There is, of course, intermarriage, when one may convert from the "religion" of one's birth. A man can also, for professional or other reasons, leave the country of his birth and settle in another country. But these are the exceptions rather than the rule. In both cases a form of conversion takes place. This is more obvious in the case of settling in another country. After a period of five years, during which he is presumed to fulfill his basic obligations to the country in which he has settled, a man who comes to America from another country may apply for citizenship. There is a formal act of "conversion" involved. Basic facts about American life must previously have been assimilated. Questions must be answered. American citizens must be produced as personal guarantors. American sancta are present at the ceremonial occasion: a judge, a verbal charge as to the implications of citizenship, the flag, the oath of allegiance: "Thy people shall be my people and thy God my God. Where thou fightest I will fight . . ." One then becomes a full-fledged member of a new people.

The moral status of a man who emigrates to America and

refuses to become a citizen is a moot point. The essence of democratic life in a modern state is participation in the political life of the country through the use of the franchise. The voting booth, another sanctum, functions in a democracy the way the Holy of Holies in the Temple was believed to function in a theocracy. In it are made those decisions which, for better or for worse, govern the future well-being and possibilities of fulfillment of the people as a whole and of the individual constituents of the people. A man who, without unusually extenuating circumstances, refuses to put himself in a position in which he can vote either in the country of his origin or in the country of his domicile behaves unethically to the extent that he is politically parasitic.

If a majority of people behaved so selfishly, organized democratic life would collapse. If an immigrant cannot find it in his heart to embrace citizenship of the country in which he lives, whose protection he enjoys and whose advantages he utilizes, he had better go home or find some other hiding place. There is more to being a good American than paying taxes and obeying traffic regulations.

Intermarriage also raises ethical considerations. In an open and pluralistic society there is bound to be intermarriage on the periphery and, frequently, in the midst of the ethnic group. Statistical evidence seems to indicate that where Jews live in dense concentrations, the rate of intermarriage is markedly lower than in a small and scattered Jewish community which exists within an overwhelmingly Gentile context. Increased opportunities for mixed dating on the campus and the general relaxation of rigid social controls among young people also lead to far greater exposure than heretofore between Jew and Gentile.

Some of this intermarriage is inevitable and unavoidable. When a young Jewish boy from the finest of Jewish backgrounds sits down at a lecture next to an attractive Gentile coed who reminds him of his mother, no theological restrictions in the world can prevent his falling in love.

If the authors of the Bible intuited a world as a family of families of families it was because they sensed that human relationships, however grandiose, whether between man and man or man and God, ultimately relate to the original family. If a man feels at home in his family the odds are that he is going to feel at home in the world. If a man feels alienated in his family the odds are that he is going to feel alienated in the world. Faith originates in the home. It was inevitable that man should view the salvational dimension of the cosmos after this fashion: "As a father has compassion on his children so the Lord hath compassion on those who revere Him." The Hebrew word for compassion is *rachamim* from *rechem*, a womb. Man's ultimate relationship with God, as well as with woman, is mediated through a reconstructed emotional sanctum of early childhood.

Perhaps the only Jews who can avoid this problem of intermarriage arising out of mere social intercourse are the *Chasidim* and their ilk. In their circles marriages are still arranged after the fashion of the old time *shtetl*, with parents playing a role unparalleled in our modern, post-Spock, antiparental era. *Chasidim* who work in New York City's diamond industry, since they do not attend secular colleges, are unlikely to sit next to attractive Gentile girls who remind them of their mothers.

Moreover those Jews who have set the Lord before them continually simply do not see what other men see. There is a power in fundamentalist Jewish education which fills the eyes with the light of the Divine so that men are blinded to all else. The authors of the biblical Song of Songs were fully aware of the blessings of female pulchritude. The Talmud tells of the famous first-century Pharisaic leader, Simeon ben Gamaliel who, while standing on a step on the Temple mount, saw a heathen woman who was particularly beautiful, and exclaimed: "How great are Thy works, O Lord!" (a quotation from the Psalms).

But under the duress of Diaspora life such outgoing attitudes disappeared. The Song of Songs was only saved for the Bible because it was given a strictly spiritual and nonsexual meaning. As the pressures of medieval Jewish existence became intolerable, rigid attitudes to sex developed. The *Chasid* will walk past an attractive miniskirted woman on Forty-seventh Street either without noticing her or with eyes deliberately cast on the ground. A quotation from the Psalms is unthinkable. He will not shake hands with a Jewish woman other than his wife, much less a Gentile. When *Chasidim* dance the men dance with each other, never with women. Mixed dancing is strictly forbidden according to traditional rabbinic Jewish law. One may not so much as touch a woman to whom one is not married. Extramarital contact of all kind is rigorously proscribed. *Chasidim* are not likely to suffer from the problem of intermarriage. The statistics bear this out. Intermarriage inevitably increases directly with distance from tradition.

But wherever Jews mingle freely with Gentiles in the modern world intermarriage will take place. Where the bond of parental memory is strong and the Jewish partner comes from an identifiably Jewish background, conversion of the other partner may take place. This can take the form of greater or lesser indoctrination into Jewish history, ritual observance and the intricacies of the Hebrew language. In more traditional circles circumcision for the male convert and ritual immersion in the *mikveh* for both male and female converts are *de rigueur*. In less traditional circles many of these requirements may be waived.

Candidates for conversion have been known to shop around for the best "deal," that is, the least irksome mode of becoming Jewish. In recent years the number of Reform Rabbis who will marry Jews to Gentiles in a Jewish marriage ceremony has decreased sharply. No Orthodox or Conservative Rabbi will perform such a ceremony. Even among Reform Rabbis these marriages are increasingly viewed with distaste. The ethnic self-consciousness of world Jewry since the establishment of the State of Israel and the Jewish blood shed in its defense seem to have strengthened the fibers of Jewish self-respect.

The most ludicrous arguments can be heard at this stage of the game: "Most of her friends are Jewish." "She looks Jewish." "She likes Jewish food." "She has a Jewish heart." They are offered as substitutes for conversion, as if the systole and diastole of a Jewish heart were somehow cardiogrammatically distinguishable from those of a Gentile heart. No self-respecting people would tolerate such a vapid species of affirmation to belong to its ranks. "I have an American heart," "I live in America," "I like apple pie," "Some of my best friends are American," cannot substitute for the legitimate residential, intellectual and moral requisites for citizenship.

The least that can be expected in such circumstances is that some formal act of conversion take place under the auspices of an authoritative and accredited synagogue body representative of at least a section of the Jewish people. Unless there are weighty extenuating circumstances, the conversion ought to take place through that religious body which requires *more* Jewish commitment rather than *less*. The purpose of becoming Jewish is to become acceptable to as much of the Jewish people as possible, not just to one Rabbi and his small congregation. Much heartbreak and anguish have been caused would-be converts by ill-considered rabbinic advice in this sphere.

The history of conversion in Judaism presents an ever-changing process. In the earliest days there was no such phenomenon as religious conversion. In the biblical period Moses is described as having married an Ethiopian woman and Boaz a Moabitess, Ruth. This was a form of ethnic or territorial conversion. One became a "Jew" by marrying a "Jew" or settling on "Jewish" territory.

But when the Jews returned to Judea from Babylon, after the Exile, in 538 B.C.E. they were no longer an autonomous people living on their own soil, subject to their own sovereignty. Henceforth the Jews would be a *church* rather than a *nation* and Jewish existence would be increasingly religious rather than political. Symptomatic of this new trend in Jewish life, forced upon the Jewish people by radically changed conditions of living, was Ezra's decree of expulsion of all Gentile wives in the middle of the fifth pre-Christian century.

A healthy man can eat and assimilate any kind of food. A man with a delicate stomach must select his diet carefully. One heavy bout of drinking and eating spicy foods will throw an ulcerous metabolism entirely off balance. By the same token a people living a normal, healthy, sovereign existence on its own soil can afford to ingest aliens. Indeed the ingestion of aliens under such circumstances can be a source of great stimulus and creativity. There are few who would deny that the ebullience, dynamism and spirited growth of American life in the nineteenth century made it possible for the American people to accept millions of immigrants from a multiplicity of backgrounds and absorb them into a common way of life. These immigrants, in turn, enriched beyond measure the country of their adoption.

Ancient Israel, on its own soil, its identity strengthened by its own national existence, had no difficulty in ingesting aliens. Some of the "political" marriages contracted by Solomon may have aroused the antagonism of the prophets, but that was because the daughters of foreign kings brought strange cults with them. As the imminent destruction of Israel and Judah approached, the prophets began to caution against the wisdom of intermarriage on the grounds that it weakened loyalty to Yahweh. Territorial proselytization was slowly disappearing. A Church has no territory which can absorb the alien, only a theology and system of ritual. But no form of religious conversion as yet existed. Ezra therefore expelled the Gentile wives.

By the turn of the millennium Pharisaic Judaism was so spiritually self-confident that it had become a vigorously proselytizing movement. A healthy Judaism was unafraid of the challenge of Roman civilization. All the evidence shows that at the time of

Jesus countless Romans, including many aristocrats, either converted totally to Judaism or were on their way to such conversion. A fully developed form of religious conversion was now available. Women especially, exempted from the rigors of circumcision, flocked to the synagogues. Men who, themselves, would not go all the way to Judaism, had their children circumcized and raised as Jews. The New Testament speaks of the Pharisees who "scour heaven and earth to make one proselyte." Rabbinic and Roman sources confirm this claim.

But with the rise of Christianity the Jews were thrown back on themselves. Many of the half-proselytes opted for Christianity, with its undemanding approach to ritual, and some even betrayed their former spiritual mentors. "Be of the disciples of Aaron," observed the famous Hillel, outstanding leader of the Pharisees at the turn of the millennium, "loving peace and pursuing peace, loving thy fellow-creatures" (that is, the Gentiles) "and drawing them near to the Torah" (that is, converting them to Judaism). It was the selfsame Hillel who agreed to teach the whole Torah to a querulous and impatient Gentile "while standing on one foot." This positive approach to conversion reflected the dominant attitude of the Pharisees.

By the end of the third century a distinguished talmudical scholar by the name of Helbo could assert: "Proselytes are as hard for Israel to endure as a sore." Three centuries of suffering and persecution separate Hillel from Helbo. Nevertheless Judaism never closed its ranks to proselytization as long as it was authentically desired. Being Jewish was never regarded by the Rabbis as a matter of blood.

Though they would not have expressed it thus, for them being Jewish meant becoming a responsible and committed member of the Jewish people. It was a matter of joining a family and living up to the responsibilities of membership in that family. Thus they observe in the Talmud:

If at the present time a man desires to become a proselyte, he is to be addressed as follows: "What reason have you for desiring to become a proselyte? Do you not know that Israel at the present time is persecuted and oppressed, despised, harassed and overcome by afflictions?" If he replies, "I know and yet am unworthy," he is accepted forthwith and is given instruction in . . . the . . . commandments . . . He is not to be persuaded or dissuaded too much. If he accepts all the rules and regulations, he is circumcized . . . As soon as he is healed, arrangements are made for his immediate baptism. When he comes up after his baptism he is deemed to be an Israelite in all respects.

One type of conversion the Rabbis never tolerated was precisely the type of conversion most prevalent today—conversion for marriage to a Jewish partner. For the Rabbis authentic conversion meant becoming a Jew for the sake of Judaism, not for the sake of marrying a Jew or Jewess. A subtle change in attitudes is taking place today even in traditional Rabbinic circles. Today conversion for the sake of marriage to a Jewish partner seems eminently reasonable and sane. On the contrary, conversion for the sake of Judaism, in an age of Holocaust and transition, seems suspect. Most Rabbis today would probably question the motives, and even possibly the psychological stability, of one who wished to become Jewish without marital reasons. Indeed, when a stranger telephones the Rabbi today and says, "Rabbi, I have a religious problem," the most apt answer could usually be, "What's his (or her) name?"

Statistics and books on the subject of intermarriage are gloomy and present a chastening picture. The rate of divorce is high in these marriages. Raising Jewish children in the absence of authentic Jewish commitment is problematic. Far too often conversion is demanded by the Jewish family as a form of blackmail for social reasons. In an age when the Jewish people can hardly be regarded as healthy from a religious standpoint the problem of intermarriage must be treated with caution. Nevertheless there are many converts who make better Jews than the native-born and the phenomenon of the formerly Gentile spouse bringing the entire family back to Judaism is not unknown to the modern Rabbi.

The evidence seems to show that as ethnic bonds loosen in the second half of the twentieth century, deliberate intermarriage is on the wane. There are now many cases of intermarriage where neither parents nor children care about the status of the non-Jewish partner. Even the desire to have, at least, a Jewish wedding for social reasons has disappeared.

Here we are dealing with Jews on the periphery, who will marry at City Hall and unless the arrival of children precipitates a problem of Jewish education (which is unlikely) will remain on the periphery. An outburst of anti-Semitism in Russia or a flaring up of a serious crisis in the Middle East threatening the existence of the State of Israel may momentarily jog their consciences to the extent of signing a check or even attending a public meeting. It is possible to cease being Jewish in the open society, at least for the individual. Ethical Culture Societies and Unitarian Churches, not to mention liberal political organizations and radical groups, have waxed fat on the idealism of two thousand years of Jewish spiritual stamina divorced, in the twentieth century, from its ethnic context.

Space travel has introduced modern man to the concept of weightlessness. If a man is propelled far enough from the center of terrestrial gravity, he will become weightless and float around in space. By the same token, the center of gravity of Jewish life is the Jewish people. It is possible for a Jew, through environmental forces, to be propelled beyond the gravitational pull of Jewish peoplehood. Such a person will become Jewishly "weightless."

America abounds with such Jews. The tragedy is that whereas for the most part they are not acceptable to the white Anglo-Saxon Protestant majority (and are Jews not so much because they themselves identify as Jews but rather because others so identify them), they have no relationship with other Jews which might afford them a sense of Jewish identity. Many of them live, procreate and die in this condition. One can get along with Beethoven and Shakespeare and without the poetry of Bialik and the stories of Sholem Aleichem. But does an American Jew, who deliberately cuts off half of his identity, live in the fullest sense of life?

Occasionally, one sees a tree which, through forces beyond its control, has become stunted and warped. A storm may have twisted its trunk in an early stage of growth, lack of sunlight may have distorted it further. It is a living tree, with leaves and bark, but not to be compared with the upright tree growing to its full height and maturity as nature intended it.

There are Jews who, through no fault of their own, are comparably stunted. There are no visible symptoms but close analysis yields a fundamental lack of fulfillment in all their relationships and a corresponding diminution of identity. Their idealism is impoverished to the extent that it is exercised on an individual or *ad hoc* committee basis, unrelated to the ongoing ethnic group of which, against their will, they are part. A man can no more run away from his people than he can run away from his parents. He can deliberately ignore them but he is avoiding part of himself by doing so. It is surely better to try to live with oneself than to spend one's life avoiding oneself.

No man can fulfill himself entirely in terms of three score years and ten. After he has eaten, slept, played and pursued his other necessary interests and needs, the amount of time left in his life for creative work for humanity is perilously limited. The greatest danger involved in any efforts to make of human society a place where all may achieve fulfillment is the apparently insuperable obstacles in the way of such a goal. Intransigent human nature, bigotry, intolerance, general apathy and indifference breed cynicism and despair. These in turn destroy hope. The greatest tragedy in modern society is found where men say: "But how can what I do make any difference?"

Only when the individual allies himself to goals which transcend the limits of his own personal life can he achieve a sense of fulfillment and an authentic identity. To be born into an ethnic group, such as the Jews, is to be associated with an ongoing cosmic operation of and aspiration for justice and mercy going back four thousand years. There is enough spiritual "uranium" in the hills of Jewish experience to move a world if only Jews mine wisely and creatively in their past for the needs of the present.

In the rabbinic period and during the Middle Ages men saw the center of gravity of life in another world. With the birth of modernism Jewish experience has come full circle. The Jew now lives in a this-worldly society, as in the biblical period, where the exclusive stage on which the drama of life is enacted is this world. The modern Jew, in common with biblical man, makes it here or makes it nowhere. Belief in a life after death is no longer a possibility for modern man. Nor is a biblical *Sheol* acceptable.

But the Bible had another conception of meaningful survival, which again makes sense in a this-worldly culture. The relationship between the individual Israelite and the people of Israel was conceived as comparable to that between the leaves of the tree and the tree. "For as the days of a tree shall be the days of My people," Isaiah says in the name of God. The author of the apocryphal Ecclesiasticus, Joshua ben Sira spells out the image more clearly: "All flesh waxeth old as a garment: for the covenant from the beginning is, Thou shalt die the death. As of the green leaves on a thick tree, some fall, and some grow; so is the generation of flesh and blood, one cometh to an end, and another is born." The tree lives on, even though the leaves come and go.

We may further elaborate the image. As the dying leaves fall to the ground they reenter the cycle of life through decomposition. In death they fertilize the soil whence they originally derived their sustenance and in substance, collectively if not individually, continue to maintain the vigor of the ongoing tree. Even so, only by participating in projects larger than our own personal lives can authentic meaning and immortality be conferred on our, of necessity, limited personal efforts.

To belong responsibly to one's ethnic group and promote, enhance and advance the values it stands for, is to achieve fulfill-

ment for self as well as to make it possible for others. To neglect
fulfilling one's ethnic dimension by refusing to participate in
the ongoing life of one's native people, to the extent that it
deprives others of the beneficence of one's own contribution, is
selfish and unethical. Freedom of speech does not include freedom to shout "fire" in a crowded auditorium. Freedom to
achieve identity within society ought not to include freedom to
squander a birthright and heritage which others need—even if one
is not conscious of that need oneself.

Of course we cannot legislate against the dissipation of spiritual
treasures any more than we can legislate people into voting.
Nevertheless bars and liquor shops are closed while the polling
booths are open in New York City and no one has suggested that
this is an infringement of liberty. It is certainly a hint as to the
direction in which civic responsibility lies. By the same token,
in a country which prides itself on the separation of Church and
State, every possible assistance and encouragement must be given
to the ethnic and religious groups for fulfilling their ethnic and
religious obligations. If public schools are closed on Christmas
Day and Good Friday, they should also be closed on Jewish and
Negro holidays.

Daniel S. lives in two civilizations. His Jewish civilization goes
back to Abraham. His American civilization goes back to the
Founding Fathers. Daniel S. sings "land where my fathers died,"
but his own "fathers" died in Minsk. Like most American Jews
Daniel's family originally came here to escape from persecution
in Europe. They have become "converted" to American civilization, originally by domicile and naturalization and now, automatically, by birth. Daniel S. identifies with those who died at
Valley Forge and Bull Run the way converts to Judaism are
renamed, in Hebrew—for example, "Ruth, the daughter of Abraham our father"—and, if the conversion was successful, identify
with the Exodus from Egypt. An old German Rabbi in England
used to ask would-be converts to Judaism: "What will you do

when Hitler comes?" It was a good question, comparable to being asked, on becoming an American citizen, whether one intends to defend one's adopted country when called upon to do so. The acid test of conversion is the willingness to lay down one's life, when called upon to do so, for the values of the group.

Can Daniel S. be fulfilled and achieve an identity merely by living in one civilization, America? Had he not been born a Jew there would have been a possibility, but born a Jew, and conscious of being a Jew, he is always a Jew. There was a cruel story current at Oxford in the forties—when, in the postwar era, innumerable scholarship candidates from poor homes entered the inner chambers of what had hitherto been a sanctuary for the overprivileged aristocracy and idle rich—that one could always tell a scholarship student by the way his hand trembled when he poured the sherry.

By the same token the Jew who, being born a Jew, is conscious of being Jewish, and yet strives to lose his Jewishness, always "trembles" a little in his striving. He is a little too eager to avoid Jewish contacts, a little too anxious to prevent his children from becoming involved in Jewish affairs. Daniel S.'s parents believed they were thoroughly assimilated. They prided themselves on being more American than the Daughters of the American Revolution. They tried just a little too hard. Their hands trembled ever so slightly as they raised their son.

Daniel S. sensed inversely through their negativism a deep void in his own soul—and theirs. His parents, better than they knew, raised him to be a potential Jew. Consciously they could never have achieved what they unconsciously did in producing a sensitive, searching soul. Unconsciously they mediated something positive of the value of the Jewish past through their own negative hypersensitivity in the present.

Most Americans are hyphenated. They bring with them from their countries of origin an ethnic and often religious background which refuses to disintegrate in the melting pot of American life. Cultural pluralism is not an accident of American life. It is a law of societal and human nature. A man cannot feel responsible to a world of three and a half billion human beings or even a people of two hundred million. People who claim to be citizens of the world first and Americans, Jews or Christians second are suspect.

The insipid dreams of those who posit a cosmopolitan world, speaking Esperanto, in which all ethnic variants have been dissolved, are dreaming of a sick world. Loyalty must be fashioned within the human context of the home and the historical ethnic group before it can be tested on the nation and the world. It is unethical nationhood which can destroy civilization. There is nothing wrong with ethical nationhood. On the contrary, only through a profound allegiance to all his born loyalties can a man grow to his full stature. Immoral, jingoistic and chauvinistic nationhood is what corrodes human life and makes the world unsafe for the family of man. Nationalism is a most wholesome and civilizing device when it is used *for* man, not *against* him. The Bible intuits this as of God. Study of the animal kingdom points to this as a basic need growing out of nature itself. The collectivity is part of nature.

The possibility of being a good Jew is, for Daniel S., bound up with his being a good American. American civilization is his primary civilization. Accident of birth has given him no alternative but to seek his fullest identity through living responsibly in two civilizations. If he does not strive to be an exemplary American his Judaism will be diminished. If he does not attempt to fulfill his Jewish responsibilities his Americanism will be diminished.

He will have to ally himself with the forces of righteousness and justice in order to be a good American. His citizenship cannot be simply a matter of getting by. It will be taken for granted that he fulfill all the responsibilities devolving on all Americans. For Daniel S. this will be but a beginning. He will not be able simply to vote, pay his taxes, contribute to sundry charities and sit back. The quality of American life depends on service on the part of the individual over and above the basic requirements of citizenhood.

Within the framework of American liberalism there are legitimate differences of opinion. Some, for example, have a gradualist approach to the Negro revolution. Some are understandably impatient and press for immediate effective action. No Jew, however, can countenance racism or bigotry in any form. Daniel S. is a Jew and by virtue of his sharing in a secondary civilization, he has more of an obligation than the next man to rise for the support of the downtrodden. Jews as individuals ought to have learned from their own experiences of suffering the need for being sensitive to the suffering of others. Reactionary Jewish bigotry ought to be a contradiction in terms. Hopefully it is the exception rather than the rule.

Daniel S. married a Jewess more by accident than by design. He and his wife were born Jews but only in a limited physical sense. They emerged from the wombs of Jewish mothers. Is that all there is to being a Jew? Of course not, but it is a beginning. A Jew is one who is either born a Jew or who becomes converted to Judaism through some recognized authoritative and accredited channel. Both Daniel S. and his wife have links going back to a time in Jewish life, two hundred years ago, when a very distinct pattern of belief and practice was involved in being a Jew. These links are attenuated in them. Their Jewishness lies dormant. It is potential rather than actual. Daniel S.'s inquiring mind grows out of his parents' attempt to silence their Judaism. Had he not been Jewish, even in this limited sense, he would hardly have started visiting synagogues searching for something. Perhaps Daniel S. married a Jewish girl because his parents would have preferred him not to, in order that their own principles might be justified.

Sometimes parental ignorance and indifference can create negative feelings. His wife's parents, unlike his, had ceased trying to destroy their Jewishness. They had forgotten all about it, only to be tragically reminded by Hitler. Jewish identity by Gentile de-

finition is the most painful form of Jewish identity but it cannot
be denied as an existential reality of the twentieth century. In this
case the rude awakening of Auschwitz and exile had bred hostility and hatred. When Daniel S. has achieved his own identity he
is going to have a long and hard struggle with his wife. Their
mutual love and concern for each other will be the lifeline along
which she will hopefully walk to find her own Jewishness.

Traditionally, being Jewish has long depended on the status of
the mother. A Jewish father and a Gentile mother produced a
Gentile child. In the modern period Reform Jews have conferred
Jewish status on such children provided the parents promise to
rear them as Jews. The linking of Jewish status to the mother has
historical reasons. In the earliest days the father was all important. But certainly for the last two thousand years the mother's
religion has generally been regarded as primary.

An additional reason is often added to justify the mother's
dominance. The mother, it is claimed, has the most intimate associations with the home. It is she whose influence permeates the
home. It could also be argued that the father is the one with
whom the child chiefly identifies. Whether or not the pedagogic
reason is claimed along with the historical, the fact remains that
in the State of Israel, and among the vast majority of affiliated
Jews, the status of the mother is crucial. By common custom,
therefore, tradition still is regarded as normative in this sphere.
Regardless of any philosophical or theological qualifications the
operative definition of Jew in the twentieth century is still for
the most part one born to a Jewish mother or one formally
converted to Judaism.

What is Jewish about someone who is born to a Jewish mother
who was born to another Jewish mother going back to a period
of rich Jewish identification in a premodern *shtetl?* Nothing visible under any microscope. Chromosomatically, genetically, blood-
count-wise, there is nothing to distinguish Jewish hemoglobin
from Gentile. But a man is not born and left on a desert island.
He is reared in a family. So long as the Jew lives in a world

where Jews are news and where the Judaeo-Christian tradition is constantly referred to by politicians, the *shtetl* will out one way or another. It is an invisible sphere which envelops even the ephemeral Jew. One cannot live in a world in which six million Jews were killed because they were born Jews, even though many had forgotten they were Jews, and not be acutely aware of being Jewish.

"Anything in the newspaper, darling?" "Some Jewish doctors have been killed in Russia." "Oh!" A long pause. "Is anything else happening?" The child sitting at the breakfast table has absorbed his first lesson in Judaism—or rather, in anti-Semitism. The "Oh" is pregnant with "I know I am a Jew but I am damned if I am going to be made to feel guilty or responsible for those stupid people who are always getting into trouble for one reason or another. It must be their own damn fault. Look at me. I am a perfectly respected member of the local Ethical Culture Society, we winter in Palm Beach and we've never had any trouble!"

Through a process of subtle osmosis the child learns to hear what his parents *are* behind what they *say* they are. Daniel S. was taught better at the breakfast table than he would have been taught at any Hebrew School about what it means to be a Jew, indirectly of course, the way a photograph is translated optically in the camera into a reverse configuration to be translated back again in the print. Daniel S. was a born developer of theological photographic negatives. If his parents had really wanted to achieve their goal they would have joined the local synagogue. That might have done the trick. Many a child has been ruined for life by five years, and less, of Hebrew School. Daniel S.'s parents were just too consistent in their rejection and handed him a perfect set of negatives to work on.

His mother had mentioned once too often that she didn't look Jewish. Once, in a supermarket, his mother had shied away in fright when Daniel S. had asked for a piece of stuffed derma. She would have indulged him with frogs' legs or octopus. A Jewish delicacy had an air of decadence about it. Daniel tabulated all these reactions. He had never set foot in a *shtetl*. He had hardly met any Jews, certainly not authentic Jews. Something subtle in the complicated pattern of family responses came to him from another world. It was not visible, but it was real all the same. There are far more things in the rearing of a child than can be touched, smelled, tasted, heard or seen.

During the Six-Day War, when the State of Israel fought for its life, thousands of this kind of Jew, world over, potentially but not actually Jews, peripheral Jews in the extreme, were suddenly reactivated. Reading a book on the Holocaust has had a comparable effect on many. The peripheral Jew is always vulnerable to being radically confronted with what he had thought he had long since left behind. The spiritual capital of the *shtetl* is not yet entirely dissipated. It crops up in the most unexpected places. It grows under the stress and strain of uncertain Jewish existence.

Daniel S. was once born from his mother's physical womb. To be authentically Jewish he must be twice born from the womb of his people. He must get to know Jews, identify with them, work with them, share their aspirations, ultimately join with them. Commitment without some kind of affiliation is like using a cookbook without any foodstuffs to make a meal. It sounds fine but it leaves you hungry. There is no use for Daniel S. to agonize privately over his Jewish identity. In isolation he will not experience the existential reality of what it means to be a Jew. To be Jewish means to belong to the Jewish people. One cannot belong through books and ideas alone. Judaism, like life, is with people —with Jews.

Daniel S. can belong in one of many ways. He can become affiliated with a synagogue, a cultural, philanthropic or welfare organization. He can study Judaism in the abstract, read books on Jewish life, think about Judaism and talk about Judaism "till the cows come home." But he will never feel Jewish in his guts until he mixes with Jews. Visiting a synagogue is not enough. That is looking in on a restaurant as an outsider with nose pressed up against the glass. It may be easy on the eyes but bad for the stomach. It arouses expectations which cannot be fulfilled.

Daniel S. must enter the great restaurant of Jewish life and absorb some of the real delicacies himself. The Jewish people must become flesh of his flesh and bone of his bone. Only thus will his academic and philosophical doubts be resolved. Only thus will the hunger in his heart be satisfied. If he is confused about what it means to be a Jew, part of the reason is that he has never been afforded by others or himself the luxury of feeling like a Jew. Only when he can feel at home with some other Jews, from whatever part of the spectrum of Jewish life, will Daniel S. belong. Once he belongs to any group, he can begin to identify with every group.

Above all, the past will then come alive. Up to now he has known of the Jews of former days as ghosts. Like the early Puritans in America, for whom there was no visible correlation between the characters in the Bible and the real-life Jews of the Colonies, so for him the Pharisees and the Jews of America seem unrelated. Daniel S. cannot afford such a schizophrenia. A house can have the finest plumbing system with all modern conveniences but if it is not attached to a water main, it is of no value. A Jew may have the finest theoretical notions about Jewish life and Judaism but unless somewhere, somehow, he is linked to a living source of real Jewish life, his conceptual system is useless. It cannot provide life-giving sustenance. A recipe is no substitute for a meal. A book on the internal combustion engine is no way of traveling. Knowing how a bicycle is constructed is no substitute for riding one.

Where can Daniel S. link up his own burgeoning desire to be a twice-born Jew in the modern world? Where are the contemporary life-giving sources of Jewish life for the searching Jew? There are many possibilities, depending upon his temperament. In visiting many synagogues, he may have found a place where he feels that he can belong.

Franz Rosenzweig, one of the greatest Jews of the twentieth century, whose theological writings and personal example of endurance in suffering have endeared him to and made him a source of inspiration for many, was once on the verge of converting to Christianity, when he visited a small Orthodox synagogue in Berlin. It was the Day of Atonement, October 11, 1913, and as a result of his experience in this small Orthodox synagogue that day Franz Rosenzweig, assimilated to the point of desiring to convert to Christianity, began the long hard trek back to his Jewish origins. ". . . after prolonged, and I believe thorough, self-examination" he wrote to a friend a few weeks later, "I have reversed my decision. It no longer seems necessary to me, and therefore, being what I am, no longer possible. I will remain a Jew." Sitting with other Jews in a sacred place on a sacred occasion was for him a crucial experience. The process of being twice born a Jew had commenced.

Jewish religion has tended, on the whole, to be somewhat leery of sudden conversions. The "St. Paul on the road to Damascus" syndrome has been suspect. Becoming Jewish, whether from a state of non-Jewishness or once-born Jewishness, is not a question of suddenly seeing a blinding light. It is the slow but sure association with Jews and Judaism, under authentically Jewish conditions, until one feels that one is a member of a living people. (Being with Jews on any level is not enough. The purpose of being together is paramount. There is a hierarchy of purposes culminating in the religious.) To be twice born, there is the need to be linked through an existential umbilical cord to the mother Jewish people, to bask in and be protected by the amniotic fluid of shared ideas and creative group experiences. If the conversion is to take, there must be a prolonged period of gestation. A flash of light on the road of Damascus turned Paul from being a violent anti-Christian into being a violent anti-Jew. Such conversions do not basically affect the inner man.

It could be a synagogue, but it need not be a synagogue. It could be any institution or organization dedicated to religion, culture, art, music, literature, philanthropy, social action or welfare. The purpose must be elevating, not degrading. It could be a visit to Israel. Perhaps there, more than in any other place in the world, Daniel S. might experience the tangible nature of Jewish peoplehood. In a little country in the Middle East whose two million inhabitants embrace Anglo-Saxon Jews from England, Canada and America, Oriental Jews from Iraq, Morocco, Yemen, Syria, Egypt and Algeria, where Jews speak every language under the sun and yet are united in one common national purpose, Daniel S. will learn more and feel more about the rock whence he was hewn. Israel reborn could be an ideal place for Daniel S. to become twice born.

It is conceivable, but unlikely, that Daniel S. will arrive at Lydda Airport and suddenly decide that he will settle on a *kibbutz* for the rest of his life. There are his wife and family to think of. Moreover, Daniel S. has had time to test his Zionistic reflexes in terms of newspaper reports. (An awareness of current trends in the Middle East is even part of the intellectual paraphernalia of civilized Western Gentiles.) Immigration from affluent Anglo-Saxon countries is negligible in comparison to immigration from countries where Jews are insecure and oppressed. In the 1930's it was customary to ask the new immigrants to Israel: *"Kommen Sie von Deutschland oder von Überzeugung?"* ("Do you come from Germany or out of—literally, from—conviction?") It was a cruel quip but not unrelated to reality.

In the early years, after the foundation of the State of Israel, the old-time Zionists who had come from Europe in the first days of settlement were angry with the Western Jews, whose lot had fallen in pleasant places, for not uprooting themselves from their countries of domicile and participating wholeheartedly in the destiny of Israel. In the two decades of the existence of the State of Israel this temper has changed. Especially after the Six-Day War, Israeli Jews realized that Jewish survival is a two-way affair between Israel and the Diaspora. The Diaspora needs Israel but Israel also needs the Diaspora. The old tub-thumping platitudes about Jews only being able to live decent Jewish lives in Israel have subsided.

A growing realization has crystallized in Israel that, while there will always be a handful of dedicated idealists who will be prepared to sacrifice everything to serve their ethnic group and their ancient homeland, most Jews living in relative comfort outside of Israel are not going to give up what they have in exchange for the avowed hardships involved in life in a young country. Israel will continue to draw largely for immigration on Jews who do not find acceptance in their countries of domicile rather than on those who do. This is not a subject for romantic rhapsodizing. It is a fact of life.

It is even a moot point, were Russian attitudes to change radically, how many of the three million Jews in Russia would emigrate to Israel. Zionist theory falls down in the face of reality. For over twenty-five hundred years the Jewish people has been a Diaspora people. The Jewish people is still a minority in the world, perhaps most vulnerable at its densest and most Jewishly creative population center in Israel. Once it was customary for Israeli Jews to warn Diaspora Jews how fragile and insecure their position was. Every outburst of anti-Semitism in the world, however minor, was taken as proof positive that Jewish existence outside of Israel was simply not viable. These arguments may still be heard but they have lost ground. Reality gives them the lie. American Jewry is the most powerful Jewry the world has ever known. And if American Jewry were to suffer the fate of European Jewry, Israel's days would also be numbered.

The State of Israel was unable to protect the rights of Jews in Arab countries in the aftermath of the Six-Day War. The existence of a Jewish state, however well armed, in the Middle East, is no guarantee of the life and limb of Jews living elsewhere unless international protocol is strictly observed. Even here, protest is probably the extent of intervention. Israel's continued existence in reality terms is posited on the goodwill of America and the continued interest and support of American Jews. Jewish survival itself, in a national sovereign state, in a world which is rapidly shrinking and where power politics are largely in the hands of the truly powerful is, in any case, as problematic as any other kind of survival. Israel's survival is as secure or as insecure as Jewish survival (or human survival for that matter) anywhere.

In the year 1850, a British Jew by the name of Don Pacifico became embroiled with the Greek government. Lord Palmerston, then British Foreign Secretary, invoked the power of the British Navy to protect him and delivered one of his most famous speeches in the House of Commons. In the course of his speech Palmerston quoted the words of Cicero: *"Civis Romanus sum"*— "I am a Roman citizen." The gist of his argument was that a British citizen, in any part of the world, whatever his ethnic origin, should be protected to the fullest extent by the power of the British government.

There was a time when Zionists dreamed that a Jewish state might perform just such a function. Wherever and whenever a Jew suffered from persecution, all that would be required would be a remonstration from Israel and the persecution would cease. At worst he could emigrate to Israel. But even the United States cannot pursue Palmerstonian foreign policies in the latter half of the twentieth century. The incident of the *Pueblo* clearly indicates the limitations of "I am an American citizen" in a nuclear age. And three million Jews behind the Iron Curtain cannot emigrate to Israel even when they want to.

The increasing realization of the limits of physical power in a world shrunk to the size of "a global village," in Marshall McLuhan's phrase, has given the State of Israel pause. In Israel there is a deeper awareness today than two decades ago that the Diaspora cannot be written off and that, in a real sense, Israel itself is part of the Diaspora. The discrepancy between Israeli and Arab birthrates will make the very Jewish majority status of Israel problematic by the end of the century. There is one Jewish people, of which the Jews living in the State of Israel are but a part—a vitally important part, but a part nonetheless.

A dangerous counterpoint is sometimes heard in Zionist circles. "Masada will not fall again." This is the oath taken by certain Israeli soldiers on initiation into the army. It is a stirring challenge but contains ominous overtones. Even outside of Israel, Jews, understandably depressed and saddened by the agony of the Holocaust and the manner in which Israel has invariably been left to fend for herself by the nations of the world, speak of the virtue, if not of being able to live as Jews, of dying as Jews. "Better to die with a rifle in the hand than to perish at Auschwitz." The alternative is not as exclusive as it is often made to appear.

If Masada is merely a romantic or poetic image there can be no cavil. Every army needs its slogans. But from a reality point of view it must never be forgotten that it was the Pharisees (who compromised with the Romans) who lived to tell the tale of Masada. It was the descendants of those who survived because of the Pharisees who were motivated to rediscover the site of an ancient defeat transmuted through Pharisaic, not Zealot, Jewish survival into a victory of the spirit. Pharisaic Judaism tended to endorse Oliver Goldsmith's aphorism that

> . . . he who fights and runs away
> May live to fight another day.
> But he who is in battle slain
> Can never rise and fight again.

The author of the Book of Ecclesiastes put this in a different way: "For to him that is joined to all the living there is hope; for a living dog is better than a dead lion." Konrad Lorenz has shown that when, in the course of a fight between two timber wolves, the stronger animal has the weaker at its mercy, the latter is able to stop the fight by deliberately exposing the bend of his neck with the jugular vein.

Less than an inch from the tensed neck-muscles, where the jugular vein lies immediately beneath the skin, gleam the fangs of his antagonist from beneath the wickedly retracted lips. Whereas, during the thick of the fight, both wolves were intent on keeping only their teeth, the one invulnerable part of the body, in opposition to each other, it now appears that the discomfited fighter proffers intentionally that part of his anatomy to which a bite must assuredly prove fatal.

What happens next is that the victor loses all desire to kill as a result of this gesture of submission and slinks away.

The entire ethos of Pharisaic Judaism is embodied in the behavior of fighting timber wolves. The Talmud records that as the Romans encircled Jerusalem in 70 C.E., and the city was already going up in flames, Yochanan ben Zaccai, the leading Pharisee of the day, had himself carried out of the beleaguered city by his pupils in a coffin to escape detection. He was taken to the Roman general Vespasian and one of the requests which he made epitomizes Pharisaic Judaism: "Give me Yavneh and her sages." Yavneh, or Jamnia, was a little coastal settlement where a school for the study of Torah already existed before the destruction of the Temple. In the person of Yochanan ben Zaccai the Jewish people exposed its jugular vein to the power of Rome. "Let us study our religious traditions and serve God after our fashion. We relinquish all aspirations to physical victory over you.". The Roman and, later, the Christian timber wolf, slunk away. The gesture of submission was adequate to take all pleasure out of total extermination. As long as the Jews maintained a submissive stance, at least in the premodern period, they would survive.

Animals act on instinct. Human beings in society must discover the path of life. Nonviolence is not an accidental quirk of the human mind. It is deeply rooted in the evolutionary process. It has a distinct survival value. The Jews, in fact, despite horrendous persecution, survive. The Romans are no more and Christianity, visibly in our day, yields its imperial pretensions in theology as well as in society. The ecumenical movement itself exhibits, in strict ethological terms, the once proudly victorious

Catholic Church offering its jugular vein to a victorious secular age.

It is argued that the Holocaust has radically altered Jewish attitudes to survival. The Holocaust, it is said, was an unprecedented attack on the Jewish people. Rather than submit to a state of affairs in which no gesture of submission whatsoever is of avail, let us die fighting. Better be wiped out at Masada than be cremated in ovens at Auschwitz. It is doubtful whether even the Holocaust can radically alter deep-seated tendencies in the Jewish people. The horrendous extermination of six million Jews while the world stood watching helplessly and, to a considerable extent, indifferently, is, indeed, an eternal blot on the human conscience.

But the Jewish people still lives. From the ashes of the crematoria the State of Israel emerged, phoenixlike, with its promise of hope and dignity for Jews the world over. Without Hitler, the State of Israel might never have been born. But we must be cautious about the nature of that dignity and its quality. Many of those who died in the concentration camps were devoutly Orthodox Jews who even *in extremis* did not lose their faith in God. Orthodox Rabbis counseled against suicide in the hell of Auschwitz. The distinguished liberal Rabbi Leo Baeck also maintained his spiritual integrity in the face of all suffering.

It would be ironic and tragic if the rightful and legitimate anger of the survivors of the Holocaust did not adequately articulate the ongoing immortal aspirations of those who, in fact, died. Daniel S. is far removed from the anguish of the Holocaust but part of the Jewish people with whom he must come to terms are the dead. His Jewish identity is bound up with the martyrs. He is part of their immortality. He must have some attitude to the catastrophe which engulfed not only peripheral and unconscious Jews such as his wife's grandparents but also the cream of West and East European Jewry.

In Israel Daniel S. will discover bitter feelings about the Holocaust. A generation of Jews raised on the firm steel of the machine gun and the whine of bullets, who have had to fight incessantly for sheer survival and know the value of the tank and jet cannot understand why millions of Jews permitted themselves to be led like lambs to slaughter. Even graphic accounts of heroic Jewish resistance against overwhelming odds, such as the staunch defense of the Warsaw Ghetto, fail to quench the stark realities of Jewish passivity.

But there is a greater danger that Jewish survival will be seen exclusively in terms of defense. A strong Israel is imperative. But an Israel which sees only Masada, and not Yavneh also, as part of the fabric of Jewish survival, is in danger of forgetting the well-springs of Jewish existence.

European Jewry was not world Jewry. The Holocaust was evil, but other inhuman acts of men and nations have been evil. Attempts have been made to wipe out other ethnic groups. The American Indians are a case in point. The Holocaust, however tragic, cannot be made a theological watershed. It must be placed within a wider historical perspective. When we have reached the ultimate point of human anguish in the individual we have reached the outer limits of the theological problem of suffering. No mother in Nazi Europe suffered more than Hannah who, in the Maccabeean story, witnessed the cruel death, one by one, of her seven sons. Multiply one toothache by a million and we are still left with one toothache, from the point of view of intensity of human pain.

It is our tragic, if understandable, insensitivity, which sees a million children deliberately burned to death as more tragic than one child deliberately burned to death. It speaks of our own spiritual poverty that one bereaved mother does not seem as tragic as a million bereaved mothers. But the numbers game has no role in theology. What are we saying—that if Hitler had only killed one Jew it wouldn't have been so bad? Then Hitler was sick but we are insensitive.

Violent emotional Jewish reactions to the Holocaust are understandable. Gentile reactions are also understandable. There is little doubt but that the vogue for things Jewish in a post-Holocaust world stems in part from feelings of guilt. Every man and woman who survived Auschwitz somewhere feels guilty. Every man and woman who escaped the burning asks, "Why did it happen to them and not to me?" But anguish and guilt can often becloud the issue of our authentic reaction to what happened. Of course the world was guilty. Recent disclosures of happenings in the State Department only underline what everyone knows—that the world regarded European Jewry as expendable.

But Jews also have a complicity in this reaction. When Jews already knew what was happening in the concentration camps there were those who still felt that there was a limit to what could be done. "America should only have declared war after Pearl Harbor. How could we have asked her to fight before then? It would have looked like a Jewish war. How could we have asked American boys to give their lives for European Jews?" How indeed? Or for Koreans? Or for Vietnamese? The Jew who survived, rightly or wrongly, in Europe, in America or in Israel, feels guilty. He has every reason to feel guilty. A sick humanity tolerated, aided and abetted the machinations of madmen.

The dead cannot be resurrected but the living can be made secure. Daniel S. must be prepared to spend more time and energy on the living than the dead. Did he ever give of his substance to Israel before? If he cannot do what others have done (settle in Israel and make a personal investment in her destiny), there are other roles he can play. Here in Israel, to a greater extent than elsewhere, the tragedy of the Holocaust is given, albeit limited, a meaning. The Law of Return, had Israel existed in 1939, would have provided the only haven in a storm-tossed and indifferent world. Here, to a large extent, the remnants of those who survived have found a haven where they can live in dignity.

But Daniel S. must also see beyond the present harsh reality to a deeper level of insight. In the year 480 B.C.E. Leonidas, King of Sparta, was sent to defend the narrow pass of Thermopylae from

the Persian army under Xerxes. Leonidas was betrayed and surrounded on both sides. Instead of either yielding or attempting to
withdraw, he and his army fought to the last man.

It is unlikely that Thermopylae could have inspired Masada.
Nevertheless the Greek parallel is too obvious to be gainsaid. But
those who vow today that Masada shall never fall are more indebted to Yavneh than they would care to admit. Daniel S. will
be tempted by Masada. In a sense, it is a Jewish heresy, since
Jews have favored survival by avoiding the self-destructive extremes of asceticism or death with glory. But the fact that
Masada is needed does not mean that Yavneh has outlived its
usefulness. It is a tragic concession to the grim realities of the
century of the Holocaust.

Daniel S. may not die in bed. His wife and his children might
conceivably be torn away from the family hearth. To be Jewish
in the twentieth century is to be marginal, in Israel as well as
outside. There is no hiding place for the Jew. History has made
of him a barometer of civilization. The Jew thrives on peace. He
is the first to suffer in war. He must accept the inevitable limitations of self-defense. To rave and rant at this minority condition
is suicidal. It must be accepted and lived with. Still it has its
advantages, for where it is acknowledged and accepted it yields
insights of much maturity and creativity. It is not without blessing. It must, in any case, be accepted. Rejection of this condition
is a rejection of one's very identity.

It is tragic that in a century which has reached a realization of
the ultimate limitation of all war, a sovereign State of Israel had
to be born with all the paraphernalia of a defense system to
which sovereignty in the modern world is heir. George Steiner
has described the State of Israel as a "sad miracle." There is a
valid pathos in this description. The Diaspora people had prayed
for a restoration to Zion for almost two thousand years. Three
times a day the Jew, after the destruction of the Temple, prayed:
"And let our eyes behold Thy return in mercy to Zion." After
every meal the Jew recited: "And rebuild Jerusalem the holy

city speedily and in our days." Every Festival and New Moon the Jew prayed: "Bring us with exultation to Zion Thy City, and to Jerusalem Thy sanctuary with everlasting joy."

There was a time when a hope for a return to Zion, under happier conditions, would mean a gathering together of Jews for the creative purposes of rebuilding their lives without the necessity of recourse to arms. Cruel world history has shattered that dream. Tragically, but necessarily, an Israel without the latest refinements of self-defense is unthinkable and intolerable.

Daniel S. will realize this tragic necessity. He will not be seduced by the blandishments of those who demand of Israel alone that she disarm herself. Israel has been the defender and not the aggressor. Even though he might never serve in the Israeli defense forces Daniel S. must sympathize with the need for security of a little people of two million Jews in a vast sea of one hundred million Arabs.

The timber wolf of Arab aggression cannot be relied upon to play the game of charitable response to submissive gesture. In the century of the Holocaust, the dramatic gestures must come from others. Once bitten in the jugular vein by Hitler, the Jewish people cannot afford the luxury of spilling more of its precious blood. The risk of yet another Holocaust is frightening. The lives of two million Jews are at stake. Vigorous self-defense, in Israel, at least, must take precedence over submissive gestures which no longer avail in desperate need. For the immediate future Masada takes precedence over Yavneh, even though Yavneh must, from a long-term point of view, especially for world Jewry, never be forgotten.

But in Israel Daniel S. will see further than the needs of physical self-defense. He will see visible results of remarkable and unprecedented creativity. He will see the desert blossoming as the rose. Almost every family he meets will have lost at least one close relative in the Nazi Holocaust. Almost every family will have suffered in the constant war of self-defense. He will witness the transmuting of the persecution of the Jewish people into the creativity of the Jewish people.

He will learn to tolerate some of the paradoxes, anomalies and inconsistencies of Israeli Jewish life, painful though they will be to an American-born Jew. The incompatibility of a modern state which aspires to be a democracy and a deeply entrenched politically conscious Orthodox rabbinate powerfully opposed to a separation of Church and State will be one of the most glaring of these anomalies. An ambivalence toward the Arab minority arising out of a fear of its ever becoming a majority will be another.

Daniel S. will learn to love the Jewish people at the Achilles' heel of its twentieth-century existence. Old states have not yet worked off or resolved all their inconsistencies and Israel is a relatively young state. Her absorbing of newcomers from so many different countries and different walks of life is a latter-day miracle. Where he criticizes, he will learn to do so with love. The Jews of the State of Israel are truly flesh of his flesh and bone of his bone. They must be loved even with their shortcomings.

Daniel S. must avoid one danger. He must not accept the notion of being an American Jew as a condition of second-class Jewish citizenship. There was a tendency in the early days, not so marked now, to an Israeli superiority not entirely untinged with arrogance directed at the visitors or tourists who only came to visit, not to settle. The notion that a Jew can only lead a truly Jewish life in Israel goes back to the archaic notion of Israel as Yahweh's territory over which He has exclusive jurisdiction. Living outside of Israel meant being unable to commune with Yahweh.

In an era when world Jewry could not, in any case, be housed in Israel nor, for the most part, would wish to be, such an anachronistic attitude is harmful and creates much ill-will. The malarial swamps of modern Zionism which need reclaiming are worldwide. A Jew in America can be just as good a Jew as an Israeli so long as he is responsibly committed to the meaningful existence and continued survival of the Jewish people. Daniel S.'s choice not to settle in Israel can be as valid and authentic as the immigrant's desire to settle in Israel and the *sabra*'s or native-born Israeli's, desire to remain.

Israel will be, for the foreseeable future, a sovereign national state in which the majority of citizens will be Jewish. Will this mean a renaissance of the Jewish religion? Theoretically, before the establishment of the State of Israel, it was hoped that, in the words of the prophet, Torah would come "out of Zion." A large Jewish community, settled on its ancient soil, would rejuvenate Jewish spiritual life. Achad Ha'am (1856–1927), a Zionist thinker and writer, spoke of the possibilities of Israel as a "spiritual center" for world Jewry.

Thus far Israel has been a source of technology for the burgeoning young African states. She has also provided emissaries for the transmission of the resurrected Hebrew language and culture throughout the world. But Torah, in the sense of religion, has not yet come from Zion. The holy days of the Jewish calendar are celebrated as national holidays on a merely secular level by most Israelis.

Many Israelis fondly imagine that the equation of national days of rest with traditional Jewish holidays makes for a rejuvenated Jewish religion. Diaspora Jewry looks for new symbols, new folkways, new liturgy, new prayers, new poetry which can be incorporated meaningfully into the worldwide celebration of Jewish holy days. Some music and some songs have emerged. There is not as yet sufficient thinking on the need for reconstructing religion. The official state-sponsored Israeli synagogue tends to preclude other versions of Judaism and thus offers no alternative for the religiously alienated younger generation. "There is only one kind of Jewish religion—Orthodox—and that's not for me." From such sweet simplicities one does not erect a spiritual center for world Jewry in an age of secular and spiritual crisis.

Hopefully Daniel S. will return home from Israel with a keener awareness of Jewish destiny in the twentieth century, an appreciation, albeit indirect, of the tragedy of the Holocaust, an awareness of the creativity which grew out of its aftermath—and a modest introduction to Hebrew.

For Judaism is not merely religion. The multiplicity of sects, viewpoints and opinions on religious and ritual matters which Daniel S. has seen in America, and now in Israel, will have confirmed in him the understanding that that which unites the Jewish people in the twentieth century is neither creed nor ritual. It is a shared concern with the ongoing destiny of the Jewish people which makes for a sense of Jewish identity.

In the premodern period, when Jews lived for the most part in enclaves hermetically sealed off from the prevailing winds of outside culture, it was possible for Jews to believe approximately in the same theology and perform approximately the same rituals. Even in this premodern period there were differences of stress and custom within the overall framework of Jewish life. But now that the Diaspora Jewish people lives in two civilizations, the influences which are brought to bear on individual Jews are too diverse to permit that kind of uniformity. Only a centripetal concern for the entire Jewish people within its historical and current context will bind together in an overriding harmony the inevitable centrifugal tendencies arising out of the modern Jewish condition. Unity in ethnic diversity rather than theological and behavioral conformity will be the hallmark of Jewish life in the democratic stage of Jewish existence.

If Judaism were merely religion, the Hebrew language would be an anachronism. What has a foreign language got to do with religion? Even the Catholic Church now bids farewell to Latin. But Judaism is the evolving religious civilization of the Jewish people and, accordingly, language plays an important role. Daniel S. has learned Hebrew the painless way. To be thrown into the vortex of a living language is the best way to learn its immediate relevance and significance.

But modern Hebrew, as it is spoken in Israel, is no radical linguistic innovation. It is grounded in the ancient Hebrew language, the tongue of prophet, priest and sage. The impassioned and untutored agony of Amos, the measured, statesmanlike oratory of Isaiah, are reflected in the modern language. Noun and verb formations are strictly patterned on the old. The word for paratrooper (*tzanchan*) for example, is built from a verb used in the Bible to describe Achsah, the daughter of Caleb, softly dismounting, with billowing skirts, from the ass she was riding (*vatitznach*). An article from *Davar* or *Ha-aretz*, leading Israeli newspapers, will carry linguistic and idiomatic overtones of Bible, Talmud and *Midrash*. The subtle nuances of modern stylists, as well as archaic, such as Nobel Prize winner Agnon, will be experienced on an impoverished level if the wealth of their historical background is not to some extent appreciated. It is a little like reading Shakespeare without the benefit of, at least, a modest acquaintance with the referents of classical allusions.

Daniel S. will not be able to appreciate this all at once. To approach the language from its colloquial end is to overlook most of its historical nuances. For him, however, a Diaspora Jew, destined to remain in America, the Hebrew language must become far more than a language of daily intercourse. It must become what it is, in fact, for all Jews, whether Israeli or not, a sanctum. If *Eretz Yisrael* is, for the historic Jew, "land where my fathers died," Hebrew is "the language my fathers spoke."

The Hebrew language, at its inception, was merely colloquial. Born in a proto-Arabic tongue, cousin to the speech of other denizens of the Middle East, Hebrew arose as one of several ancient Semitic languages. But the God-intoxicated prophets put their stamp on the language. After Chopin played the piano it was never the same instrument again. After Amos had proclaimed, "Let justice well up as waters, and righteousness as a mighty stream," and after Micah had declared, "It hath been told thee, O man, what is good, and what the Lord thy God doth require of thee, only to do justly, and to love mercy, and to walk humbly with thy God," the Hebrew language was never the same again. It had truly become a holy language.

The Bible is not a book but rather a library of books. The span of time in which the books of the Bible were written extends over almost a thousand years. But the Bible is only a small part of ancient Hebraic literature. The prophets and scribes preserved only that part of the total literary output of the ancient Hebrews which spoke of God and man's search for God. As the top tenth of the iceberg points to the nine-tenths submerged below the surface, so the Bible points to a vaster and wider literature left behind.

What was this ancient literature which the prophets did not deem worthy of preservation? It is not that they deliberately destroyed it. They simply declared, in the fact of their editing, that it was not holy enough to deserve being preserved by the scribes. That was tantamount to destroying it. In the ancient world, papyrus could not guard the literary insights of the past unless generation after generation of painstaking scribes were prepared laboriously to transcribe from one manuscript to another in order to preserve. Even those traditions transmitted orally would to some extent be determined by official criteria of worth.

The Bible itself refers to some of the missing material. It seems that much of it was historical reportage, books describing battles, secular history as we might describe it today. A Zionist documentary of the thirties, called *One Suitcase*, purported to show the anguish of some East European Jew who was being assisted to emigrate from his country to Israel but who, understandably, because of the exigencies of expense, was only permitted to take one suitcase with him. The documentary showed the agony of having to leave behind treasures, mementos, *objets d'art*. All had to be relinquished in the interest of survival.

The history of the biblical canon might also be described as "One Suitcase." (The word "canon" is from the Greek and means a straight rod, and hence, norm. It was used by the Christian Church from the fourth century on to describe those books handed down from the past which were officially regarded as normative. Although the Jews never used this word, the concept is derived from a distinction they made between holy books and extraneous books, that is, books not deemed to possess the same authority as the most ancient and, therefore, most holy books.) As the prophets foresaw the imminent destruction of Israel and Judah, they intuited that the people was destined for a long dark night of wandering Diaspora existence. Under such circumstances it was impossible to carry along all the people's cultural belongings. An anguished choice left behind poetry, history and treasures we can only estimate, all in the interest of survival. Only that part of Hebraic literature which could be fitted into "one suitcase," one book, one Bible, could be taken along. To be encumbered by too much "extraneous" and "irrelevant" material would be a potential source of great danger. As on a ship which is in danger of foundering in a storm, all had to be jettisoned save only that which was of utmost importance. Only what could reasonably be carried under dire circumstances of stress, which possessed the inspirational and spiritual qualities making for survival, could remain on board if the ship of the Jewish people were to endure the squalls and perils of Diaspora existence and remain afloat until it could reach a safe harbor of redemption and freedom.

The Bible thus became a holy book, "holy" meaning "supremely important and valuable for meaningful survival." Those who believe in a God who is a Person maintain that only those objects or persons touched by such a God are holy. Reconstructionist, or religious humanistic Judaism, insists that the category of the holy operates outside of such a supernaturalistic universe of discourse. If we observe the way the ancient Israelites used the word "holy," we readily see that, despite their ancient universe of discourse, they meant that which is of supreme importance for human fulfillment. One does not have to believe in God as Person to appreciate the role of the holy in human life. God conceived as Process, as Power making for salvation, also presupposes the need for holiness and its reality.

Daniel S. will thus not be able to rest with a merely colloquial acquaintance with Hebrew. In his search for a deeper Jewish identity he will seek to master, to the best of his ability, the Hebrew language in all its dimensions. It is the language of the Bible, of the prophets and, because the traditional prayerbook is largely a mosaic of biblical quotations, the language of the liturgy.

We must not overwhelm Daniel S. with the richness of his heritage. We must create in him a realization that, as a Jew, Hebrew as a sanctum is his language in a salvational sense. Acquaintance with it will elicit from him his deepest aspirations and fulfill his deepest needs. The rebirth of modern Hebrew is a miracle only made possible because the role of Hebrew was central in Jewish consciousness long before Theodor Herzl ever wrote *The Jewish State* or the earliest Orthodox settlers left Europe for Palestine in the late nineteenth century. An old Jewish lullaby, which the *shtetl* mother sang to her infant, speaks of the tears that lie in the letters of the Hebrew alphabet, which he would soon learn. Tears, persecution, joy, sorrow, anguish, spiritual elation, suffering and repentance—all these are enshrined in the holy language.

Hebrew may today be a modern colloquial language for two million Jews in the Middle East but for the Jewish people as a whole, including the Israeli Jews, Hebrew remains holy. It is not merely a language in which one may order a very dry martini at the Kateh Dan Hotel in Tel Aviv. Nor is it merely a language in which one may discuss the problems of Arab-Israeli tension. It is a language in which the soul of the Jew communes with God and total Jewish destiny, a destiny which transcends any particular community of Jews, even of the Jews living in Israel. For all Jewish communities are part of one people.

Nor is Hebrew the only holy Jewish language. One of the best known Jewish prayers, even for the peripheral Jew, is the *Kaddish*, or the sanctification. This is a doxology recited by mourners. It is not written in Hebrew. It is written in Aramaic. Aramaic was the lingua franca of the Jewish people at the time of Jesus. By that time, Hebrew had ceased to be a colloquial language and had become a language reserved largely for sacred purposes. Some Rabbis, notably Judah the Prince (135–220), editor of the *Mishnah*, spoke it in their homes, but they were the exception rather than the rule.

An Aramaic translation of the Bible was widely used in synagogue and school in the rabbinic period. Prayers were recited in the vernacular. The *Mishnah* was written in Hebrew as was the *Midrash*, not the Hebrew of the Bible but an academic Hebrew of the schools. Both the Jerusalem Talmud and the Babylonian Talmud were written in Aramaic. The *Zohar* was written in Aramaic. The traditional prayer book, largely Hebrew, still contains remnants of ancient vernacular Aramaic prayers. The opening declaration of the traditional *Haggadah*—the order of service for the eve of Passover, or the *Seder*—"This is the bread of affliction which our ancestors ate in the land of Egypt," is couched in Aramaic. So is the delightful fairy-tale folk song *Chad Gadya*—about the goat which father bought for two *zuzim*—which concludes the *Seder* service.

As the center of gravity of Jewish life moved from the Middle East to Spain, Italy, France and the Rhineland, the "one suitcase" syndrome repeated itself. Aramaic ceased to be a vernacular and colloquial language. Only those sections of Aramaic deemed of supreme value in the spiritual life of the people were carried to the new countries of settlement. To this day the Orthodox Jew devoutly reads the weekly portion of the Torah in its Aramaic translation. But Aramaic has long since ceased to be a living language. In the Middle Ages Jews communicated with each other largely in a scholastic Hebrew. Maimonides wrote his philosophy in Arabic but his legal codes in Hebrew. Within the framework of scholasticism, he raised the Hebrew language to new heights of simple lucidity. His Code is a linguistic gem.

Nor are Hebrew and Aramaic the only holy Jewish languages. The Middle Ages gave birth to two new holy languages, Ladino, among the Sephardic descendants of those expelled from Spain, and Yiddish, among the *Ashkenazim* or French and German Jews. These languages are an amalgam of, in the case of Yiddish, Hebrew and middle German and, in the case of Ladino, Hebrew and Spanish. A comparable phenomenon existed among Persian Jews.

Yiddish may have arisen out of the colloquial use of German by Jews who later moved to different parts of Europe. But from the earliest times, written in Hebrew letters, it became inextricably bound up with the Jewish spirit. Through a voluminous literature which had a special appeal to the masses of downtrodden Jewry, and through the labors of such literary giants as Mendele Mocher Sforim, Isaac Leib Peretz and Sholem Aleichem, Yiddish became a dimension of the Jewish soul. The Jew who created Yiddish at a time when his own collective destiny was reaching a low ebb blended into the language the deepest resonances of his own ideal yearnings and aspirations. There are things that the Jew can say in Yiddish for which no other language, not even Hebrew, will suffice. If Hebrew is the head and the heart of the Jew, Yiddish is his soul.

Poor Daniel S. is overwhelmed. He has had more than he bargained for. He would like to withdraw. Is there no other place to go? Couldn't I belong to an ethnic people with just *one* thousand years of history, thinks Daniel S. Do I have to have warriors *and* kings *and* prophets *and* Rabbis *and* politicians *and* the rest? Wouldn't just the Bible do? Do I have to have the Bible *and* the *Midrash and* the *Mishnah and* the Talmud *and* the Codes? Do I have to have the Hebrew language *and* Yiddish *and* . . . ? Couldn't I have just *one* tragedy, not the war with Rome *and* the Crusades *and* the Inquisition *and* the Pogroms *and* the Holocaust?

Daniel S. is four thousand years old. He is his people. His identity is bound up with theirs. He thought he was only thirty-odd years old. Now he realizes that every Jewish child is born with all this history behind him. There is no cause for concern. Daniel S. should take to heart the words of an ancient Rabbi: "It is not thy duty to complete the work, but neither art thou free to desist from it."

Daniel S. must have some idea, however vague, of the magnificence and scope of the canvas of which he is part, the Jewish people in its historic and current reality. Only then can he pursue his purposes in the particular area of his choice. An awareness of the historical and societal parameters of his potential Jewish existence gives depth to his own personal commitment. He does not have to be an astronomer to appreciate the sun. He must, however, expose himself to its rays if he is to bask in its health-giving warmth.

A visit to Israel in depth, an ongoing creative association with the Hebrew language on as many levels as time and energy permit, will afford Daniel S. a sense of the outer limits of his search. It will place him within the focus of Jewish identity. Back in America he must decide to belong.

His quest is not merely a social quest. It has distinct spiritual overtones. It is unlikely that Daniel S. will join the *Chasidim* of Spring Valley—not impossible, but unlikely. In American life one of the possibilities open to him will be the synagogue. This much-maligned institution still has a potential viability in the twentieth century. It suffers from certain inherent defects and certain difficulties born of living in an age of transition. If Daniel S. cannot find a synagogue which answers his needs he will have to participate actively in trying to create one. He will have to join the synagogue closest to his heart's desire and, together with others of a like mind, attempt to fashion it in his own image.

Erstwhile peripheral Jews, like Daniel S. before his visit to Israel, are often full of religious protest. They violently oppose the vulgarity of million-dollar edifices on Long Island dedicated to the greater financial security of the caterer. They hate the pomp and circumstance of Jewish fund-raising. They resent the theological anachronisms of synagogue and Hebrew School. They find all Rabbis venal and all Cantors prima donnas. If they ever attend services in synagogue or funeral chapel they are loud in denunciation. If the Rabbi speaks on a relevant subject he is out of his depth; if he speaks on a traditional subject he is an anachronism.

Protest is good for the stomach but bad for the soul. It helps to externalize aggression and, as all readers of the *Marjorie Morningstar* type of Jewish novel will know, the modern Rabbi and the modern synagogue are stand-by Aunt Sallys for the brickbats of the disgruntled intellectual anxious to witness the total collapse of a Jewish community in which he personally cannot and will not try to feel at home. But blind protest is immature and destructive. What the synagogue needs today is creative dissension. Dissension is responsible. It participates in the democratic process. It follows the rules of the game. It lays itself open to being overruled but, at the same time, to overruling. A church in England once ran a billboard outside:

> THE TROUBLE WITH THIS CH RCH
> IS THAT U ARE NOT IN IT.

The typographical inexactitude has merit. The trouble with the "synagog e" is that the protestor stays outside instead of dissenting responsibly from within. With all its defects, the synagogue remains a viable focal point of Jewish life in America. When John F. Kennedy was assassinated it was to the synagogue that Jews thronged. When the Six-Day War erupted it was the synagogue which proved the prime vehicle through which succor was channeled to beleaguered Israel. The synagogue is admittedly weak but by no means totally devitalized. It still possesses considerable societal charisma.

We must arm our hero with some criteria of judging what a

synagogue ought to be like in an age of transition, when Jewish civilization is moving from a rabbinic and supernaturalistic other-worldly stage into a religious humanistic democratic stage. If we cannot recommend that he join any synagogue as it is, the least we can do is to suggest to him the kind of synagogue that it ought to be. Armed with such guidelines Daniel S. will at least know what he is looking for. Having made his choice, he will then know what to work for.

The Rabbi will be a teacher rather than a preacher. He will not give ex-cathedra pronouncements on the basis of an infallibly revealed law which Daniel is supposed to obey or feel guilty about regardless of whether or not it engages his inner assent. There is no "hot line" to God in the twentieth century and Daniel S. will be wise to avoid all places where the truth, the whole truth and nothing but the truth is purveyed under the guise of eternal Judaism or eternal Jewish values. There is no infallibly revealed code which can answer for all times our modern nagging doubts about God, man, human life and destiny.

The synagogue will primarily be a place for meeting—a place for meeting with Jews for worthwhile purposes. On some level the synagogue must be involved not only in prayer, worship, philanthropy and study but also in social action. A synagogue cannot be expected to tackle singlehanded the major issues of crime, war and poverty. For these purposes it must be associated with some "umbrella" organization through which its own voice may more significantly be heard. It must, however, have some rapport, however modest, with Jews and Gentiles who live in its immediate neighborhood, of whatever race, color, creed or denomination. And it must constantly goad, urge and spur its individual constituents to morally responsible action within society at large.

There is a sickness in being preoccupied, for example, with the problem of apartheid in South Africa—about which the average synagogue can do very little by itself—and overlooking poverty, crime and inhumanity on one's own doorstep. The American Jew cannot be a whole Jew if any American is half an American. The Negro's plight, if ignored, diminishes the Jew's religious integrity. Nor are the dispossessed assisted merely by the signing of a check. Human concern must be expressed. Personal, not only fiscal, involvement is called for.

Where the synagogue is deliberately exclusive, catering only to one social grouping, it cannot mediate for the Jew an awareness of the Divine. The relationship between the individual and God is a secondary relationship. The primary relationship between man and God is through the collectivity. The Jew qua Jew experiences God through his committed and responsible involvement with the Jewish people. Clearly the synagogue can represent the entire Jewish people only symbolically and in thought.

But if the synagogue only caters to the rich, its possibility of mediating an awareness of the Divine to the individual is severely hampered if not totally suppressed. A synagogue is not a private club. It is a collective sanctuary, a home for the Jewish people. If any Jew feels rejected therein the synagogue is not fulfilling its prime socioreligious function. No fiscal-, intellectual- or even religious-means test can be applied in the synagogue. It must be a supreme example of an open society in miniature.

Chief among the activities of the synagogue are its acts of worship on Sabbaths, Festivals and other special occasions. Four elements must be present in any act of modern worship if the Jew, in coming to the synagogue, is to be strengthened in his resolve to lead a responsible Jewish life. The quality of all his other associations with the synagogue—education, culture, philanthropy, social action, interpersonal relationships—will be governed by the depth of commitment which the central act of worship arouses in him.

A prime element in the act of worship is *davvening*, or the rote repetition of traditional prayers from the past. When these traditional prayers were first written they were meaningful affirmations for their authors. The author of the twenty-third Psalm, for example, if not a shepherd himself, lived in a culture where shepherds and sheep were as common sights as cabs on Fifth Avenue are in New York today. In a prevailing idiom and metaphor culled from everyday life, he expressed his faith in God and the cosmos, in God conceived of as a Supreme Father. "He restoreth my soul."

When the modern Jew recites the twenty-third Psalm, or any other Psalm or combination of verses from the Psalms or from the Bible, he does not affirm, at firsthand, but rather quotes at secondhand. All the Hebrew *davvened*, or prayed, in the modern synagogue, save in those rare instances where modern Hebrew prayers have been introduced into the act of worship, is quotation, not affirmation. The traditional Hebrew sections of the synagogue service are all in quotation marks, whether the praying Jew is aware of this or not.

Davvening is a basic element in Jewish worship because only by identifying with his past can the Jew gain strength in the present to strive toward the future. An awareness that countless generations expressed a basic faith in the cosmos, and strove to overcome the defects in themselves and in their society through an ongoing relationship with their ethnic group, is a source of strength in present trouble. The traditional prayer book reflects the three stages through which Jewish civilization has already passed, the biblical, the ecclesiastical and the rabbinic. Strength in an age of radical and often disturbing transition is gained from an awareness that the Jewish people has undergone metamorphosis in the past but still maintained its identity in change by reconstructing its sancta. *Davvening* is a prime sanctum of Jewish life.

A perfect example of this metamorphosis may be found in the ninety-second Psalm recited in the synagogue on Sabbaths:

> *It is good to give thanks to the Lord*
> *And to sing praises to Thy name, O Most High;*
> *To proclaim Thy lovingkindness in the morning,*
> *And Thy faithfulness every night . . .*
> *How great are Thy works, O Lord!* ˎ
> *How very deep Thy designs!*

A stupid man does not know,
Nor does a fool understand this,
That when bad men thrive like grass,
And evildoers flourish,
It is that they may be destroyed forever.

The Psalm, as it stands, clearly articulates the ancient prophetic theodicy. This world is the exclusive stage of life. Man makes it here or he makes it nowhere. So it is intolerable that good men should suffer. If they suffer they cannot be good. This is the main burden of Job's comforters. "Think, Job. You must be doing something wrong. It figures. Otherwise you would not be suffering."

Evil is more easily visible. A good man may be good on the surface but a man visibly and manifestly bad can hardly be good within. Basic to the prophetic theodicy found in the Bible is the nemesis which must overcome the bad. True, they flourish for a while, muses the Psalmist. But, then, "the bigger they come, the harder they fall." In the third pre-Christian century, when evil was rampant and the Jewish people was undergoing a radical change in its inner being (from which the Pharisaic movement would ultimately spring), the old theodicy suddenly became transformed into a new and challenging concept stemming in part from Persia and in part from Greece, but embraced in a creative synthesis by the Jews and appropriated as their own. This world could not be the exclusive stage of human destiny. There must be another world where the patent injustices of this world are rectified in a higher reconciliation. It was at this stage that an addendum was made to the ninety-second Psalm—a superscription was added designating the Psalm "A Song for the Sabbath Day."

Why? What on earth has theodicy, the justification of the works of God to man, got to do with the Sabbath? On the contrary, in terms of the slow but sure reconstruction of the Sabbath during those centuries from a day of gloom to a day of delight, one would have thought that the apparent irreconcilability of the principle of terrestrial justice with the manifest success of the wicked would be precisely a subject to be avoided on the Sabbath. Surely it could only make the Jew miserable to reflect on the disparity between his faith and reality.

But as the ecclesiastical period of Jewish life moved in the direction of a sophisticated eschatology, the Sabbath no longer meant merely the seventh day of the week, on which the Jew rested. It also meant the Sabbath of the next world of bliss, the "Day which will be entirely Sabbath," the Cosmic Sabbath of the world to come. A radical metamorphosis of a this-worldly Psalm into an other-worldly Psalm rendered an apparently un-Sabbath-like excursion into theodicy a most highly appropriate reading for the Sabbath. Terrestrial Sabbath now affords a foretaste of the bliss of the world to come.

But how, thinks Daniel S., am I supposed to know all about this? Clearly Daniel had better find himself a synagogue where Judaism is not presented as a static once-and-for-all revealed faith but rather as a dynamic response to the present in terms of the past. But granted that this is all very interesting, thinks Daniel S., what does a metamorphosed Psalm have to do with me? What is it to me that the ninety-second Psalm was translated, over two thousand years ago, from a this-worldly key into the key of other-worldliness?

The modern Jew can neither accept the original biblical theodicy nor its ecclesiastical and rabbinic reconstruction. True, the modern Jew again lives in a this-worldly civilization, but he cannot accept the biblical theology. Where God cannot be accepted as a Person, as a Supreme Being, who can, as in the Bible, interfere with all happenings, He cannot be held responsible for the good men suffering and the bad men prospering. The question then becomes: What are the cosmic implications of a world in which good men may suffer and bad men prosper? One of the prime prerequisites for not being depressed by the evil in the world is to have faith in man's ability to withstand that evil. "Though He slay me," affirms Job, "I will have faith in Him."

Such faith may be born in the synagogue where an awareness

of the majestic evolution of Jewish existence is spelled out clearly. The Jew is heartened not so much by the fact that his ancestors solved the problem of evil (which they did not) as by the fact that they were not dismayed or confounded by it. Thus as he chants, in quotation, words which enshrine two distinct and outmoded levels of spiritual approach to the problem of evil, he adds his own reflections on the miracle whereby man's indomitable spirit refuses to be cowed by the apparently insurmountable and insuperable. It is a holding of hands over the centuries, the living with the dead, in the dark face of evil.

But that, exclaims Daniel S., is fantastic but impossible. It is like being a juggler with three or four world outlooks at the same time. Fine for the circus but not for the synagogue. Does not one have to be an expert to do this? Does it not take years of study and meditation? Do I have the time to learn how to sit in a synagogue and *davven* in this fashion? Can I leap from the faith of the past to the affirmation of the present?

It is very difficult and the difficulty is compounded by living in an age of transition. Most synagogues, apart from the Reform (and even they have their orthodoxies), follow so faithfully the traditional patterns of prayer that the service is almost exclusively *davvening*. This defeats its own purpose. Only a modicum of *davvening* is feasible in a modern synagogue. It is all a matter of proportion as well as perspective. And the appropriate attitude to *davvening*, like the appropriate attitude to almost everything in Jewish life, will have to be taught and learned in the synagogue.

Every student of art and music knows the difference between merely *looking* at a painting and *listening* to a symphony and understanding both art forms within a historical, formal and conceptual framework. One should no more assume that one can jump into a *davvening* experience than one can jump into a duodecimal or Dadaist experience. The River Thames in London has been described as liquid history. The traditional prayer book, as quotation, is spiritual history. There are profoundly different levels of nuance and meaning.

The poignancy of Lear is enhanced for those who live in a republic by the fact that poetic genius is expressed through the anachronistic universe of discourse of monarchy. Hamlet is the more awe-inspiring because he and his colleagues, unlike modern man, believe in "angels and ministers of grace," that is, supernatural beings. Neither play would be as compelling if Lear were in the White House or Hamlet the son of a Senator. Distance lends both charm and depth to art no less than to religion. When the Jew *davvens* to God, the Just King, on the New Year and Day of Atonement, a comparable translation from a supernaturalistic to a religious naturalistic universe of discourse inspires through a historical recapitulation, as well as edifies through a spiritual one.

Davvening is but one element in the synagogue service. Praying is another. Prayer is the articulation of human aspirations in the idiom of everyday life. In the mere course of living, the Jew inevitably becomes desensitized to the challenge of his higher self and to that extent becomes dehumanized. Praying in the synagogue, in the vernacular, is the supreme occasion for restoring a sense of moral priorities. There is a tragic shortage of good prayers in the English vernacular. Much of what passes for prayer is quotation in English of what was originally spontaneous affirmation in Hebrew. An anachronistic theology with references to a deity conceived as the last vestige of animism is invoked. But the noises from the secular world outside and the realities of the secular world within render such prayer almost irrelevant. Quotation is valid only when it is consciously recognized as such.

In many areas of the life of the spirit the presence of a time lag between present and past assists man in his search for spiritual orientation. In the days of the printing press and electricity the *Sefer Torah*, which rests in the Ark in the synagogue, is still written on parchment with quill and ink made according to ancient prescription, and the Sabbath lamps, if not oil lamps, are still candles. Ancient technology carried over from the past develops a patina of spiritual purpose and ethnic identification. The Jew would not derive the same moral encouragement from a contemporary edition of the Pentateuch or from an electrified Sabbath candle. By the same token the *Chasid* in the twentieth century wears the one-time contemporary clothes of the Polish aristocracy of a bygone age. But in the articulation of the Jew's innermost hopes, affirmation in contemporary mood is an imperative adjunct to quotation of the old. The Jew must worship *his* God as well as the God of Abraham, Isaac and Jacob. There must be an authentic spiritual dynamism in the present as well as an identification with the past.

The creation of a new liturgy is the work of ages, not just of one generation. In an age of transition the Jew must patiently wrestle with the problem of articulating religious insights in compelling language of immediacy. An example culled from the Reconstructionist Prayer Book merely points in the direction in which modern religious humanistic prayer must go. It directs the worshiper's attention to the Divine process at work in life rather than to God, conceived of as a Supreme Being. If God is to be addressed as "Thou" in the modern world, the ascription of personality on the human level must be taken for what it is—a poetic summing up in an age-old metaphor of the sum total of all those aspects of the cosmos which help man to become more fully human. Liberty cannot be equated simply with the lady slowly oxidizing in New York harbor.

Even in a post-Copernican age, it is still legitimate to speak of the sun rising and setting. And it is totally impossible to pray to an abstraction. The tendency to reify is natural. Abstract thought is the most difficult of all thought. Even in a sophisticated age of analytic philosophy we still "follow" an argument, "see" a meaning and "grasp" a point. Reifying is valuable so long as the reification is not given an existence of its own beyond the reality in religion which it crucially symbolizes.

God is in the faith
By which we overcome
The fear of loneliness, of helplessness,
Of failure and of death.

God is in the hope
Which, like a shaft of light,
Cleaves the dark abysms
Of sin, of suffering, and of despair.

God is in the love
Which creates, protects, forgives.
His is the spirit
Which broods upon the chaos men have wrought,
Disturbing its static wrongs,
And stirring into life the formless beginnings
Of the new and better world.

Even in the traditional benediction the Divine is referred to only briefly as "Thou" and is then referred to in the third person. "Be praised, O Lord, our God, Sovereign of the Universe, who brings forth bread from the earth." Another traditional prayer runs, "Praised be God who has created us for His glory." So a religious humanistic prayer for *Chanukkah*, taken from the Supplementary Prayer Book of the Society for the Advancement of Judaism (the "mother synagogue" of the Reconstructionist Movement), reads:

Eternal

Who has commanded us to kindle the lights of Chanukkah, commencing with one light and adding one further light each night of the festival, let us never forget that even so is the Truth made manifest in the world by individuals such as Judas Maccabeus who, by their courage, add man to man and brother to brother until in the fullness of time Thy word is accepted from family to family and from people to people. Let the Festival of the Eight Lights which commence with one teach us to see the potential in the smallest acts of courage, that we, too, may be emboldened to help build the Kingdom of God.

In addition to *davvening* and praying, study plays a profoundly important role in a Jewish act of corporate worship. The pattern of the traditional liturgy is based on the Temple service. The very names given to the different orders of service: *Shacharit*, or morning service, *Mussaf*, or additional service, and *Minchah* or afternoon service, all relate to the fact that, originally, the traditional formulations of prayer were meant to be surrogates for the different daily stages of sacrificial worship in the Temple. When the Temple fell, and it was no longer possible to serve God with sacrifices, words of prayer were offered as a substitute for the animals which could no longer be sacrificed and burned on the altar. "So will we render for bullocks the offering of our lips."

But even before the Temple was destroyed, the Pharisees had broken through to a new concept of service of the Lord, *Talmud Torah*. Neither they, nor the prophets who preceded them, wished to abrogate the sacrificial system. The prophets, who castigated the people for a narrowly ritualistic approach toward the sacrificial system, are often accused of having wanted to abolish it. "For I desire mercy and not sacrifice, knowledge of God rather than burnt offerings." Such harsh indictments, seen within their context, speak of a desire for ethical refinement in terms of the Torah, not an uncompromising attack against its central ritual prescriptions. Neither prophet nor Pharisee could have asked for the cessation of sacrifice. It was part of the vocabulary of worship of ancient religious man.

Nevertheless, the Pharisees built on the ethical critique of the prophets. Long before the Temple fell they had arrived at a mode of worship considered by them to be at least as important as sacrifice—study. When the Temple fell, study rose in the Pharisaic schools to a level of preeminence unparalleled in the history of religion. "Apart from the direct intercourse of prayer," writes R. Travers Herford, "the study of Torah was the way of closest approach to God; it might be called the Pharisaic form of the Beatific Vision. To study Torah was, to the devout Pharisee, to 'think God's thoughts after him' as Kepler said." "The careful student," writes Louis Finkelstein in a study of one of the greatest Pharisaic teachers, "will soon recognize the close relationship between Spinoza's *Amor Dei Intellectualis* and Akiba's teaching that worship is an expression of love, and that study is the highest form of worship."

Christian religion has tended to place a premium on simple faith. St. Augustine (354–430) wrote in his *De Civitate Dei:* "A man shall say unto me 'Let me understand that I might believe' and I will reply to him 'Believe that you might understand.'" Tertullian (160–225) claimed of the Christian faith: "It is certain because it is impossible." Hillel, leader of the Pharisees at the turn of the millennium said: "An empty-headed man cannot be a sin-fearing man, nor can an ignorant person be pious." Jewish religion in its Pharisaic formulation could never endorse the idea of *"Credo quia absurdum"*—"I believe because it is absurd." The Jew was commanded to know God as well as love God. The act of faith in itself had little saving efficacy. But then the Pharisees were merely articulating an ancient insight of the prophets that God is known through His ways—ethical behavior in action. Jeremiah speaks for the prophets:

> *Thus saith the Lord.*
> *Let not the wise man glory in his wisdom,*
> *Neither let the mighty man glory in his might;*
> *Let not the rich man glory in his riches;*
> *But let him that glorieth glory in this,*
> *That he understandeth, and knoweth Me,*
> *That I am the Lord who exercise mercy,*
> *Justice and righteousness in the earth;*
> *For in these things I delight,*
> *Saith the Lord.*

Torah is neither for the ignorant nor for the narrowly educated but for those who strive for education of the conscience. Torah study leads to living the good life.

It is unlikely that Daniel S. will be satisfied with an outmoded concept of Torah. Torah is a sanctum. In the earliest, or biblical, stage of "Jewish" existence the term "Torah" merely referred to the *ad hoc* teachings of priest, prophet and sage. In the ecclesiastical stage of Jewish existence, the term "Torah" developed

further to refer to the concept of a Written and an Oral Torah
providing, through the interpretations of the Pharisees, a comprehensive way of life for the Jew. In the rabbinic stage of
Jewish existence, when a Jewish legislative body no longer functioned and the Rabbis had become jurists, interpreting a law they
were no longer empowered to alter, Torah became synonymous
with the massive Codes and commentaries prescribing for the
Jew the minute details of his everyday life.

In the democratic stage of Jewish existence Torah, as in previous stages in Jewish history, will be reconstructed as a sanctum.
An ancient term which has already undergone radical metamorphosis will be further expanded. In the past the reconstruction of
sancta took place unconsciously. The Pharisees were unaware
that they had read into the Torah, which had come down to
them from the past, much which the authors of that Torah
would not have accepted, let alone understood. The twentieth-
century Jew is aware of the psychodynamics which lead to this
unconscious process of reading into ancient texts ideas which do
not exist there. He is therefore unable to emulate previous generations of Jews in the reconstructing of sancta. The new meaning
of the sanctum Torah for the modern Jew will be deliberately
read *out of*—that is, added to the traditional concept of—Torah.
There will be no pretense made of reading such a meaning *into*
Torah. There will be an equivalence of function, not of literal
substance.

Ancient insights often adumbrate modern concepts. The authors of the Bible and rabbinic literature often, even with their
limited knowledge of reality, groped remarkably close to ideas to
which only the twentieth century has been able to give adequate
theoretical foundation.

The account of the creation of the world and the Garden of
Eden is a case in point. The story is couched in the idiom of a
universe of discourse in which God is conceived as a Spiritual
Being who can communicate with man and convey His pleasure
or displeasure in accordance with whether man, His creature,

obeys or disobeys His behest. That universe of discourse is no longer available to modern man, even with a supreme act of will. Yet there are certain permanent needs of human nature embedded in the story of Eden which transcend the limitations of the outmoded universe of discourse in which the story is couched. The separate creation of man points to an intuition that man is destined to transcend the limitations of bestial existence.

Adam and Eve lived in the Garden of Eden without children. Only in the most recent decades have psychiatrists and psychotherapists been able to spell out how marriages which exist for ulterior motives, even such as having children, are diminished. The full value of marriage lies in a creative relationship of mutual comradeship. Where that is present, everything else follows. The ancients sensed, in the story of Eden, that if love between man and woman cannot be all embracing, love between parent and child is correspondingly constricted. The very idea that man and woman were both created by God and placed in a garden points to the intuition that the basic unit of civilization is not the individual but the family unit, ordained by God. Modern psychiatry, in its analysis of the different stages through which the child must develop in order to achieve ego integrity, reflects on a theoretical level the implications of this ancient intuition. Civilized values presuppose the family.

Another example of how the biblical authors reached through gropingly to modern insights is afforded by the story of the dialogue between Abraham and God concerning the impending doom of Sodom and Gomorrah. God is slowly forced to yield to Abraham's insistent demand that a city cannot be destroyed if it contains a certain number of righteous men. The cities are finally destroyed but only because the quota of righteous men is not found. But the numbers game played by Abraham is revealing. He diminishes his claim from fifty righteous men to forty-five, forty, thirty, twenty, ten. "Shall not the Judge of all the earth do justly?" There are not even ten righteous men in Sodom and Gomorrah!

In terms of its context the story is obviously unacceptable to modern man. Yet it enshrines profound insights. What seems to have happened is that two cities were destroyed by natural means —an earthquake. In accordance with the ancient prophetic theodicy there was no such thing as a natural catastrophe. An earthquake had to be a manifestation of God's displeasure. The greater the catastrophe, the greater the reason for it. Folk memory of a terrible natural holocaust at the time of Abraham became transmuted into the grisly story of two cities so bestial and wicked that their very names have come down in Western culture as synonymous for all that is vile.

We moderns cannot accept the prophetic theodicy and argue backward from "punishment" in the shape of natural catastrophe to guilt. But the author of the story had no other philosophy of life available. Within the context of this—to the modern mind —horrendous doctrine he comes as close as possible to an intuition of religious humanism. "Shall not the Judge of all the earth do justly?" The cities were in fact destroyed. But at least the author wants the impossible assurance that every man, woman and child was steeped in iniquity. If there were even ten righteous men there, the calamity would not have happened. God's standards of behavior must at least measure up to what man considers just. This is a humanistic insight, one of a series of such insights which may be found throughout the Bible and rabbinic literature. This should hardly be surprising. The modern Jew and the ancient author both live in the same universe.

This is not to say that the Bible presents us with fully developed theories of human life or religious humanism. The ancient authors, however, undoubtedly foreshadow the modern ideas. When the husk of the ancient universe of discourse is carefully removed, the life-giving kernel of the spiritually nutritious insight remains.

But that is a far cry from asserting that the ancient texts contain the full-fledged modern ideas. That is what the Pharisees did. They read their own advanced ethical insights *into* the Torah.

They did not know better. The modern Jew, when he observes the Torah anticipating modern insights, must at all times be conscious that he is extracting from an outmoded universe of discourse those insights which relate to permanent needs of the human being. The ancients were probably not even aware of many of these insights. When they are gifted, men invariably write more than they know. Modern and more clearly articulated insights of this type can clearly, but consciously and deliberately, be subsumed under the concept of Torah.

Daniel S. is relieved. He had always been given to believe that the ancients knew far more about God, man and human destiny than the moderns. God, after all, only spoke to men in the biblical period. He has observed a remarkable reticence ever since, permitting the Rabbis to speak for Him. That, at least, is what Daniel S. had gleaned in his wandering from synagogue to synagogue and from desultory discussion with sundry Hebrew-School-up-to-Bar-Mitzvah-age-educated Jews. The thought that the situation might be the reverse appeals to his sense of historical perspective and general attitude to life.

It stands to reason that a people which did not know the meteorological dynamics of a simple rainfall could not conceivably have fathomed all the dimensions of Godhood. Since God is a Power making for salvation or human fulfillment in the cosmos, the more learned about the cosmos and the more ascertained about human fulfillment, the more will be learned about God. Modern schools of psychology, which speak of a child's need for the early "ingestion" of values on the same level of importance as a child's need for the early ingestion of vitamins, are important sources of such knowledge.

Suddenly Daniel S. no longer feels totally overwhelmed by the size of the past. Looking at Judaism in terms of an evolving world he begins to see more clearly how he, too, can play an important role in his own generation insofar as he is aware of the basic trend and direction of Jewish development. In one sense he is traveling uncontrollably on a vast river of Jewish ethnic identity. But in another sense, with a knowledge of what the past means for the present, he is able to see the possibilities of controlling the direction in which he, in conjunction with other Jews, can take in the future. The democratic stage of Jewish life, sees Daniel S., is a time for directing rather than drifting.

Torah, for Daniel S., will include all those elements of premodern Jewish sacred literature in which the Jew strove to embody his highest ideals and satisfy his deepest needs. It cannot include, except by way of quotation (for purposes of identification with the past), those areas of error where, on the basis of limited knowledge, the Jew misinterpreted the nature of reality. Ancient meteorology is passé but then so also is the ancient decree, for example, that homosexuals should be stoned to death. Even if the modern Jew elicits from this injunction the ancient intuition that heterosexual sex is central for the wholesome transmission of civilization, he still must reject the Bible's cruel affirmation of this insight. The Bible may have been right in elevating sex within a family context to a central civilizational role, but it was wrong to attempt to achieve that state of affairs by such—to our way of thinking—unacceptable means. But then, in the absence of any knowledge of the nature of homosexuality, it is difficult to see how the ancients could have achieved any compassion or understanding for those afflicted by it. To be able consciously and deliberately to reject part of the past is the first stage in authentically accepting the present.

But Torah for Daniel S. will also include any and every insight in the modern world, regardless of its source, which will help him to make the most of his life as a Jew. Literature, art, music, psychological insights, insofar as they lead to greater human fulfillment, will all be embraced under the concept of Torah for the modern Jew. The ancient Psalmist declared: "The Torah of the Lord is perfect, restoring the soul." The Reconstructionist Jew affirms: "That which is perfect, and that which restores the soul, is the Torah of the Lord."

The switching of subject and predicate effects the transition from the premodern to the modern universe of discourse. Functionally it achieves identical results. That is what the Pharisees did, even if they could not have articulated it thus. Whatever they themselves found perfect in terms of their own advanced ethical insights, they read into the Torah of the Lord. The modern Jew will do consciously what the Pharisee did unconsciously. It is in the nature of the sanctum mechanism.

Moreover, by placing the center of gravity of Torah in human conceptions of perfection (which is what the author of the story of Sodom and Gomorrah was doing in his own limited way), the path is left open for further future development. What was generally considered perfect in 1950 is, hopefully, more than what was considered perfect in 1900 and less than what will be considered perfect in the year 2000. The sanctum of Torah thus is made to embrace the ethical relevancy of the modern without losing the ethnic efficacy of identification with the past. The past is thus creatively harnessed in terms of present needs to serve the future.

Davvening, praying and study are important elements in the corporate act of Jewish worship. By sharing an awareness of common needs with the past, the Jew is encouraged and inspired to continue the work of ages, regardless of frustration or setback. No disappointment can efface the awareness that one is part of the ongoing creative life of a total people. But Daniel S. will need more than this sense of historic destiny. He will need a sense of existential holiness if he is to make the most of his life as a Jew. This, hopefully, he will achieve through the fourth and, perhaps, most crucial element in the corporate act of worship, the public celebration of rites of passage.

In birth and death, in joy and sorrow, in sickness and health, Daniel S. will not be able to achieve consolation, satisfaction or fulfillment if he lives unto himself and his immediate nuclear family. At those crucial points in the development of his own personal life and the lives of those he most intimately loves, he will need the benediction of the extended family of the Jewish people.

As the luster of the diamond is only fully shed in the appropriate setting, so the celebration of the rites of passage of his and his family's life will only truly be brought to fruition if enacted against the backdrop of the Jewish community. It is through the synagogue, conceived as symbolic of the total Jewish people, past, present and future, that the Bar Mitzvah of his son, the marriage of his children, the burial of his loved ones, the anniversaries of life and death, the anticipation of hospitalization and recovery therefrom, will be given a transpersonal meaning. Authentic identity is rooted in the soil of collective life.

Traditionally the celebration of these rites of passage is associated in the synagogue with the reading of the Torah. In the modern synagogue which will satisfy Daniel S. the reading of the Torah will, in a sense, function primarily as an act of celebration rather than an act of affirmation. Much of the Torah, narrowly conceived as Pentateuch, is literally meaningless to modern man by virtue of its outmoded universe of discourse. Some of it, from a modern standpoint, is ethically offensive. But the study element in corporate worship will elicit the ancient insights and elaborate on the spiritual and intellectual equivalences of past and present. Here is where allowances will be made for the context in which the Torah, in terms of its own age, was actually in advance of the then contemporary ethic. But the Torah reading itself will serve primarily as a peg on which to hang the emotions of men and women who wish to affirm their existential reality in moments of crisis within a context larger than life. The *Sefer Torah*, with all its blemishes from the modern standpoint, still serves as the historic canvas in terms of which contemporary Jewish life develops. It was the original constitution of the Jewish people.

Traditionally seven men are called to the Torah. Daniel S. will expect women also to participate in the rite, as is the custom in all Reconstructionist synagogues. The readings are traditionally lengthy and should be shortened in the interests of the contemporary function of this dimension of the act of worship.

To the Torah reading are called those who observe *Yahrzeit* (the anniversary of the death of a loved one), those who are to be married in the coming week, those who have been blessed with a child and wish to name the child, those who are to undergo surgery, those who have recovered from sickness, those who celebrate wedding anniversaries and birthdays.

The involvement of the individual celebrant and his immediate family is only a part of the value of the acts of celebration which cluster around the traditional Torah reading. The middle-aged married couple, struggling with the tensions that all marital flesh is heir to in the modern world of stress and strain, secretly renew their own marriage vows as they see the rejuvenating freshness of young love being pledged on the *bima*, or dais, in front of the holy Ark, to the eternal and ever-renewed challenge of Jewish marriage: "May they establish in Israel an abode of love and loyalty, peace and holiness, a home in which children can grow up in health and happiness, in the knowledge of Torah and in the practice of good deeds."

The father or mother who is struggling with the problem of raising a recalcitrant adolescent is supported in the sight of a young mother clutching her child, reciting with the proud father —the love of each other and of their newly born offspring in their eyes—in front of the open scroll of the Torah:

Eternal God, we have come to this synagogue with overflowing hearts to offer our praise and our thanksgiving to Thee, who in Thine infinite wisdom renewest the marvels of creation.

Send the blessings of a strong body, an alert mind, and a true and kindly spirit upon this our beloved child. Help us to be worthy of this our responsibility and our joy; help us to cherish, to protect, and to guide our child in ways of righteousness and peace. Help us also to find in our little one yet another bond drawing us closer to each other in mutual understanding and helpfulness. Teach us to carry on, through our child, the noble heritage of Israel, that our family may thereby become a source of blessing to us, to the Jewish people and to all mankind. We are truly grateful that we have been kept alive, sustained, and enabled to rejoice in this happy occasion.

There is no place in the modern synagogue for petitionary prayer to an all-powerful supreme being. The prayer of the young parents is a poetic outpouring of deep feeling stressing the sense of gratitude and communal responsibility which parenthood properly brings. This feeling is expressed through a prayer which is part affirmation and part, insofar as it addresses God as Person, quotation.

Especially in the realm of sickness is theurgic prayer to be avoided. Attempts to influence a supernatural being to change the course of sickness are profoundly superstitious. Yet when a Jew is involved in the ongoing life of a congregation the expression of hope for recovery or gratitude for recovery articulated from the *bima* elicits a sense of deep identification and empathy on the part of the gathered congregation.

The sick man, for whom prayers are offered by members of his family or, in their unavoidable absence, by friends, is then informed that his name was mentioned in a holy place at a holy time. He is also informed that it elicited that response in the hearts of many which, on previous occasions had, in similar circumstances, been elicited from him. He is correspondingly sustained and fortified. That kind of prayer in public is efficacious.

Prayer cannot reverse an incurable cancer. But in an infinity of psychosomatic disorders and in borderline cases, where the will to survive is crucial, such prayer can effect remarkable cures. But the efficacy of such prayer is related to the prior participation of the sick man in the life of the congregation. The wise sailor checks his lifeboat before leaving harbor and facing the risk of squalls.

The same identification and empathy takes place when a *Yahrzeit* is observed, when a Bar Mitzvah is celebrated. The pressures of life in the modern world tend to dehumanize men and make them insensitive to the pulsebeat of their souls. In the synagogue the celebrant not only affirms the profound dignity and meaning of his own personal crisis. He is the cause of the affirmation of a sense of dignity and meaning in others.

Daniel S. always thought that the Jew went to synagogue to

get something out of it for himself. It occurs to him that one might, under certain circumstances, go to synagogue to put something into it. It even occurs to him that, on the occasions when he himself is hale and hearty and has no need for the synagogue, someone else may actually need Daniel S.'s physical presence there to sustain him in his hour of need. Daniel S. had always thought that the purpose of religion was to satisfy the needs of the individual. The thought that, in addition to his own needs, he is needed to satisfy others' needs places his demands in a new perspective. "Ask not only what you need from the Jewish people. Ask what the Jewish people needs from you." It is a provocative thought.

The People of Israel, the land of Israel, the Torah and the synagogue are all sancta. Sancta are the fixed points of reference in the heavens of Jewish religious civilizational existence. They serve as means whereby the Jewish people collectively and individually plot their course in life and discover their cosmic position. They are not meant to be reached in any literal or specific sense. They are guidelines seen and experienced differently from different points of the collective Jewish spiritual compass. They are not reached, but the course of Jewish life in each generation is inevitably plotted by them. They are the basic childhood experiences of Jewish existence which fix for all time the parameters of the Jewish search for meaning and purpose in life. They are reconstructed and reinterpreted. To reject them is to reject the Jewish people. It is to reject one's parents and the formulating experiences of childhood within the parental and domestic context. It is to reject oneself.

The people was once a loose-knit federation of seminomadic Semitic tribes. But the concept of Israel underwent radical metamorphosis. Israel became aware of itself as the Chosen People of God, exiled from the Promised Land but destined to return. Israel became, under this outlook, a church, a theocracy under

God. Later the Jews were a Diaspora people, patiently waiting
for God to redeem them.

Zionism was a secular movement. It violated ancient theology
in that it permitted Jews to take the matter of the return to Zion
into their own hands, without waiting for the Messiah and God.
The modern secular world in general has made of the Jewish
people outside of Israel a people living in two civilizations.
Radical metamorphosis from the people as nation, church,
Diaspora people, has now, in the modern world, yielded to a
democratic and humanistic conception of the Jews as the bearers
of Judaism and of Judaism as the evolving religious civilization of
the Jewish people.

The land of Israel was originally a land conquered by the
ancient Hebrews from the Canaanites. Later it was invested with
a religious role as the territory controlled exclusively by Yahweh.
As the minds of the prophets reached out to a universal conception of God, the land of Israel underwent a spiritual hypostasis. It
was more than a national territory, even for God's Chosen People. Its spiritual significance transcended its geographical role in
the life of a single people.

> And it shall come to pass in the end of days,
> That the mountain of the Lord's house
> Shall be established as the top of the mountains,
> And shall be exalted above the hills;
> And all nations shall flow unto it.
> And many peoples shall go and say:
> "Come ye, and let us go up to the mountain of the Lord,
> To the house of the God of Jacob;
> And He will teach us of His ways,
> And we will walk in his paths."
> For out of Zion shall go forth the law,
> And the word of the Lord from Jerusalem.

The foundation of the modern State of Israel has given a section
of the Jewish people a national existence coterminous with the
land of Israel. But for the foreseeable future the vast majority of
the Jewish people will not be Israeli nationals. The land of Israel
will play a spiritual and not a political role in their lives. The land

of Israel, *Eretz Yisrael,* thus functions in an unprecedented fashion
in modern Jewish life. Jerusalem is a capital only to some but a
spiritual focal point to all.

The synagogue has also traveled a long way since the early
agonizing reappraisals of Jewish existence which took place in
isolated conventicles in Babylonia in the years following the destruction of the Solomonic Temple in 586 B.C.E. From being an
adjunct to a sacerdotal system it flowered into a Pharisaic house
of study. In the medieval period it was the very heart of Jewish
life. Study, prayer, philanthropy and acts of loving-kindness and
mercy were all performed there. Jews even ate and slept there.

In the modern period the synagogue, as a sanctum, is again
reconstructed. It must deliberately be fashioned into an institution which serves the authentic current needs of Jews. It must
become a laboratory for experimentation within the framework
of past patterns, present needs and future hopes. It cannot remain
merely a museum for the recapitulation of tradition.

Daniel S. must make his peace and come to terms with all these
collective and communal sancta. They are the warp and woof of
the fabric of his ethnic identity. Which synagogue or Jewish
organization he will belong to or attempt to fashion is his own
personal choice. History provides a context. Daniel S. will have
to participate creatively in the making of the content if he is to
find his true role as a member of the Jewish people in an age of
transition.

"I can't do it," says Daniel S. He is facing the agonizing problem of behaving as a Jew. Belonging was bad enough. There was
a long labyrinthine tracing of ancestral paths through distant
lands and far-off concepts. Ideas and experiences he had regarded
as utterly alien had suddenly entered into his blood stream.
Strange tongues and exotic overtones had made his pulse beat. He
suddenly found an unexplained affinity with cadences he had not
known and company he had never kept.

Or was it so? There were two Daniel S.'s. There was the

Daniel S. he thought he knew, born of his mother, and the embryonic Daniel S. emerging slowly and not without pain from the
womb of the Jewish people. There had been ties and links with
far-off countries and remote communities which he seemed to
have known about all the time. Where had these links been kept?
Where had these unconscious memories been sheltered? In his
skin, in his blood, in his bones? Or in an invisible environment
surrounding his Jewish body which bound him in time and space
to all Jews alive, all Jews who had died and all Jews as yet
unborn?

"I can't do it. I can't carry on. Enough is enough." Daniel S. is
weary. He is emotionally exhausted. There is too much happening. His world has been turned upside down. Before his visit to
Israel his reading had been desultory and patchy. It could not
have been his random forays into Jewish culture which had made
the homeland of his other being suddenly assume such a compelling fascination.

His wife had reluctantly agreed to accompany him. Her love
for him and her sensitivity to his deepest needs transcended her
own latent anti-Semitism. Unlike many of her friends who could
tolerate Judaism, but not Jews, she had found both the civilization *and* the people repulsive. She was constantly wrestling with
ghosts from the attic of her childhood. But she, too, was moved
by the visit to the land of the ingathering of the exiles, though to
a much more limited extent than Daniel. She was honest enough
to admit to herself, if not to her husband, that she felt more than
she was prepared to admit about the old-new land.

Grandmother S. had snorted on hearing about the impending
visit. She had heard of restaurants in Tel Aviv where nonkosher
food was sold brazenly. How could they be Jews over there if
they didn't "eat kosher"? Grandmother S. had even heard of
collective settlements where pigs and rabbits were bred and,
"God forgive us," eaten.

Not all the gallantry of the Six-Day War and the recapture of
Jerusalem could entirely obliterate for Grandmother the image

of a *kibbutz*-ic pig wallowing in some Hashomer Hatzair sty. The casualty reports mollified her somewhat. Paying in blood for eating blood, in some archaic and atavistic sense, yielded her a modicum of "measure for measure."

Daniel S. had gone to Israel without any intellectual or emotional reservations and the impact on him had been cataclysmic. He wept unashamedly, much to the embarrassment of his wife, as the El Al aircraft nosed over the Israeli coast and prepared to land at Lydda Airport. For a moment he could not see the image of live Israelis moving around on the ground, Jews all: porters, customs men, cab drivers, policemen, brands plucked from the burning. He could only see the legions of Vespasian marching on Jerusalem and hear the overtones of rabbinic voices lifted in heated discussion.

From Israel, Daniel S. had gained a sense of belonging. He had begun to recognize who he was. Some of his nagging questions about his identity had been muted, if not silenced. A sense of belonging seemed to place formerly agonizing questions into a new perspective. That sense had been heightened by wide and voracious reading after his return home.

His wife had since given birth to a baby girl and he had registered his son in an afternoon Hebrew School which had been recommended to him by some friends. He still did not entertain the notion of belonging to the synagogue. When he thought of belonging, he suddenly felt claustrophobic. It would limit his freedom. Part of him wanted to sink deep into the ocean of Jewish ethnicity. Part of him still wanted to fend off the Jewish people. Daniel S. had a feeling that there was no "halfway house" for him and Judaism. He would be a total Jew or nothing.

"I can't do it," says Daniel S. He had been strangely moved when he visited the synagogue on the occasion of his child's induction into the Hebrew School. It was the first time in his life he had ever been in a synagogue as a participant rather than as an onlooker. His parents had not sent him to Hebrew School, so that a Bar Mitzvah had been out of the question. His wedding had been in a hotel.

The parents had been invited to stand with the children on the *bima* and, as he stood next to his son, age-old emotions suddenly welled up within him and choked in his throat. An invisible assembly had suddenly entered the synagogue. "Be praised O Lord our God, Sovereign of the universe, for having preserved us alive, sustained us, and enabled us to reach this season." He knew that his son was also experiencing a sense of belonging. This was his people.

A week earlier Daniel S. had read a story from the Talmud which described how, when a Jew goes home from the synagogue on Friday evening, the eve of the Sabbath, two angels accompany him, a good angel and a bad angel. If the Sabbath table is decked with a white cloth, the candles are burning and a spirit of Sabbath peace pervades the home, the good angel says: "Amen. So may it be next week." But if the television is blaring and the children are squabbling and the dinner is not ready and the wife hasn't changed her clothes, the bad angel says: "Amen. So may it be next week." Suddenly the synagogue is filled with good angels nodding and saying: "Amen. So may it be next year." The sages, martyrs, priests and prophets, Moses, Jeremiah, Hillel, Akiba, the dead of Auschwitz, look down invisibly from the walls as Daniel S. leaves the *bima* with his son: "Amen. So may it be . . ."

"I can't do it," says Daniel S. He has learned to belong as a Jew, at least peripherally. That has taken a long time. He is shortly going to be forty. He knows a little Hebrew and a lot of Jewish history. He is already participating, albeit marginally and somewhat vicariously, in the life of a congregation. But he is having intolerable difficulty in behaving like a Jew.

Daniel S. has always regarded ritual of any kind as a nuisance. How can he create what he knows must sooner or later be a real Jewish home? His son is already being taught in Hebrew School about what Jews do on the Sabbath. Jews recite *Kiddush*, or sanctification, over wine. The candles are lit. Bread is broken with the traditional benediction. The Jew does not talk about the dignity of man. He is meant to demonstrate it in life and celebrate it in symbolic ritual. Jews do this, Jews do that, Jews do the other thing. "What Jews?" thinks Daniel S. "Not me. I can't do it."

It is not that he would encounter, at this stage, any serious opposition from his wife. She was not prepared, at first, to admit to him the extent of the effect that their visit to Israel had made on her, although Daniel S. was not the kind of husband who would say, "I told you so!" It was an inability on her part to admit that her negative attitude to the Jewish dimension of her personality was grounded on hatred, a hatred of Hitler who had disrupted the life of her family, a hatred of her historical situation which forced her into being something over and above an average American.

It was her maternal instincts which reconciled her to the fact that she, too, would have to join with Daniel S. in a joint quest for Jewish identity. The boy had been a different child since going to Hebrew School. Some deficiency in his spiritual diet seemed to have been deeply satisfied. His eyes glowed in eager anticipation of each visit.

His mother was at first surprised. She had assumed the child would reflect her own sense of boredom. She noticed that among his peers attendance at the school was regarded as a cachet, a little extraordinary and bizarre at first but a unique distinction nonetheless. When the news traveled around the Public School grapevine that the son of Daniel S. was attending Hebrew School two other mothers made inquiries and promptly registered their children. The boy's cup now ran over.

A mood of initial displeasure moved through reconciliation to positive acceptance. Her joy was intensified when the teacher spoke highly of the boy's enthusiasm and ability. But the problem of the Jewish home remained. At a PTA conference, when the Rabbi spoke of the need for the parents to participate in the Jewish education of their children by striving to exemplify practically in the home what could only be taught theoretically in the school, both Daniel S. and his wife felt that the remarks had been directed to them personally. "I can't do it," said Daniel S. to himself. But as he thought of his son, his resolve was weakening.

The traditional Jewish home is the creation of the Pharisees and the Rabbis. When Daniel's grandmother speaks of *Yiddish-keit*, or Jewishness, she is thinking of the kind of warm Jewish home her own parents and grandparents enjoyed in Europe. Grandmother S. thinks that the sanction for this Jewish home goes back to the Revelation of God on Mount Sinai. Actually it emerges much later than that.

The Jewish home is a sanctum. Like *Am Yisrael*, or the People of Israel, *Torat Yisrael*, or the Torah of Israel, *Eretz Yisrael*, or the land of Israel, the Sabbath and the Synagogue, it is a focal point of ever-changing holiness in the ongoing life of the Jewish people. From the earliest times, as reflected in the opening chapters of the Bible, the nuclear family, initially made up of husband and wife, was regarded as the basic unit of the people. If there are no children in the Garden of Eden, neither are there grandparents, brothers or sisters, nieces or nephews. After Eden, as myth merges into legend, and legend into history, the centrality of husband and wife, or wives (in accordance with the fashion of the age), and children is seen more clearly.

In the Bible the ideal is monogamy, though polygamy often prevails. "Therefore shall a man leave his father and his mother and cleave to his wife, becoming one flesh." The greatest panegyric in world literature to woman, from the thirty-first chapter of the Book of Proverbs—"A woman of worth who can find? Her price is far above rubies . . ."—clearly presupposes the monogamic ideal.

The Book of Hosea could not have been written in the absence of this ideal. Hosea (eighth pre-Christian century) marries a prostitute who constantly betrays him with other men. Nevertheless he still loves her and takes her back again and again. In his

own love for his recalcitrant wife, Hosea sees reflected the love
of Yahweh for wayward Israel:

> *And I will betroth thee unto Me forever;*
> *Yea, I will betroth thee unto Me in righteousness and in justice,*
> *And in loving kindness, and in compassion.*
> *And I will betroth thee unto Me in faithfulness;*
> *And thou shalt know the Lord.*

Such language of the relationship between Israel and God clearly
indicates that monogamy, and not polygamy, was the norm.

Spinsters and bachelors must have existed but they play no
significant role in the ongoing life of the people. Biblical Hebrew
has no word for bachelor. "Give me children," says Rachel to
Jacob, "or else I die." The intuition implicit in the story of the
Garden of Eden that the relationship between man and woman
has intrinsic merit regardless of procreative prowess is over-
shadowed by the reality of the conquest of Canaan and the need
for population growth.

It has even been surmised that Jewish sex laws, deriving from
the Bible, which permit sexual relations between husband and
wife only at that time in the menstrual cycle when the woman is
most fertile, are also geared to the problem of population expansion. "And it shall come to pass when your son asks you tomor-
row 'what is this?' " observes the Exodus narrative, in connection
with the departure from Egypt. It is assumed that a man will
have a son. The epitome of blessing in the Bible is couched in the
image of the extended family:

> *Happy is everyone that feareth the Lord,*
> *That walketh in His ways.*
> *When thou eatest the labor of thy hands,*
> *Happy shalt thou be, and it shall be well with thee.*
> *Thy wife shall be as a fruitful vine, in the innermost parts of thy*
> *house;*
> *Thy children like olive plants, round about thy table.*
> *Behold, surely thus shall the man be blessed*
> *That feareth the Lord.*
> *The Lord bless thee out of Zion;*
> *And see thou the good of Jerusalem all the days of thy life;*

And see thy children's children.
Peace be upon Israel.

The modern mind finds capital punishment for sexual mis-
demeanors unnecessarily harsh. It was common practice in the
ancient world. And if the ethical insights of the Bible—often far
in advance of ancient custom in labor relationships, civil law and
tort—fail to protect the adulterer, the homosexual, the sodomite
and the willingly deflowered virgin from being stoned to death, it
can be said, at least, as extenuating circumstance, that belief in the
centrality of the family for the civilizing process made all sexual
practices which interfered with licit, potentially procreative sex
abhorrent in ancient Israel. It was a harsh way of expressing an
important insight. Canaanite sexual profligacy was linked with
gross immorality on all levels.

Biblical civilization was a this-worldly civilization. This world
was the exclusive stage of human endeavor. Clearly this influenced the tangible reality of leaving children behind as one's
immortality. Because Judaism began in an other-worldly civilization, even when, in common with the rest of the world, it underwent transformation into an other-worldly civilization at the turn
of the millennium, it never lost sight of the realities of this world.

Monastic orders existed among the peripheral sects of the
Essenes but never in the mainstream of Pharisaic Judaism. Bachelors among the Rabbis were virtually unknown. A typical rabbinic comment on marriage runs: "A man without a wife is without joy, without blessing, without goodness." A man's home and
a man's wife were rabbinic synonyms. The Rabbis even believed
that a bad marriage was better than no marriage. "It is better to
sit with a load of grief than to sit as a widow."

In the biblical period, religious life seems to have clustered
around the sanctuaries. One of the main approaches to God was
through a family sacrifice. On a holiday, the whole family would
march up to the top of the nearest hill on which there was a
sanctuary available, serviced by a local priest. They would take
the sacrificial animal along with them, no mean financial burden

in an age when wealth was measured in terms of heads of cattle.

The central act of familial worship would be the slaughtering of the animal in accordance with traditional ritual prescription. This would be done by the father. The blood, believed to be the source of life, especially, would be drained onto the altar, which consisted either of unhewn stones or a pile of earth. The family would have brought along wine and possibly oil, portions of which would be poured on the altar. Giving part to Yahweh was believed to make permissible consumption of the remainder. Parts of the slaughtered animal, which by now had been skinned and sectioned, would then be dedicated to God and burned on the altar. Parts of the animal, in accordance with tradition, would be reserved for the exclusive use of the priest, his "honorarium" as it were. The rest would be roasted and eaten by the family.

After the family had eaten and drunk, musical instruments would be produced—the shepherd's flute and the harp—and dancing ensue. Snatches of traditional songs praising Yahweh would be uttered. It would be far into the twilight before the family would take their leave of priest and sanctuary with formal courtesies and slowly wend their way down to the valley. Within the security of the village they would sleep at ease, reassured of Yahweh's favor and Divine Concern. Had they not obeyed His law? Had they not sacrificed in accordance with tradition? "Behold, He that guardeth Israel shall neither slumber nor sleep."

Archeological evidence indicates that the average Israelite house was little more than a hovel. Luxury artifacts were reserved exclusively for the affluent minority. Nevertheless, within his humble abode the ancient Israelite, with his wife and children, truly experienced bliss. His relationship with Yahweh through his family, and through his family—especially his sons (who hopefully would survive him)—with his people, gave him a deep sense of belonging.

> *Lo, children are a heritage of Yahweh;*
> *The fruit of the womb is a reward.*

As arrows in the hand of a mighty man,
So are the children of one's youth.
Happy is the man that hath his quiver full of them;
They shall not be put to shame,
When they speak with their enemies in the gate.

The average age span of the ancient Israelite was probably not much more than half a century. It has been estimated that, on the average in ancient Israel, a man would be a father at nineteen, a grandfather at thirty-eight and a great-grandfather at fifty-seven. Marriage would have been relatively early in an agricultural economy for the Psalmist to value so highly "the children of one's youth." Being a great-grandfather would have been a special privilege. Infant mortality was high.

Blessing within the family was thus derivative. One source was in the blessing of Yahweh through appropriate worship at the sanctuary. Yahweh gave children, especially male children, to those who revered Him. Another source of blessing was in the status and dignity afforded by children within the context of the community. The biblical "gate" was the center of gravity of ancient Israelite society. But in the biblical period there was nothing comparable to the Jewish home which Daniel S.'s grandmother remembers. The biblical home derived its status from external sources. Grandmother would have found little to commend it.

In the process of time, the local sanctuaries yielded their prerogatives to the central sanctuary of the Temple in Jerusalem. Whether this was accomplished before the destruction of the Solomonic Temple in 586 B.C.E. is doubtful. The later biblical authors and the Rabbis found the plurality of sanctuaries clearly recorded by tradition offensive to their disciplined and systematic minds. They tended to project the reality of a central sanctuary back to a period in time when such a centralization of religion would have been inconceivable. Nevertheless, after the Jews returned from Babylon in 538 B.C.E., the Temple which was subsequently rebuilt (516 B.C.E.) became the exclusive center of sacrificial worship. The quality of family life was now determined by reference to the Temple in Jerusalem.

It was during the ecclesiastical stage of Jewish history that the ancient injunction which called upon all males to present themselves before Yahweh three times a year reached a high level of spiritual development. The Pilgrim Festivals of Passover, Pentecost and Tabernacles became three focal points in the year for entire Jewish families from the furthest parts of the Diaspora to present themselves in the Temple and there offer up the requisite festival sacrifices. Even families who could not make the journey themselves participated in the life of the Temple by making annual fiscal contributions, *shekalim*, from which money the regular sacrifices would be purchased. Thus, symbolically at least, all Jews could worship at the Temple.

The offering of the Paschal Lamb, with the traditional stress on its consumption by an entire family, underlines the centrality of the Temple in the spiritual life of the family. The glow of meeting in the courtyard of the Temple, thronged with visiting pilgrims, was what afforded the ancient Jew an authentic experience of the reality of his people and through that reality, the reality of his God. Here was where he derived his own and his familial identity.

The very notion of appearing before God in Jerusalem, a "local" God, a God primarily experienced at a point where masses of Jews gathered together for holy purposes, made all the more poignant the memories and recollections brought back by the family to their own homes to sustain them in the months ahead. God was everywhere, He was the Omnipresent, but was especially to be experienced at His abode in Zion.

Just as the prophets had anticipated the fall of Israel and Judah and provided, in their radically new evaluation of the meaning and purpose of Israelite existence, a means of national survival, so also had the Pharisees, anticipating the fall of the Temple, made provision for providing a bastion of Jewish security which would weather the storms of Diaspora existence removed entirely from national territory.

Perhaps "anticipate"—for the fall of both Israel and the Temple—is the wrong word. Neither the prophets nor the Pharisees were conscious of what they were doing. Had history turned out differently, neither the prophetic nor the Pharisaic mutation would have endured. In retrospect, however, the Pharisaic attempt to extend the aristocracy of the priest to the aristocracy of the learned, the holiness of the Temple to the sanctity of the home and the priestly responsibilities to the religious obligations of the average Jew effected a change in stress in Jewish life which enabled Judaism to survive in the absence of the Temple and a national territory.

The Pharisees decentralized Jewish life theologically and ritually. The Temple could only stand in Jerusalem but a synagogue could exist wherever there was a quorum of ten males, or a *minyan*, literally meaning "number." Only a priest could offer up a sacrifice but every Jew could study Torah and perform the *mitzvot*.

After the fall of the Herodian Temple in 70 C.E. the Jewish home (within the wider context of the synagogue and community) became both Temple and national territory for the Jew. In the steppes of central Russia deep snow might be on the ground, but on Passover the Jew would assiduously celebrate the spring festival of a land he had never seen nor was ever likely to see. He would pray in the synagogue for the dew to fall on a distant land in which his ancestors lived long ago. On Tabernacles he would pray in the synagogue for rain to fructify the fields of ancient Israel, not of the land of his domicile. And for eight days he would live in a frail *Sukkah*, or booth, a temporary home, remembering the wanderings of olden days.

The Jewish home had become a miniature Temple and microcosmic homeland. The meticulous ritual of the abattoir had been transferred to the domestic hearth in the minutiae of the dietary laws. The father of the house was the High Priest. The table

around which the family gathered for sacred meals was an altar.
The presence of salt on the table of the traditional Jew goes back
to ancient Temple custom. The Bible prescribes the offering of
salt with all sacrifices. This may have had a preservative value. It
certainly had a symbolic value. The ancient Canaanites, as part of
their fertility rites, offered leaven and honey, symbolic of the
growth and sweetness of sexual desire, with their sacrifices. The
Hebrews were enjoined to use only unleavened bread and salt,
symbolic of their astringent discipline in this area.

From the moment the rabbinic Jew opened his eyes in the
morning until he closed them in sleep at night, week in week out,
month in month out, year in year out, his life was rigorously
governed by rules and regulations. These rules, precepts, commandments or *mitzvot* were believed to have been ordained by
God.

In her conversations with Daniel S., Grandmother S. often
refers to *Yiddishkeit*. This is a Yiddish word and means "Jewishness." By it Grandmother S. means the whole complex of ritual
and ceremonial governing the Jewish home. Under the category
of *Yiddishkeit* she includes many ceremonies and rituals which
she herself has long since abandoned. There is something about
eating which makes the keeping of a kosher home and observance
of the dietary laws, even though not as strictly as her own
mother or grandmother would have liked, somehow central to
her Jewish life.

Daniel S. has noticed, in his forays and skirmishes into Jewish
life, that Jews who have long since stopped adhering to traditional Jewish behavior patterns still seem to be preoccupied with
eating as Jews, although vast numbers of Jews are totally indifferent to these behavior patterns. He heard a joke about a man from
the Midwest who became a Rabbi without ever hearing the word
"kosher." Daniel S. also knew of synagogues where the serving of
shrimp cocktail had become a necessity on public occasions, a

matter of principle, as it were, to assert emancipation from tradition.

Somewhere in his reading he had stumbled on other anomalies where gross ignorance of Jewish dietary practice had led to some weird historical quirks and turns. It was said that a famous break in Jewish denominational life occurred in America because someone served a wrong menu. Daniel S. couldn't quite remember whether this had been accidental or on purpose. Some traditional Jews had been offered food which offended them and they had walked out. Daniel S. also enjoyed the joke about the correct *berachah*, or benediction, for bacon. The Orthodox Rabbi who had been asked didn't know what bacon was and the Reform Rabbi didn't know what a *berachah* was.

Daniel S. knew enough about psychology to realize that people only joke about things which worry them. He was often perplexed, in his discussions with committed and involved Jews, by how often the matter of food cropped up. "Do you eat kosher?" or "Do you keep a kosher home?" seemed like a Masonic criterion of entry into the charmed circle. In some Jewish circles keeping a kosher home seemed a liability. In others it appeared to be an asset. In both cases it was a problem. Even where Jews didn't keep kosher any longer they still seemed to talk about it a great deal. Depending upon how peripheral the Jew was, keeping or not keeping a kosher home seemed to make for a certain insecurity and anxiety in others as well as in self.

Daniel S. couldn't quite fathom why food should take priority. From his reading, though not from his own direct experience, he knew that a kosher home, though profoundly important from a traditional point of view, was only one dimension of the Jewish home. To be sure, the kitchen had to be run in accordance with tradition. That meant separate sets of crockery and cutlery for meat and milk, duplicated for the eight days of Passover (when no bread could be eaten and no crockery used with which bread had come into contact.)

But there were other things. There were Sabbaths and Festivals. There were prayers. There were acts of hospitality and charity. Daniel S. had never heard Jews discussing the merits of Sabbath observance as assiduously as he had heard Jews discussing the merits of kosher food observance. Moreover, he had occasionally participated in Bar Mitzvah celebrations where the crass vulgarity and superfluous ostentation of the food served seemed to transcend in ethical impropriety any ritual appropriateness of the "correct" cuisine.

Until Daniel S. began to worry about what being Jewish truly meant to him, the problem of kosher food had never even occurred to him. He had always been accustomed to eating anything that had been put in front of him. Since his visit to Israel, as a sign of some identification with the Jewish past rather than the Jewish present, he had decided to abstain from eating pork products and shellfish. It was something of a sacrifice, for he had particularly enjoyed them. But the pig seemed to have functioned so negatively in the traditional Jewish sources that Daniel S.'s personal discomfort was outweighed by the sense of historic belonging he gained.

He had simply woken up one day to find that he could no longer eat with impunity an animal whose flesh his ancestors had resisted eating to the point of death. He could not share their theology but found a strange peace in sharing their aversion.

He had a problem at home. The idea of keeping a kosher home had not even been discussed and his wife happened to be extremely partial to lobster. A faint nagging at the back of his mind made Daniel S. realize that on the one hand his wife was an individual in her own right, with a right to do as she pleased. On the other hand he felt increasingly a disparity between the world of his intellectual aspirations and spiritual dreams and the reality of his home life. He and his wife were one insofar as their—potentially as yet—Jewish home was concerned.

After his initial decision to abstain from pork and shellfish Daniel S. agonized for a year before raising the matter at home. He had prepared himself thoroughly. He tended to minimize the

problem of individuality of husband and wife. Instead he spoke
about the historic reality that where a kosher butcher existed the
Jewish community existed and that where the butcher closed
shop that invariably pointed to the demise of the Jewish community. He spoke of the need of supporting, as Jews, institutions
which, even if one didn't need them oneself or even believe in
oneself, other Jews needed and believed in. Almost embarrassing
himself, he evoked the memory of the murdered millions of the
Nazi Holocaust, most of them from devoutly Orthodox centers
of Jewish life.

He was just about to launch into a defense of symbolism from
the standpoint of the children and to argue that being different
as Jews, even to a small extent, deliberately and consciously,
helped to affirm a sense of belonging, when his wife interrupted
him quietly. He had expected anger and rebellion. He had
anticipated at least an argument about equality of the sexes in
marriage. His wife said very softly that if it meant that much to
Daniel S., she would buy meat from the kosher butcher where
Grandmother S. went.

Daniel S. almost reacted violently to this suggestion until he
realized that just because Grandmother S.'s kosher home was
almost obscene in terms of its limitation of religion to one ritual,
that did not mean that he had to follow suit. The symbol could
be creative as well as corrosive. Everything depended on the
context. *Kol hatchalot kashot*, all beginnings are difficult, mused
Daniel S. to himself, in Hebrew. It was one of the first phrases he
had learned. It seemed to fit the occasion most appropriately. He
was amazed to find himself quoting in Hebrew.

Grandmother S. was wrong not only in limiting the meaning
of the Jewish home to the origin of the meat served from the
kitchen but in limiting *Yiddishkeit* to the Jewish home. Rabbinic
Judaism was more than a home. It was a home within the framework of an organic community. That community had provided

for a total set of Jewish needs, not domestic alone. Jewish law had, indeed, once been coterminous with the whole of life.

The Pharisees and the Rabbis had spoken of a sum total of six hundred and thirteen *mitzvot*, as having been given by God to the Jewish people. "Six hundred and thirteen commandments were revealed to Moses," observed Rabbi Simlai, a third-century Palestinian scholar, "three hundred and sixty five being prohibitions equal in number to the days of the year and two hundred and forty eight being mandates corresponding in number to the bones of the human body." Rabbi Simlai was echoing an ancient tradition. Its obvious artificiality conceals a reality. Jewish religious genius in the rabbinic period lay in the area of behavior patterns. The Romans created law, the Greeks philosophy and the Jews *mitzvot*.

There was no absolute unanimity among the Rabbis as to the specific nature of these commandments. Many different lists were drawn up. Even the most famous tabulation by Moses Maimonides in his *Sefer Ha-mitzvot*, or *Book of the Commandments*, was subject to later criticism and modification. Nevertheless there was a large measure of agreement over the bulk of the obligations falling on the Jew.

What could not be denied, however, was that the vast majority of these obligations had, in the process of time, become inoperative. With the destruction of the Herodian Temple, all those commandments relating to the sacrificial system and other priestly matters fell into desuetude. When the Jews were largely living in Exile, under Diaspora conditions outside of Palestine, all those laws which related to conditions in the Holy Land ceased to be relevant. Slowly, up to the modern period, the area of reference of operative Jewish law dwindled from the whole of life to but a part.

With the entry of the Jew into the modern world following the French Revolution, a final death blow was struck to the system of *mitzvot* as developed by the Pharisees and the Rabbis. The price which the Jew paid for the privilege of living as a citizen in a modern state was the right to control absolutely marriage, divorce and civil law in general. In the rabbinic period the Jews had largely functioned as a people within a people, a state within a state. The Rabbi was a jurist who interpreted the law and applied past precedent to current condition. With the Emancipation all this was swept away. Jewish marriage and divorce would henceforth have a moral and religious but no absolutely binding legal relevance.

A Jew could now be married and divorced without recourse to rabbinic law. Even when he married according to that law, this had to be preceded by secular civil marriage. And if he was to be divorced, secular divorce had to precede rabbinic divorce. Since the rabbinic law, unlike the civil law, could no longer be enforced as in the rabbinic stage of Jewish life, it became largely superfluous. Among the extremely Orthodox Jews and in the State of Israel, where there is an Orthodox religious "Establishment," the old patterns are rigorously followed. But even in these circles a dying struggle is being waged against the inroads of secularism.

The Israeli rabbinate now accepts conversion for the sake of marriage—which was absolutely prohibited during the rabbinic period. Outside of Israel, if an Orthodox Jew finds the rigors of orthodoxy too harsh, he can always be accepted by the Conservative movement. Beneath the façade of denominationalism, Jews today, in the post-Emancipation world, are Jews voluntarily. Rabbinic law in all these areas is dead even if, in those circles of Jewry dedicated to supporting the past, no admission of this demise is possible as yet. But death does not depend upon the writing of an obituary notice.

When the reality of the new situation becomes truly apparent, there will undoubtedly be a need to erect a new system of Jewish law, which takes cognizance of the radically changed conditions under which the modern Jew lives. Every society, even a voluntary organization, requires rules of procedure for admission and internal control. But until a need for such a system arises among a sufficiently large number of Jews, representative of the Jewish people as a whole, the pretense will continue that there is a Jewish law operative in the twentieth century. The rabbinic conception of Torah, which enabled the Jew to survive for almost two thousand years, is dead but has not yet decided to lie down.

Nowhere is this demise of rabbinic law more visible than in the area of civil law. For almost two thousand years, the Jews possessed their own autonomous civil law administered by the Rabbis. Jews were forbidden to take their litigation before Gentile courts. But in the modern world even the most Orthodox of Jews take their litigation to the civil courts. A vast section of the traditional six hundred and thirteen commandments has thus been deliberately permitted to fall into disuse.

It is sometimes argued, in defense of rabbinic law, that the bulk of it is inoperative simply because the Jews can no longer administer it. God will one day render all of rabbinic law, now for the most part unavoidably in desuetude, operative again. But this argument does not apply to large areas of civil law which could be utilized if there was a genuine desire to invoke rabbinic law. Nor, in a majority Jewish state in control of Jerusalem, does it apply to the reintroduction of the sacrificial system and the rebuilding of the Temple. If Orthodox Jewry appears reluctant to reintroduce the sacrificial system could it not be that Orthodox Jewry has no stomach for this institution? But then, for it, too, must rabbinic law be dead.

The sacrificial system forms a prime segment of rabbinic law and, to this day, the traditional prayer book includes prayers asking for the restoration of the Temple and its service.

May it be Thy will, O Lord our God and God of our fathers, to lead us up in joy unto our land, and to plant us within our borders, where we will prepare unto Thee the offerings that are obligatory for us, the continual offerings according to their order, and the additional offerings according to their enactment.

This prayer was never intended to be metaphysical poetry. It enshrined an aspiration for a restoration of past religious glory.

But perhaps the worst thing that can happen for some types of prayer is that they are answered. It then becomes a "calling" of a theological "bluff." The only truly consistent Orthodox Jews today are those who regard Zionism as a pseudo-Messianic movement. After all it was not God and his Messiah who led the Jews up in joy to their land but Theodor Herzl, Ben Gurion and Moshe Dayan. Until such a time that God redeems His people personally, the question of rebuilding the Temple is academic. That, at least, is the position taken by the fanatical Jerusalemite sect of the *Neturei Karta,* or guardians of the city, and also of many Orthodox Jews throughout the world, who refuse to recognize the "religious" existence of the State of Israel.

Grandmother S. speaks of *Yiddishkeit,* but she is totally unaware that *Yiddishkeit* was once a vast river of life which has now dwindled to a small trickle of water in a dried-up river bed. Apart from the laws concerning the ritual and ceremonial governing the home and personal life, a few dozen at the most, the six hundred and thirteen *mitzvot* in their rabbinic framework are of the past. The Jewish home, under rabbinic law, as part of a wider organic community, was a living reality. The Jewish home in this context was a veritable fortress of Jewish life in an alien world. But the Jewish home as a last defense of an anachronistic system of law, neither applicable nor valid for modern conditions, exposes Judaism to great danger. Modern secularism corrodes its very foundations.

The only authentic sovereign body which could, in the twentieth century, give a new lease on life to Jewish law and Jewish religion would be the international Jewish people which, outside of Israel, lives in two civilizations. In the past, Jewish law and custom evolved out of the total civilizational needs of the entire people. But the Jewish people is one only in theory in the modern world. There is often unity in purpose but rarely unity in organization. To give substance to such peoplehood sovereignty, the Jewish people would have to reconstitute itself as a people, rewrite its "Constitution" in terms of the demands of modern Jewish life and reformulate thereby the meaning and purpose of contemporary Jewish existence.

No one has done more to draw the attention of world Jewry to the tragic and dangerous state of fragmentation and denominationalism in modern Jewish life than Mordecai M. Kaplan, the founder of Reconstructionism. Foremost in Kaplan's mind is the recollection of that crucial event in the fifth pre-Christian century when, after the traumatic experiences of the destruction of the Temple in 586 B.C.E. with its ensuing Exile and the equally traumatic experience of the Return to Zion in 538 B.C.E., the people collectively accepted the Torah, systemized and edited in Babylon under the spiritual guidance of priest, prophet and scribe, as their Divine Constitution. The Holocaust of European Jewry and the rebirth of Israel constitute two twentieth-century traumas which cry out for a contemporary restatement of Jewish purpose.

In terms of his own avowed religious naturalistic assumptions Kaplan desires the Jewish people collectively, once again, to accept a constitution reflecting the new conditions governing Jewish life in the twentieth century—a Diaspora Jewish existence of living in two civilizations for the bulk of world Jewry and a national autonomous existence for a crucially important segment of world Jewry which Kaplan calls Zion, the Jewish majority of the sovereign State of Israel. In these new circumstances lies the great divide between premodern rabbinic Judaism and the realities of modern Jewish life.

Kaplan envisages a world Jewry, recognized by the United Nations, with consultative status, in the symbolic form of a wheel. The Diaspora communities would consist of *kehillot*—from *kehillah* or community—or organic communities, performing functionally equivalent spiritual and moral purposes for modern Jewry as did the old premodern organic communities of the rabbinic period. These organic communities would center on the "hub" of Zion, the only Jewish community which lives in a primary Jewish civilization.

All Jews in a particular geographical area would belong not to a particular denominational synagogue or independent philanthropic, cultural, educational or even social institution. All such Jews, who voluntarily wished to be considered Jews, would deliberately affiliate with the *kehillah* or organic community, of the region, which would be organized on democratic lines. There would be organizational links between *kehillot* throughout the world. The *kehillah*, in turn, would sponsor religious and other institutions to satisfy the needs of its constituents in terms of democratically expressed criteria. Belonging to the *kehillah* would be voluntary but its standards would obtain in the spirit of the aphorism that free men live by the rules that they themselves have ordained. The Jew would feel that his prime sense of belonging stemmed from the *kehillah* and not from the synagogue or other subsidiary body.

In Diaspora organic communities, where the Jew of necessity experiences his national and not his Jewish civilization as primary, Zion would be looked upon as a focal point for Jewish spiritual rejuvenation. Where Jews live in a majority Jewish culture and a primary Jewish civilization, a new lease on life could be afforded old ritual and symbol and new modes of religious expression developed.

The advantages of such a *kehillah* organization are self-evident. Instead, for example, of four inferior congregational Hebrew Schools, divided denominationally, failing to meet their budgets and struggling for existence in a ten-block area of a big city, a *kehillah* could determine areas of need for the highest quality educational projects to be set up.

All shades of the Jewish spectrum could be serviced but the servicing would be done on a rational and realistic basis. Organization, administration, salaries, could all be improved by an overall planning for the needs of the entire community, not for the fragmented aspirations of minority factions.

The greatest value accruing from a reconstituted Jewish people would be that Jews would know who they are. That sense of belonging, so profoundly important for Jewish identity, purpose and faith would be clearly defined. The God of Israel would once again have a recognizable and clearly defined "constituency." The question "Who is a Jew?" could be definitively answered in the way "Who is an American?" can be definitively answered. A Jew would be one who formally belonged to the Jewish *kehillah*. One could even opt out of being a Jew (although whether anti-Semites would accept such a definition is dubious).

Basic to Kaplan's Reconstructionist philosphy is the idea that the quality of Jewish faith in God is ultimately bound up with such a reconstruction of Jewish peoplehood. Religion does not exist in the abstract. It inheres in the ongoing life of a particular people. In the past, Jewish peoplehood created Jewish religion as part of a total Jewish civilization. If the Jewish religion is again to be healthy it must grow from the total body of the Jewish people, not merely from some denominational limbs. If the Jewish religion is theologically sick in the twentieth century, that is because the Jewish people is organizationally sick. As physical health is a prerequisite for personal well-being, collective health is a prerequisite for religioethnic well-being.

Kaplan is aware of the strength of denominationalism. He envisages the term "Reconstructionist" as a hyphenate. Reconstructionism will cut across all denominational and organizational barriers. The "sixty-four-dollar-question" in Jewish life will be couched neither in religious, cultural, ritual, nationalist nor philanthropic terms but in terms of belonging.

It will not be a matter of "Do you believe in God?" or "How much Hebrew do you know?" or "Do you keep a kosher home?" or "Are you going to settle in Israel?" or "How much do you contribute to the UJA?" The only question will be, "Do you want to belong to the Jewish people and enhance and advance the quality of its life?" All other considerations will be secondary.

As Kaplan sees it, those who can answer that question in the affirmative, be they Orthodox, Conservative, Reform, Zionist, secularist or Yiddishist, are, in addition, hyphenate Reconstructionists. Not the *manner* of their belonging—at least as a first step—but the *fact* of their belonging is paramount. The concern of Orthodox Jews with the total Jewish people, for example, regardless of the supernaturalistic universe of discourse in which they wish to conduct their religious dialogue, would link them, in reality terms, with the religious naturalists. The common denominator would be Jewish peoplehood.

A consideration, at least, of the reconstitution of the Jewish people, cannot be indefinitely postponed. But in the foreseeable future a sense of Jewish identity will have to come from participation and involvement in the ongoing life of some particular denominational yet, hopefully, not exclusively parochial Jewish organization. The reconstitution of the total Jewish people is, regrettably, not yet on the agenda of world Jewry. A community of purpose will, for the time being, have to substitute for a community of organization.

As at the University of Oxford, where one may only belong to the university by first being accepted into one of the individual colleges, so Jewish identity, in an age of denominationalism, will primarily continue largely to be achieved through the denominations. By belonging to such an organization the Jew, hopefully, will feel a sense of belonging to the entire Jewish people. The greater the community of purpose with world Jewry, the greater the sense of belonging.

This is far from the ideal but well within the realm of the possible. Within the various denominations, the work must proceed apace for the ever wider recognition that it is the university, and not the college, which confers the degrees of authentic Jewish existence. Nothing less than Jewish peoplehood experienced on ever higher levels will afford the Jew that sense of meaningful identity without which his Judaism is a liability rather than an asset.

In an imperfect Jewish age of transition, Daniel S. will aspire to authentic peoplehood but will have to work for it from the ground level up. No latter-day Theodor Herzl seems to be in the wings, ready to summon a new world Jewish peoplehood conference, however desirable such a goal may be.

There are, however, some problems involved in the concept of *kehillah*. The inherent defects of government in a mass democracy would be compounded in a "government" within a voluntary organization. "Professional" politicians, conveniently limited within a denominational Judaism, would be untrammeled on a worldwide scale.

Moreover it is to be doubted, for example, whether the Rabbi would feel any freer were his salary to come from the coffers of a central *kehillah* than from the pockets of the members of the parochial congregation. The problem of the Rabbi "running scared" with a local constituency would not necessarily be enhanced by a situation in which preferment would undoubtedly be afforded the organization men who tended not to rock the boat.

There are no cut and dried answers for Daniel S. He must belong as a Jew to the best of his ability. He must behave as a Jew within the context of his past environment, current needs and future aspirations. Without a solid and responsible effort at both belonging and behaving as a Jew he will never believe as a Jew.

Believing without belonging and behaving is like attempting to swim in an empty pool. One may avoid being hurt if one is careful and even go through the appropriate motions but there is no future in it. The crucial medium is lacking. It is an exercise in emptiness. Belief is the fruit, not the seed.

The modern Jewish home of Daniel S. cannot be hermetically sealed off from reality, attached to the past by an unrealistic theology and to the present by a negative and nostalgic defensiveness. It must be part of the modern world and modern Jewish reality if it is to be a celebration of the present as well as a commemoration of the past. Daniel S.'s Jewish home must be a Jewish home for today. It will be a reconstructed Jewish home. For the Jewish home as a sanctum has passed through three radical metamorphoses, from the biblical through the ecclesiastical and rabbinic stages of Jewish life. It will maintain its identity in change only by building on the past rather than by burying itself there.

Daniel S. will observe the Sabbath, for example. The Sabbath is the day on which the Jew traditionally commemorates the dignity of man. Perhaps the greatest spiritual invention of all times was the institution of a day of rest. The Romans poked fun at this idea and called the Jews who rested every seventh day a lazy people. But that institution, reflected in the Creation story that even God Himself, after working for six days, rested on the seventh, ultimately captured the imagination of the civilized world.

Daniel S. will observe the Sabbath, for example, but it will not be a replica of the rabbinic Sabbath. The traditionalist Jew observes the *mitzvot* associated with the Sabbath as fiats from a Supernatural Being. God, the Commander, ordains the commandments. Violation or infraction of the many "do's" and "don'ts" of the Sabbath arouse Divine displeasure. Personal evaluation of the merits or demerits of the various *mitzvot* does not enter into consideration. The "slave" does not question or comment upon the "Master's" orders. This does not prevent the Orthodox Jew from experiencing joyous spontaneity in his observance of the Sabbath. The ultimate sanction of that experience, however, resides not in him but in his Maker.

Daniel S. does not believe in that kind of God. For him *mitzvot* cannot any longer be regarded as Divine laws which are related to some Supreme Lawgiver. For Daniel S. the *mitzvot* will be regarded as behavior patterns evolved and developed by the Jewish people over four thousand years of history to confer holiness on life through the sancta of the Jewish people. Because he was

born a Jew, holiness for him as a Jew will be achieved through
these sancta, not through others.

The dignity of man, the need to cease from labor and rest as a
mark of self-respect, are all part of one universal value theme.

Daniel S. cannot live generalities. He is a particular part of an
ongoing historical living people. For him, the universal value
theme of the dignity of man will be refracted through the folkways of the people into whose destiny the accident of birth has
cast him. Since he lives in an age of transition, when Judaism is
moving from its rabbinic stage into its democratic stage, his Sabbath will reflect something of that transition. It will be tentative
rather than dogmatic, flexible rather than rigid.

Daniel S. will have to experiment with the Sabbath. He will
learn as much as he can about how Jews observed the Sabbath in
the past and how Jews observe the Sabbath in the present. This
learning process is never ending. It is an ongoing experience deriving from the world of Jewish books and the book of the
Jewish world. In the process of learning, Daniel S. will have to
make certain responsible judgments. He cannot live in a vacuum
until he has made up his mind. He cannot argue that he has to
wait until he has more information available before he can make a
judgment.

Every decision made by modern man, ethical, spiritual or
moral, is of necessity based on imperfect knowledge. There are,
equally, no absolute ritual judgments. Within the basic framework of the Sabbath, which is the historic matrix of the Jew's
expression of human dignity, Daniel S. will draw on all sources of
information, living and dead—but he then must make a decision
how to act this coming Sabbath. The Sabbath as a sanctum is the
constant; the method of observing the Sabbath, in an age of transition, is the variable. Daniel S. must himself be involved, with
millions of other Jews, in the process of that transition.

Perhaps the crucial difference between *mitzvot* conceived as
fiats of a Supreme Being and *mitzvot* conceived as folkways
evolved by the Jewish people over the ages to confer meaning on

life lies in the attitude to their infraction. Daniel S. will develop a strictly nonobsessional attitude toward the performing of *mitzvot*. He will not feel guilty if he fails from time to time to observe even those *mitzvot* which he selects as being particularly meaningful for him. He is not doing a personal favor to a Supreme Being by performing them, nor incurring the wrath of such a Being by not performing them. If anybody is let down it is himself insofar as he gains from the incorporation of the ritual symbol into his and his family's life. A folkway is meant to enhance the quality of life, not to detract from it by engendering morbid feelings of guilt.

The vast mansion of rabbinic Judaism has fallen. This much is evident to Daniel S. A few corners and niches are still left standing which will continue to provide warmth and shelter for the few. The traditionalists, like the *Chasidim*, will continue to gather around these remaining livable areas of the once magnificent mansion of premodern rabbinic Jewish life. They will create therein a semblance of the glory that once was by turning their backs on the widespread ravage and ruin. By such subterfuges they will satisfy a limited number of Jews in an age of transition. But most Jews who, like Daniel S., strive to create a modern Jewish home in the *spirit* of the past but not in the *image* of the past, will have to live in the drafty ruins of reality until a reconstruction can be effected, making it possible for all Jews (not merely the select few who still are able to cherish the old illusions) to live under the wide roof of an authentic Jewish peoplehood.

The independent experimentation of many Daniel S.'s, within the context of the needs of the present as well as the norms of the past, encouraged by other experimenters, will lead to the creation of the modern Jewish home. Even where Daniel S. behaves like a rabbinic Jew, the rationale for his behavior will not be rabbinic. It will derive from his deepest needs to be a Jew. Daniel S. needs the Sabbath more than the Sabbath needs him. That is why his own creative involvement is paramount. He finds the rough and tumble of modern life dehumanizing. Even man in general requires a pause, a moment for introspection and for rest. Daniel S. will seek the antidote to his own life-torn soul in the healing balm of Jewish sancta in whose reconstruction he himself will participate.

Daniel S. will strive to create a Jewish home for himself as well as for his children. Far too many Jewish parents introduce Jewish symbols and rituals into the home "for the sake of the children." But if Daniel S. and his wife cannot treat these symbols and rituals seriously for themselves the children will soon sense that the Jewish home is for the children—"kid's stuff." If the parents are to be the vehicle through which Jewish values are to be transmitted to the children it must be an adult, not an infantile, appreciation which is conveyed. Children, unlike adults, are never deceived.

Daniel S. will have to try for the impossible if he is to achieve the possible. Some form of Jewish articulation must be in his home on every day of the week. The modern spirit wearies of the endless repetitions to which the rabbinic world was prone. To recite all that a rabbinic Jew had to recite left little time in the day for anything else. Unlike the rabbinic Jew of the premodern era, Daniel S. lives in two civilizations. Paradoxically he has to become less Jewish than a rabbinic Jew in order to become more authentically Jewish as a modern Jew. Jewish religion, by no longer being his exclusive interest, can now become a creatively important interest. But it is still a great deal more than he has been accustomed to—or, at present, wants.

There is a vast world of difference, thinks Daniel S., between *davvening* three times a day as the traditionalist Jews do and having some modest form of home worship. It is going to be difficult enough for Daniel S. to involve his family in any ritual celebration, even on holy days. Every day is out of the question.

There is the recitation of the *Shema*, an extract from the Book of Deuteronomy, which has played a central role in Jewish liturgy for well over two thousand years. "*Shema Yisrael*—Hear O Israel, the Lord our God, the Lord is one. And thou shalt love the Lord thy God with all thy heart, and with all thy soul, and with all thy might." The prayer is a quotation, couched in an archaic idiom. God is conceived as Lawgiver. It has been on the lips of generations of martyrs and saints. It is part of the traditional confession on the deathbed. It has developed an aura over and above the literal meaning of the words. It is a living torch of Jewish faith. It expresses a belief that against all the evidence to the contrary we live in a *universe* and not a *multiverse*, that meaning and purpose in however small an area of human life has cosmic implications for all other areas of human life. The unity of God is the archaic way of expressing faith in the potential unity of life, not canceled out by any human aberrations.

Like all modern Jews, Daniel S. had been overwhelmed by the reality of Auschwitz. The evil perpetrated by man against man rose in the concentration camps to unparalleled heights. Yet Daniel S. remembers that millions of Jews died there with the *Shema* on their lips. It seemed paradoxical for those who did not endure Auschwitz to betray the faith of those who perished there by constructing philosophies of nihilism out of their ashes.

From his reading he has learned that the affirmation of the unity of God became strong in Jewish history in the face of affirmations to the contrary. Zoroastrianism was such a contrary affirmation. In the face of evil this religion affirmed that the world was not a unity. There were two principles operating in the world, two Gods, a God of light and a God of darkness. Evil came from a different source than good. Against this ancient heresy Judaism had thundered, in the words of Isaiah, that one God created light and darkness, peace and evil.

Daniel S. could not accept the Nazi Holocaust as a radical innovation in cosmic evil. *Men* had permitted Hitler and his henchmen to perpetrate their foul deeds. Men must prevent any future occurrence of such evil. The thought that evil was an independent, uncontrollable force which brooked no human interference struck terror in his heart. It took away all hope for the future.

Daniel S. looked into his own heart and saw good and evil struggling for mastery. The affirmation of the unity of God, albeit couched in archaic language—precisely *because* couched in archaic language—doubled his resolve in the context of an age-old Jewish cosmic stance not to permit Hitler to destroy Jewish faith as well as Jewish bodies. The ancient insight endorsed his own inner belief that evil often does, but need not inevitably, dominate the human scene. To take away hope was to paralyze human endeavor and utterly inhibit human creativity. He had always felt that atheistic existentialism came from men who had suffered in childhood. Betrayal in the nursery led to a profound subsequent feeling of cosmic betrayal.

Daniel S. came home late one night. His son had run out of the bedroom and, at frantic pace, had rushed into his father's up-sweeping arms, almost knocking him down in loving haste. Legs were flung gripping around waist, arms pinioned neck—a little body pulsating with love. Nothing spoken, only felt. Freud could explain some of this and Darwin more, thought Daniel S. later of this glowing experience. *Adonai echad*, he mused. God is one. If love of this intensity can exist in this little body, in this fleeting human contact between father and son, we live in a love-producing cosmos. The part somehow pointed to the whole. Man is also part of one Nature. *Adonai echad*. What the Jew experiences as a love of his people and, through his people, as the power that makes for salvation which is God, also has cosmic implications. This is an experience-of-the-Divine-producing cosmos, thought Daniel S. He had begun to recite the prayer with the children before they went to bed, for him as much as for them. He felt like a fool to begin with, but the foolishness soon wore off.

The famous Pharisaic leader of the second century, Akiba, had died with the words of the *Shema* on his lips. The Talmud records that when the Roman government under Hadrian (117–138) issued a decree forbidding the Jews to study and practice the Torah, Akiba, who insisted on lecturing in public as was his wont, was imprisoned by the Romans and sentenced to death.

When Rabbi Akiba was taken out for execution, it was the hour for the recital of the *Shema,* and while they combed his flesh with iron combs, he was accepting upon himself the kingship of heaven. His disciples said to him: Our teacher, even to this point? He said to them: All my days I have been troubled by this verse *with all thy soul* which I interpret "even if he takes thy soul." I said: When shall I have the opportunity of fulfilling this? Now that I have the opportunity shall I not fulfill it? He prolonged the word *echad* (one) until he expired while saying it. A heavenly voice was heard saying: Happy art thou, Akiba, that thy soul has departed with the word *echad.*

Daniel S. knows from his reading that Akiba was not the only Jewish martyr who died with *echad* on his lips. Throughout the medieval period, and in the Nazi concentration camps, millions died with *echad* on their lips. This prayer had represented to them the sublime quintessence of the martyr's aspirations. The Jew loves God for being a Jew even if that must entail death *al kiddush ha-shem,* for the sanctification of God's name. The Jew cannot avoid his fate. He must accept it with love. It is the price paid for being a member of a marginal minority. This status also has its advantages. The very richness of Jewish experience stems from it. Powerful men wage wars. Marginal men create values. There is a price to be paid for everything.

Somewhere Daniel S. had read that Keats' *Ode on a Grecian Urn* was more beautiful in the twentieth century than in the early nineteenth century when it was written, because millions of lovers had since then read it and experienced through it all the pain, anguish, agony and keen joy of young love.

> *Bold Lover, never, never canst thou kiss,*
> *Though winning near the goal—yet, do not grieve,*
> *She cannot fade, though thou hast not thy bliss,*
> *For ever wilt thou love, and she be fair . . .*
> *More happy love! more happy, happy love!*
> *For ever warm and still to be enjoy'd,*

For ever panting, and for ever young;
All breathing human passion far above,
That leaves a heart high-sorrowful and cloy'd,
A burning forehead, and a parching tongue.

The words of the *Shema*, in their constant repetition over two thousand years, had become encrusted with comparable cadences of joy and sorrow which transcended the literal meaning of the original text. The Hebrew words had become "leitmotifs" in which the music of a whole civilization was now composed. More than Daniel S. knew was conveyed to his children as he falteringly pronounced the sonorous Hebrew phrases. He was the inarticulate mouthpiece of generations, unknowingly communicating the incommunicable.

The traditional Jew recited a *berachah* before and after eating food. Enjoyment of the good things in life had to be an occasion for praising the Creator with traditional formula. But an ancient rabbinic author points to a modern equivalent for Daniel S. "If a man says, 'How beautiful is this bread! Praised be God who made it!' that is his benediction." The true purpose of the benediction was to evoke a sense of wonder and awe in the Jew at the munificence and beneficence of God in nature.

Daniel S. will strive to re-create that sense of awe and wonder at food in him and his family. If it can be linked with traditional formulae so much the better. In the Jewish home, food will not be taken for granted. "What a beautiful piece of bread!" God does not necessarily have to be conceived as Creator for a sense of awe and wonder to be elicited from the Jew. God as the principle of creativity can also elicit such a reaction. The world and its blessings are a reason for blessing. They must never be taken for granted. At root the *berachah* is a cosmic "Thank You." There is a cosmic courtesy and etiquette governed by traditional protocol. In one sense even the *Shulchan Aruch* is a ritualistic Emily Post.

There are many other occasions when Daniel S. will be able to perform concrete Jewish acts in the modern Jewish home he strives to create. They need not be performed in a spirit of obedience to an external authoritative law. They can be freely chosen against the background of that law, which is the past, but performed with an entirely different motivation deriving from the present. They will be viewed as folkways and deliberately utilized to foster a sense of meaningful Jewish existence.

That they create a warm, sentimental attachment to Judaism and ultimately a feeling of nostalgia is derivative and secondary. A deliberately created Jewish domestic tradition, based on the past, but made to serve the needs of the present, makes the home a place where the experience of God becomes a living reality. This is its primary justification. The home becomes a prism through which the light of God, streaming from Jewish experience past and present, becomes refracted into the warm colors of domestic custom and ritual.

Often this independently creative approach to what was originally a tightly organized system of rabbinic law yields, from the viewpoint of the traditionalist outsider, some strange combinations and results. There is the custom of kindling the Sabbath candles at sundown on Friday. Adherence to the rabbinic tradition leads to a movable time for the performance of this act, ranging from early afternoon in winter, to relatively late in summer. The movable time is unquestionably related to the origin of this custom, in an agricultural society of antiquity when, as with farmers in general, the end of the workday coincided with the setting of the sun.

But Daniel S. lives in an industrial civilization. The end of the day is the time when the office closes and the workers in city and suburb return to their homes. This is the temporal pulsebeat of the modern world. It is infinitely more important for Daniel S. that the candles be kindled at the same time throughout the year, at the time when the day is significantly felt to end, than that he and his family should self-consciously observe a temporal phenomenon which no longer functions for them as it did for their forebears. The act of kindling the candles when it is feasible for all the family to be present makes a much greater spiritual impact than when one simply sees the candles already lit on returning home. The new version is, from a modern point of view, infinitely superior to the old.

In the frame of reference of rabbinic Judaism such behavior is, of course, rigorously proscribed. But Daniel S. no longer lives either in terms of the rabbinic universe of discourse or in terms of rabbinic law. The law viewed as folkway must now responsibly be made to suit his purposes. Similar logic can lead him to the regular performance of the beautiful *Havdalah* ceremony every Saturday night throughout the year. Indefensible from the rabbinic standpoint (which requires the appearance of three stars for the performance of this ceremony), and requiring great effort to begin with, especially for beginners like Daniel S., the custom can become a powerful challenge of dedication to the five senses at the beginning of a new week. The religious experience involved ultimately becomes its own self-justifying rationale. *Havdalah* means making a distinction. It is the name given to the ceremony which "makes a distinction" between the holy Sabbath and the secular week. A plaited candle, a spice box and a cup of wine all blend together in a ceremony which culminates in the singing of traditional melodies.

Equally strange combinations and results can appear in other areas of Sabbath observance. Daniel S. will not be able to avoid them. Rabbinic law rigorously prohibits the use of public transport, regardless of purpose and destination, save in matters relating to life and death. Daniel S. will have to learn to draw a distinction between activities which promote the Sabbath spirit, an admittedly subjective criterion (the application of which will without doubt differ from his family to another), and activities which detract from the Sabbath spirit. Thus, as a suggestion, neither private nor public transport should be used for mundane purposes—to market, to visit downtown stores or the hairdresser. But where attendance at synagogue is involved or a trip to a museum on the Sabbath afternoon or even a visit to a beauty spot for quiet relaxation, both private and public transport, as well as the use of money, should be sanctioned. Daniel S. lives in a different world from that of his ancestors and, accordingly, his conception of calling the Sabbath a delight will be different from theirs. He will use their bricks but his own structural patterns.

Some form of meaningful involvement with the Jewish people is an essential component of the Sabbath spirit, though different families might understand this in different ways, depending on their point of origin. Involvement in at least one corporate act of Jewish worship would seem to be a vital prerequisite for placing all other Sabbath activities into a wholesome perspective. This could be on the eve of the Sabbath or, since the eve of the Sabbath is a time for the family, on the Sabbath day itself. The Sabbath is a day for the Jewish people, not just for the individual Jew.

There is no rabbinic objection to the use of radio and television on the Sabbath so long as they are not switched on or off. The rabbinic category of work under which the use of electricity comes is the operative factor and the content of radio or television program irrelevant from a strictly rabbinic legal point of view. Thus, in some traditional homes, television and radio are switched on and off by the use of special clocks set before the Sabbath.

Daniel S., who should have no problem in connection with the use of electricity on the Sabbath for light, heat and even for the preparation of food, should judge the use of these communication media on the Sabbath in terms of their content, not in terms of the rabbinic framework against which they are permissible. He might just find their use on the Sabbath, except on very rare occasions, when a spiritual factor is involved (e.g., the death of a great leader or some outstanding cultural or educational program), as totally alien to the spirit of the Sabbath.

Daniel S. will find no justification in a form of casuistry being used to justify filling the Sabbath hours, destined for creative rest and a foretaste of eternity, with the bustle and clamor of the market place and the outside world. The Sabbath is a day for family creativity, singing, talking, discussing, reading. In fact it is a time for a deliberate effort to *use* time rather than merely to *spend* time.

If Daniel S. truly wishes to create an authentically modern Jewish home every effort will be made to involve eyes, ears, nose and throat in the delight of Sabbath and Festival. "All my faculties shall say, Lord, who is like unto Thee." Many of the best-known traditional rituals and customs connected with these days grew peripherally out of the strict observance of rabbinic law. Most of the dishes, for example, which are traditionally associated with the Sabbath, developed out of the specifically rabbinic legal requirements of refraining from cooking on the Sabbath and avoiding the use of heat, save where a cooked dish was kept warm under rigorously controlled conditions.

Daniel S., and certainly his wife, will find the minutiae of these observances totally out of place in the modern home. They will see no objection to making a cup of coffee or preparing a light breakfast. But some of the individual results of these legal minutiae led to the creation of some interesting types of food which, even with changed rationale, can still engender a Sabbath spirit. The traditional dish known as *cholent*, for example (probably from the French *chaleur*, or heat), a succulent mixture of beans, barley, meat and potatoes, arose entirely from the rigors of rabbinic legal requirements. It was the best way of having a hot meal for Sabbath lunch when cooking itself was forbidden on the Sabbath. But even without that legal context, its preparation and consumption fulfills a social, psychological and religious function which could not have been anticipated in terms of its rabbinic legal origin.

In the first place, there is a great psychological value in that the housewife is released on the Sabbath from the worry over what is to be served at lunch on returning home from the synagogue. An element of relaxation is thus introduced into the kitchen, not only because the Sabbath lunch is ready and prepared, but because both the serving and the clearing involved demand minimal domestic chores. Moreover, the whole house is pervaded by a delicate aroma which children and adults soon irrevocably associate with the Sabbath, with all its plethora of subtle associations of goodwill, release of tension and general delight.

In the *shtetl* it was customary to bake *challah* each week, for the Sabbath, primarily for religious purposes. The term *challah*, which is now used to designate the twisted loaf used for Sabbath and Festival, originally meant, in terms of rabbinic law, that part of the dough which, in preparation, the baker separated and gave to the priest. It is referred to as such in the Bible. When the Temple was destroyed and its "taxation" system of tithes and other levies went out of vogue, it became the custom to take a piece of dough away from every baking (*challah*) and burn it in the fire as a substitute for giving it to the priest. No longer ritually clean in the absence of the Temple, the priest could not accept it himself.

According to strict rabbinic law one should only eat bread from which *challah* has been removed, and to this day strongly traditionalist Jews will eat such bread not only on Sabbaths and Festivals but also throughout the year. However, rabbinic law does permit other kinds of bread to be eaten so that in most traditional circles one finds a relaxation of the strict rule during the week. In some circles, an extra stringency is introduced between *Rosh Hashanah* and *Yom Kippur*. During this period, known as the Ten Days of Penitence, only bread from which *challah* has been removed and burned, is permitted. On Passover, *challah* is invariably removed by the manufacturers of *matzah*.

For Daniel S., none of these laws relating to portions of food to be burned in fire as a substitute for giving them to the priest will be spiritually convincing. He will not find the priestly distinctions relevant nor the custom, at this historical remove, meaningful. Yet from an entirely different rationale than the rabbinic, the regular baking of bread by hand in the home for Sabbath and

Festival is to be strongly recommended in the modern Jewish home.

First, there is an element of creativity involved, for home bread-making is something of an art. Second, there is an element of human challenge involved to the prepacked, prewrapped, prechemically treated, presliced, synthetic apology for bread which is of staple supermarket provenance. Children who see the miracle of water, flour, yeast and salt rising weekly before their eyes are in a better position to develop a sense of awe and wonder at the miracle of food than children who believe that the source of all life resides in the deep freeze. Bread is still the staff of life and the object of our most frequent benediction.

There can also be family participation (the children will want to assist in its preparation) which, commencing on Thursday, serves to highlight the anticipated Sabbath delight. In this day and age, when almost everything in the food line can be done for one by others, personal involvement in the Sabbath table adds to the spiritual dimension of the day of rest. Father, mother and children give of the fruit of their own labor to a day dedicated to God and man.

There can be experimentation which involves introducing into the home traditions which one has read about in books or heard about indirectly from other people's experiences. There are profound spiritual implications for parent and child in the traditional custom of fathers blessing the children on the eve of the Sabbath. It is an invocation, coupled with the priestly benediction, which pours out the fervent aspirations and hopes of parents for their children through time-honored references and phrases:

> *The Lord bless thee and keep thee.*
> *The Lord make His face to shine upon thee,*
> *And be gracious unto thee.*
> *The Lord turn His face unto thee,*
> *And give thee peace.*

At such a moment, the humblest abode on the Sabbath fills with an incandescent light as generations of the past jostle each other, crowding around the Sabbath candles and echoing, with the visiting angels of tradition, "So may it be next Sabbath . . . and the next."

The Seder service on the eve of Passover is a paramount occasion for family celebration. But there are other occasions in the Jewish calendar also. The tradition of a festive meal on *Purim* has assumed new meaning since the Nazi Holocaust and the establishment of the State of Israel. *Purim* is the quintessence of thanksgiving to God for all those occasions when the Jewish people were miraculously delivered at the "eleventh hour" from almost certain destruction. Such sentiments deserve the finest setting for their full affirmation.

Formally observing *Purim* by serving a festive meal in the afternoon, the traditional time for the celebration, with suitable prayers, readings and songs, transforms the holiday into an occasion for deep gratitude. When we reflect on the million Jewish children murdered by the Nazis, we have cause to mourn bitterly, but we also might well rejoice that the Nazi tyranny was squashed before all Jewish children suffered a like fate. The Jewish child, like the adult Jew is, in the twentieth century, always a potential victim. The home is the place where the family must acknowledge both tragedy and deliverance. *Purim* is a prime occasion for this. In recent years a special day commemorating the Holocaust, *Yom Shoah*, has also been instituted and is widely celebrated in synagogues if not in the home.

The New Year of the Trees, or *Tu Bishevat*—the fifteenth day of the month of Shevat—is another occasion "off the beaten path" of Sabbaths and Festivals when experimentation can yield rich results. Grandmother S. had told Daniel S. of the custom of children planting trees in Israel (then Palestine), vicariously, of course, and receiving boxes of almonds on this day. She also had told him how her family used to obtain, on this day at least, some new fruits and recite the customary benediction over fruit, with the added benediction of *Shehecheyanu:* "Be praised , O Lord, for having preserved us alive . . ."

The *Shulchan Aruch* speaks of Jews who eat fifteen different kinds of fruit on that day, corresponding to the fifteen Songs of Ascent in the Book of Psalms, and even of some who eat thirty different kinds of fruit. A formal celebration of *Tu Bishevat,* through a deliberate attempt to gather the widest possible variety of fruit available in what is virtually midwinter, provides a most suitable occasion for expressing gratitude, not only for the rising of the sap in the trees of Israel, but for the teeming productivity of nature in general through which we are constantly, and for the most part, unconsciously sustained. This is especially meaningful in an affluent civilization where refrigeration has all but obliterated the demarcation of seasons and formerly seasonal fruits may be purchased throughout the year.

New York will yield even the average enterprising shopper over forty different varieties of nuts and fruits. When one contemplates their various countries of provenance, their remarkable variety and their pleasure-giving qualities, one discovers ample grounds for gratitude for the marvelous world in which we live.

To become conscious and aware of what we tend so much to take for granted is a prime means of sensitizing the conscience to the spiritual and physical needs of others as well as our own. When this can be done through the vehicle of a time-honored Jewish tradition which has a temporal relationship to our most ancient past as well as a geographical dimension of reality in terms of modern Israel in our present, the home truly becomes a vehicle for becoming aware of and making aware of the meaning of Jewish existence.

The expression of thanksgiving and gratitude must be kept constantly alive in our hearts and minds if we are not to become insensitive to the more spiritual dimensions of life. Jews express these reactions to life through Jewish traditions. The Festival of Tabernacles can be a supreme occasion of thanksgiving for the harvests of life, not merely the agricultural harvest with which most of us in our industrial society are only remotely involved, but the harvests of mind and spirit which, when garnered, if we do not wholesomely acknowledge, lose their spiritual efficacy and potency.

The power of the *Sukkah*, or booth, in the back yard is something which no family which has the facilities to provide will ignore. Yet even for apartment dwellers every effort should be made to avoid celebrating this most beautiful of Festivals vicariously, in the synagogue *Sukkah* alone. A domestic *Sukkah*, even one constructed indoors (despite its rabbinic legal indefensibility), is better than no *Sukkah* at all.

Experimentation need not always involve introducing traditions which have not previously been observed. An element of innovation can also be present. There has perhaps never been an age when so many toys and good things were available for children. The eves of Sabbath and Festival are best reserved for receiving such gifts. This is an unashamed, avowed, deliberate Pavlovian attempt to make the child associate the sancta of Jewish life with the good things in life.

Perhaps this is not a modern innovation after all. There was a medieval custom, at the commencement of the Jewish education of the child, of smearing with honey a slab on which were inscribed the first and last four letters of the Hebrew alphabet and some biblical verses, "which the child might lick off and taste, as it were, the sweetness of instruction." The Rabbis of old also knew of the value of associating early impressions of Jewish experience with oral satisfaction. These early associations are of prime importance in the Jewish home. They lay the basic foundations of a lifelong love of Jewish values and traditions.

There are parents who complain that they are too sophisticated for all this ritual paraphernalia involved in Jewish home life. It would make them self-conscious, they argue, to light candles and bless them, to lift up a goblet of wine and make *Kiddush*, to conduct a modest home Seder. Daniel S. himself is in the throes. It is often not symbolism that such parents are opposed to, merely Jewish symbolism. They or their Christian secular counterparts will spend hours decorating a Christmas tree or preparing for a cocktail party. The gastronomic "rabbinic legal" minutiae involved in the "Orthodox" preparation of a dry martini never embarrass them, yet even the medieval commentators rarely demanded such attention to detail.

It is, in fact, not ritual that such parents are opposed to, merely Jewish ritual. When it comes to the observance of the *Shulchan Aruch* of white Anglo-Saxon Protestantism, based on some of the more spurious snobbish social values of our secular society, they manifest an enthusiasm out of all proportion to their sophistication. Sophistication need not, however, preclude a warmly traditional Jewish home.

The home which enshrines Jewish symbolism is not only a responsible Jewish home, loyal to its past, present and future. It is also a healthy home, for an early training in symbolism grounded in spiritual values is of vital import in the emotional development of the child. There is undoubtedly a correlation between the breakdown of the Jewish home in our own day and the rise of Jewish divorce, juvenile alienation, narcotics addiction and delinquency.

It is as if religion had preached "God is love" for over three thousand years and modern science, appending theoretical foundation to ancient intuition, had added: "It's good for your ulcers too!" The paramount importance of love in human beings is, indeed, no more a matter for mere faith. It can be demonstrated in the operating room. The man who hates has a different kind of visceral function from the man who loves. There is a visible internal dimension of hate in terms of gastric juices.

It has equally been demonstrated that parental involvement in religious symbolism is a powerful factor in the emotional development of the child. Such involvement cannot develop overnight for those who never received a solid grounding in Jewish values in their own childhood. But it can be worked at, like learning to drive a car, and constantly improved, like a handicap in golf.

There is nothing spontaneous about religion any more than there is about authentic love. An element of preparation, striving, artificiality perhaps, inevitably enters into our most intimate relationships. As it is between man and woman and man and man, so also is it between man and God. "Prepare to meet thy God, O Israel!" Daniel S. prepares himself. The road is long but slowly he becomes certain that the path he is attempting to follow is in the right direction.

The truly Jewish home will spare no effort in the adornment and beautification of the Jewish folkway. At its simplest this means that Daniel S. and his wife cannot expect their children to take their own religious commitment seriously if they do not spend the same kind of lavish care, foresight and consideration when selecting a Hebrew School, or preparing for Sabbath and Festival, as they do when selecting a car, a television set or a hotel for their summer vacation. (Hard, thinks Daniel S. Too hard. Perhaps.) The Jewish home, in addition to being a place where Jewish prayers and sentiments are audibly articulated and where Jewish rituals are tangibly performed, will also be a place which in its physical presence will proclaim the glory of Jewish existence from every bookshelf, reading desk, wall and breakfront.

What the ancient liturgy did for the premodern Jew—affording a vivid sense of Jewish identity—can often be performed today by a responsible Jewish magazine or news release which makes the Jew aware of what is happening to the Jewish people outside of the home. For the family cannot be an encapsulated, hermetically sealed-off cell. The welfare of the Jewish people is ultimately the family's welfare, even as it reciprocally enriches the Jewish people through its own devotion and responsibility to Jewish values.

The Yiddish poet who "davvened" his Yiddish newspaper on the subway, as a contemporary functional equivalent for a secularist Jew of the premodern Jew's praying from a prayer book, precisely expressed how knowledge and consciousness of Jewish peoplehood can function on a spiritual level today. A Jewish home is, above all, a place where the state of the Jewish people the world over is of prime importance, not merely as an academic concern but as a ground for action and personal involvement. What is happening to Jews in Russia and Israel is what is happening to the family. Books, *objets d'art*, paintings, records, prints, which bring into the home the historical and current challenge of Jewish peoplehood thus fulfill an important function.

By the same token the modern Jewish home must be a home in which, outside of Israel, the welfare of the primary national civilization in which the Jew lives is acknowledged, consciously and deliberately. Living in two civilizations and sharing two religions, one with fellow Jews and the other with fellow nationals, the Jew must be loyal to both if his loyalty to either is to be meaningful. The truly Jewish home will thus richly express American as well as Jewish sancta.

Thanksgiving Day will no more be thought of merely in terms of a family gathering around turkey and cranberry sauce than Passover will be thought of merely in terms of a family gathering around *matzah* and *kneidlach*. These days are sacred occasions of highest spiritual expression. Indeed the more spirituality the Jew can inject into his majority culture American sancta, the more meaning will he derive from his Jewish sancta. For God operates through the American as well as through the Jewish people, and the Jew who lives in America and cuts himself off from either one of these sources of the Divine, causes the other also to atrophy.

The twentieth-century Jew who deliberately chooses to live in a spiritual as well as cultural and social ghetto is retrogressing, not progressing, religiously. By turning his back on the twentieth century he merely succeeds in avoiding the challenge of God in the twentieth century. No matter how virtuous he may consider himself to be or how traditionalist he may be in his observance, his behavior places a stringent limit on his ultimate spiritual potential. Paradoxically, in a secular age, by striving to become more of a Jew he becomes less of a Jew.

Perhaps the most difficult, as well as the most vital, expression of the modern Jewish home, is the manner in which Jewish values are exemplified in daily life both on and apart from specifically Jewish occasions. If the values supposedly enshrined in the sancta of Jewish life are honored in real life more in the breach than in the observance, we have a travesty of a Jewish home. Nachmanides, a distinguished medieval Jewish philosopher (1194–1270), spoke of the *naval birshut ha-Torah*, the man who scrupulously observes all the minutiae of Jewish law, yet manages to behave like a pig. The same is true of the Jewish home. Unless the values implicit in the Jewish observances selected from the past or developed in the present, are endorsed in action, we will have the hypocritical or the immoral but never the truly Jewish home.

One of the areas where great care will be exercised in the modern Jewish home will be parental attitudes to material things. Jewish religion, linked as it is with family celebrations, involves food and drink. These mainstays of life will be treated with respect and with perspective. Excess of any kind, wastage of any kind, will be avoided at all costs. Even the needless squandering of water and of fuel involved in washing, heating and cooking will be scrupulously avoided. The classic benedictions of Jewish home worship thank God as the Author, with man's cooperation and involvement, of the food with which we are sustained. Any waste of these commodities is a veritable blasphemy, not so much because of the economic, as of the spiritual harm involved.

The child who sees his parents recklessly squandering life's blessings will not learn from them the reverence for all parts of the Creation which must be a prime element in Jewish home life. Traditional Jewish religion, which prohibited the throwing away of bread, understood the significance of benediction in this respect. In some homes a loaf of bread, which accidentally fell to the floor, would be kissed, like a prayer book in similar circumstances, on retrieval. The problem is enormous in our modern affluent society based on wastage and built-in obsolescence.

Respect for the material things in life presupposes a perspective on them. There will always be some discrepancies between luxuries and necessities and the child will not fail to observe them. A Bar Mitzvah present involving a family trip to Israel may cost more than a lavish party at a downtown hotel. It will, however, give some indication of the scale of values of the family.

By the same token, a parent may find expenditure on a good Jewish summer camp, or some equivalent educational experience, excessive and yet almost bankrupt himself in an act of conspicuous consumption in connection with a vulgar Bar Mitzvah celebration. This is more common in modern Jewish experience, where the celebrations of this type, in their exorbitance, extravagance and waste, directly challenge every ethical insight implicit in the whole process of Jewish education. The child from the very earliest age senses how the family dollar is spent and what values are enshrined—or denied—by that expenditure. The checkbook is a barometer of familial values.

The Jew was never a drunkard, that is, until recently, when he became fully emancipated. Traditional Judaism introduces the child to wine at the age of eight days in the circumcision ceremony. Later, on Sabbath and Festival, alcohol is imbibed, in moderation, and sanctified. Certainly, until very recently, statistics indicated that among Jews drunkenness was almost unknown. In the Jewish home the use of liquor and tobacco will have to reflect the ethical and moral challenge implicit in its style of life. The statistics with regard to smoking are too impressive to be ignored. The parent who smokes and drinks heavily in the presence of children is not only flouting common sense and intelligence; there is an element of self-destruction involved. But although the *mitzvot* were not ordained for reasons of health, tribes which created unhealthy tabus simply did not survive to tell the tale.

And changing circumstances can often make laws healthy in one age, unhealthy in another.

The way in which the family dollar is spent will reflect attitudes toward people as well as toward things. A father or mother who spends money freely on self but repeatedly forgets to honor, even modestly, birthdays and anniversaries, is showing a sense of values—or lack of values. The family which can afford to visit foreign shores for a sumptuous vacation but finds it difficult to visit or support an aged or needy parent or member of the family, or contribute to charity, or support a synagogue or other Jewish institution, is expressing a clear value judgment.

The actions of the family which takes advantage of its domestic help, whether in regard to the kind of wages paid, type of living conditions provided or food served, will not go undetected by the children. Many a healthy—and sick—attitude to the color problem, to the problem of integration, to the non-Jew, is born in the parental home from parental attitudes. The child detects in the parent's voice in the kitchen, as on the telephone and in the street, the delicate nuances for the people who "matter" and the people who don't "matter." A world of healthy values is lost in the home where lies are loudly proclaimed, ill-gotten gains applauded, shady practices bragged about and children told to "do as I say, not as I do."

The child will also note how the family hour is spent. The man who spends a grossly disproportionate amount of time on the golf course as compared with the synagogue or in the office and on extended business trips as compared with the home and his children will not go unnoticed. The man who has infinite time for bridge, skiing, yachting and other pleasure pursuits but is unable to find time to serve on a worthwhile committee or do some work for the community is clearly manifesting his values.

On the other side of the scale, of course, there are those homes where parents spend time on communal affairs to the detriment of their own family life and this, too, has its own "immorality." The specter of the demands of Jewish organizational life must have been raised from many a psychiatrist's couch as a competitor with the child for a mother's love. It will be a matter of proportion. There can be too much of a good thing. In the Jewish home there must be a proper balance in the hour and a perspective on the way it is spent.

In the modern Jewish home, the unit of energy will breathe ethical and moral values. The mother who devotes time to preparing the Sabbath meal is teaching the value of effort and energy as well as money and time; the mother who goes nearly berserk in preparation for a purely social event does likewise. Indiscriminate watching of television programs (and, even more important, indiscriminate response to the seduction of its commercial advertising pressure) will teach one scale of values; spending money, time and effort on reading good books, or registering for an educational course, another. There is not a single aspect of the day-to-day life of the Jew who wishes to create a modern Jewish home which will not reflect a choice of values fraught with ethical and moral consequence. As Henry Frederick Amiel has written:

The religion of a child depends on what his mother and his father *are,* and not on what they *say* they are. The inner and unconscious ideal which guides their life is precisely what touches the child; their words, their remonstrances, their punishments, their bursts of feeling even, are for the child merely thunder and comedy; what his parents *really* worship, this it is which his instinct divines and reflects. The child sees *what* we are, behind what we *say* we are, *pretend* to be. He is a magnifying mirror. This is why the first principle of education is: train yourself; and the first rule to follow if you wish to possess yourself of a child's will is: master your own.

And as the supreme Value of values, the modern Jewish home will not be able to avoid confronting the meaning of God in the home in particular and in life in general, for the challenge of God in the twentieth century is the supreme challenge which it faces. Mordecai Kaplan has written:

The most important element in the social heritage which parents transmit to their children is a conception of God. Failing to teach their children both directly and indirectly what is meant by believing in God they leave their children spiritually stranded and disoriented, and a source of disintegration and weakness to their people.

But how does one teach children about God before their minds can grasp the abstract without inculcating in them ideas which they will only later have to unlearn? Many parents talk to children about God anthropomorphically, only to discover that this causes more complications than it provides solutions. God "up there" or "out there" may have been all right for *their* parents, but with spaceships whizzing in all directions "up there" and "out there," spaceships whose launching our modern children can actually see on television, the physical idea of God becomes of limited value, even as a first stage. The best approach to teaching children about God is to limit rigorously the use of the term "God" and to concentrate instead on those tangible experiences which we identify with God and those real emotions and feelings which we believe are grounded in God.

Sigmund Freud observes, somewhat caustically, in *The Future of an Illusion:* "I think it would be a very long time before a child who was not influenced began to trouble himself about God and the things beyond this world." This is, of course, true, but a child who was not thus influenced would equally not trouble himself about toilet training or learning how to speak. More important for our purposes, Erik Erikson has shown that the basic ego strengths or virtues, such as hope, will, purpose, fidelity and love grow and emerge from the emotional regularities of a properly organized home. The modern Jewish home will be a home where the regularities, not only of human life in general but of Jewish life in particular will, at the early crucial formative stage of the child's life, become part of the very pulse of existence.

The great Jewish ego strengths are born and nurtured in this fashion and, as prime vehicles to the Jew of the God of his people, the time-honored Jewish traditions are those for which even the child can offer thanks. "Thank you God for *Shabbat* and *Kiddush* and *Zemirot* and *Havdalah*." These can be as real to the child as record player and teddy bear. In the Jewish home they will be more than real. They will point to a reality about the cosmos beyond the home. No child is ever too young to grasp this inarticulate message through his very emotional pores by a process of spiritual osmosis—that the universe is a place in which we are meant to fulfill ourselves to the highest human level. If he is made to feel at home in his own home he will feel at home in the world. The home is a cosmos in miniature. Awareness of God, like charity, begins at home, the home conceived and experienced as part of a living people.

"Is there a God?" That question, as Mordecai Kaplan has suggested, can best be transposed into a different mode for modern man. "Is there a reality—entity or process—that helps man make the most of his life individually or collectively?" It is in the spirit of this transposition that the child may have his attention drawn to all those aspects of his life which, on his own level, afford him fulfillment. It is through authentic human fulfillment on all levels that we experience God as the power in the cosmos making for fulfillment. Belief in God as such a power is an act of faith but an act of faith grounded on empirical fact. For man is a fulfillment-seeking animal.

A lively sense of gratitude can be engendered in the child for nature, sun, moon, stars, wind, trees and parks; for his home and for his beloved possessions, whether extrinsically or intrinsically valuable (a child may find in a chewed-up rag doll a *summum bonum*); for loved ones, relatives and friends; for his people, his American people and his Jewish people; for things to eat and for things to drink.

A sense of gratitude is learned and taught. It is not something which arises spontaneously. So also is an awareness of loyalty, responsibility and integrity. Through responsibility, above all, is the Divine made manifest in human affairs. On the child's level these manifestations of God in life can be pointed out, in the home, in the school, and for the older child, in the nation, in the world. A child benefits from, enjoys and assimilates creatively health-giving food long before he can articulate the words which designate it. And there is a time when he has the concept but lacks the physiological and mental know-how to articulate it verbally.

Even so it is with God. We must strive to teach our children what is meant by believing in God pragmatically rather than by simply using the term. If we are on the right track, then, when the child is old enough, he will suddenly discover, like Monsieur Jourdain in Molière's *Le Bourgeois Gentilhomme*, that he has been believing in God all his life—without really knowing how to describe his belief as such. The reality is all-important. The word "God" is relatively unimportant until much later. A child does not need to know about vitamins. He must simply eat them. The term "God" becomes functionally and operatively potent in the collectivity of responsible adults.

There are no specifically Jewish values. There are only particular refractions of universal human values through four thousand years of Jewish tradition. The ideal Jewish home will therefore strive to be a home where husband and wife live together, not in a symbiotic relationship, or in domination or subjection of one by the other, but where the value of personal identity and human fulfillment is not only visible but constantly endorsed.

Ideals, it has been said, are like stars. We never reach them. We plot our course by them. So it must be with the modern Jewish home. As the mountain climber who, no sooner has he scaled one peak, than he finds that it was but a foothill and that a whole range of mountains challenges him ahead, so will the Jewish home set its goals on a short-term basis, patiently endeavoring to progress within terms of its own strength, yet never losing sight of the main goal, *tikkun olam be-malchut shaddai*, or the perfection of the world under the kingship of God. The noblest citizen of the world achieves that exalted level by first being a patriotic citizen and a responsible member of his historic people. Even so is the challenge of eternity mediated through the domestic hearth.

The rabbis, in a story already referred to, spoke of two angels who accompany a Jew home from synagogue on Sabbath eve, a good and a bad angel. If the table is laid and all is ready for a meaningful observance of the Sabbath, then the good angel says: "Amen. So may it be next week." If everything is unprepared, then the bad angel says: "Amen. So may it be next week." But the Jew who strives to build a modern Jewish home has more than one good angel to encourage him and endorse his efforts. All the great spirits of the Jewish past exhort him as he permits them to live through him while he passes on the torch of meaningful Jewish life to the next generation.

The Jew has traditionally been concerned more with actions than with ideas. The operational factor in life, supremely important in modern science, is surely adumbrated in the ancient Jewish concept of *mitzvot maasiyot*, or practical precepts—the pragmatic implications of a religious idea. For the meaning of a religious idea is not what you say about it or believe about it but how it operates in your life. With Tolstoy, the Jew would agree that "it is easier to write ten volumes of philosophy than to put a single precept into practice." In this spirit, these recommendations are suggested for Daniel S. as possible guidelines in building a modern Jewish home. In an age of religious pluralism and, especially, of transition, no particular set of recommendations will bear the hallmark of authority. The Jewish home of the future will be a multiple product of many Jewish homes, all striving to be loyal and responsible to Jewish identity, past, present and future.

"Next thing, you'll be deciding to become a *Chasid* and move to Spring Valley," his wife teased Daniel S. one morning as she cleared away the breakfast table. The Hebrew word still sounded a little awkward on her lips. But there was no malice or rancor in her voice and her warm, sparkling eyes revealed her true feelings.

The family of Daniel S. had undergone a minor revolution. The elder boy had become Bar Mitzvah the previous year. Instead of a party, he had asked for a trip to Israel with a group of his Hebrew School friends. Daniel S.'s wife had grumbled at first but she could not help feeling proud as they saw him off on the plane. He was a young man already. He had ideals of his own. He might have all the burgeoning problems of adolescence on his shoulders but at least he knew who he was.

She thought back reluctantly to her own youth, where no special rite of passage had marked off childhood from womanhood. In spite of herself she had been strangely moved by the intensity with which her son had approached his Bar Mitzvah. For what seemed like months the corridors of the house had echoed with the ancient cantillation. She had first resented it as something alien. Were not the cadences of Europe good enough for her? As the day approached she found herself humming the tune and even the words to herself over the kitchen sink. She was captivated and caught in the web of tradition.

Her ancient antipathy to the clergy reared its head in momentary anger as she saw the Rabbi perched high above the congregation during the service. "Pompous ass," she thought to herself. "Why do these men have to dress up and pretend they are God?" But when the boy had finished chanting his portion, which the mother now knew by heart, and the Rabbi, after a few stumbling words, well meant but poorly articulated, put his hands on the child's head with the selfsame words of blessing which Daniel S. had begun to use at home on Friday evenings, something gave way inside her. Tears began coursing down her cheeks as she realized with a sudden burst of flame that she, too, had come home.

The boy returned from Israel a young man. He had learned to converse competently in Hebrew. He had been deeply moved by what he had seen. Utterly dedicated to his historic people he insisted on continuing his Jewish education. Daniel S., who had been reluctant to insist, not wanting to destroy through enforcement what so laboriously and painfully had been built up over a period of many years, was relieved. He was as happy to find that his son had a mind of his own as that he was going to continue to learn more about what he was and where he came from.

At his secular school his friends decided that he was a "square." Anyone who wanted to study Judaism *after* Bar Mitzvah should have his head examined! The boy was unperturbed. Daniel S. marveled. He himself, as a child, had always tended to be a conformist, even denying the things he loved and wanted. He had waited too long to assert himself and the price had been high. He was grateful that his son had the strength to walk alone.

That December their celebration of *Chanukkah* took on a new and richer dimension. The pressure from the children had been constant and growing. Together they selected a new *menorah*, or eight-branched candelabrum. Daniel S. had experienced great difficulty in introducing ritual into the home. It had at first been so alien to the secular atmosphere which pervaded all things. Slowly and with great effort, novelty yielded to custom and custom to habit. Holding the *shammash*, or the servant candle which lights the others, he chanted the benediction. Everybody joined in the singing of "Rock of Ages":

> *Rock of Ages, let our song*
> *Praise Thy saving power,*
> *Thou, amidst the raging foes,*
> *Wast our shelt'ring tower.*
> *Furious they assailed us,*
> *But Thine arm availed us,*
> *And Thy word broke their sword*
> *When our own strength failed us.*

They also sang one verse in Hebrew, *Maoz Tzur* . . . Mother merely hummed. For her, Hebrew lessons were still in the future.

Grandmother S. had vigorously resisted all this fuss and bother. She was highly critical of all this nonsense. According to her, a Jewish home was a *kosher* home and the rest was commentary.

Daniel S.'s home didn't qualify because they didn't keep separate dishes for meat and milk. They merely bought meat from the kosher butcher. Grandmother resisted, but not too strongly. She was now in her ninth decade and didn't have too much resistance left anyway. Secretly she both resented and admired Daniel S. for "calling her bluff." She had always felt a little hypocritical inside at her "pot and pan-theism." But she would carry her secret with her to the grave. She could never admit her nagging doubts openly.

The little candles glowed as the family opened their gifts and embraced each other. A great miracle had happened there. And here. Over two thousand years ago a handful of Jews had fought for religious freedom against the Syrian Greeks and won. Mankind still had a long way to go before all would achieve religious freedom. In the meantime the lights of *Chanukkah* would remind the Jew where his obligation and responsibility lay. *Chanukkah*, which began as a festival of religious freedom for Jews, now spoke of religious freedom for all. On a smaller scale Daniel S. felt he had fought the Syrian Greeks all on his own.

Suddenly Daniel S. realized how weary he had become of the blandness of cosmopolitan ethics and of the *ad hoc* societies springing up overnight, of the homes which were hotels serving sandwiches, where the focal point was the television set and the latest best seller the prime topic of conversation. The source for his own sense of ethical responsibility was here. Not one life span but untold billions hovered over the *Chanukkah* candles.

> *How far that little candle throws his beams!*
> *So shines a good deed in a naughty world.*

The way to the future is paved with obstacles of human nature. The old ethnic traditions provide a soil in which a man can sink his roots deep against the fear of the unknown and the evil hidden in man's heart. They cannot protect him. They can sustain him. There are no absolute guarantees in this world, for the

Jew or for the Gentile. Daniel S. had set out to find roots. He had discovered hope and faith.

Grandmother S. was in the kitchen critically examining the way in which the *latkes*, or traditional potato pancakes, were being cooked. She hadn't quite decided whether to compromise her "kosher" soul and eat one. Daniel S. smiled. The Lubavitcher Rebbe would certainly not eat in his house. But then it was doubtful if Daniel S. would ever have occasion to invite him. The path of the past for Daniel S. was but a guide. He admired, but respectfully dissented from, those who sailed through life under the colors of a bygone age. His own participation and involvement was what made his home—for him—a Jewish home. He had learned to think of himself as a potentially first-class citizen of the Jewish world. There were many different paths to God in the twentieth century.

A whole way of life had changed. Judaism had crept in through the window of a heart and was now presiding at the family table. Many of their old friends now seemed colorless and uninteresting. They lived in a vacuum, an endless treadmill of existence in which even recreation and vacations became systematic and routinized. Even the quality of their ethical striving now seemed suspect. It was of the moment, not of eternity. It was a hobby rather than a lifelong pursuit. The Jewish calender had given him an anchorage in the harbor of history.

By deepening his Jewish identity, by mixing in circles where men and women took it for granted that their time and their substance belonged to others as well as to themselves within an ethnic context, Daniel S. suddenly experienced the religious challenge of being an American. There was much work to be done to bring about a better world. He had millions of allies, the living, the dead and the unborn, in this enterprise. His arms were strengthened. He was no longer alone. He had sought others and found himself.

A paragraph he had once read in a book by Erik Erikson came back to him. What is maturity? What is ego integrity?

It is the acceptance of one's one and only life cycle as something that had to be and that, by necessity, permitted of no substitutions: it thus means a new, and different love of one's parents . . . Although aware of the relativity of all the various life styles which have given meaning to human striving, the possessor of integrity is ready to defend the dignity of his own life style against all physical and economic threats. For he knows that an individual life is the accidental coincidence of but one life cycle with but one segment of history; and that for him all human integrity stands or falls with the one style of integrity of which he partakes.

". . . a new and different love of one's parents . . ." Daniel S. had found himself by finding his family. Not alone his parents, and his grandparents, but his ancestors, the Jewish people in time and space. "Our God and God of our fathers," he murmured. "God of Abraham, God of Isaac, God of Jacob, God of Daniel S."

BIBLIOGRAPHY

Adar, Zvi, *Humanistic Values in the Bible*, New York, Reconstructionist Press, 1967

Aharoni, Yohanan, and Avi-Yonah, Michael, *Macmillan Bible Atlas*, New York, Macmillan, 1968

Albright, William F., *From the Stone Age to Christianity*, New York, Anchor Press, 1957

——, and Freedman, David N., eds., *The Anchor Bible*, Garden City, N.Y., Doubleday, 1964, etc.

Ardrey, Robert, *African Genesis*, New York, Delta Press, 1963

Bellin, Mildred, *The Jewish Cookbook*, New York, Bloch Publishing, 1966

Bickerman, Elias, *From Ezra to the Last of the Maccabees*, New York, Schocken Books, 1962

Buber, Martin, *Moses*, New York, Harper & Row, 1958

Cattell, Raymond B., *Personality*, New York, McGraw-Hill, 1950

Cohen, Jack J., *Jewish Education in Democratic Society*, New York, Reconstructionist Press, 1964

Commentary Magazine, eds., *The Condition of Jewish Belief: A Symposium*, New York, Macmillan, 1966

Davis, Moshe, *The Emergence of Conservative Judaism*, Philadelphia, Jewish Publication Society of America, 1965

Dawidowicz, Lucy S., ed., *The Golden Tradition: Jewish Life and Thought in Eastern Europe*, New York, Holt, Rinehart and Winston, 1967

Eisenstein, Ira, *Judaism Under Freedom*, New York, Reconstructionist Press, 1956

——, *What We Mean By Religion*, New York, Reconstructionist Press, 1964

——, ed., *Varieties of Jewish Belief*, New York, Reconstructionist Press, 1966

Eisenstein, Judith, and Prensky, Frieda, eds., *Songs of Childhood*, New York, United Synagogue of America, 1955

Erikson, Erik H., *Childhood and Society*, New York, Norton Press, 1963

Fineman, Irving, *Woman of Valor* (The Story of Henrietta Szold), New York, Simon and Schuster, 1961

Finkelstein, Louis, *Akiba, Scholar, Saint and Martyr*, New York, Meridian Books, 1962

Frankl, Viktor E., *The Doctor and the Soul*, New York, Knopf, 1965

Friedlander, Albert H., *Out of the Whirlwind: A Reader of Holocaust Literature*, New York, Union of American Hebrew Congregations, 1968

Fromm, Erich, *Psychoanalysis and Religion*, New Haven, Conn., Yale University Press, 1950

Gezari, Temima, *Footprints and New Worlds: Experiences in Art with Child and Adult*, New York, Jewish Education Committee by Arrangement with Reconstructionist Press, 1964

Ginzberg, Louis, *Legends of the Jews*, Philadelphia, Jewish Publication Society of America, 1938

Glatzer, Nahum, *Franz Rosenzweig: His Life and Thought*, New York, Schocken Books, 1961

Glazer, Nathan, *American Judaism*, Chicago, University of Chicago Press, 1962

Glueck, Nelson, *Rivers in the Desert*, New York, Farrar, Strauss & Cudahy, 1959

Goodman, Philip, ed., *The Passover Anthology*, Philadelphia, Jewish Publication Society of America, 1961

——, ed., *The Purim Anthology*, Philadelphia, Jewish Publication Society of America, 1960

——, and Goodman, Hanna, eds., *The Jewish Marriage Anthology*, Philadelphia, Jewish Publication Society of America, 1965

Guide to Jewish Ritual, New York, Reconstructionist Press, 1962

Heaton, E. W., *Every Day Life in Old Testament Times*, New York, Scribner, 1956

Herford, R. Travers, *The Pharisees*, New York, Schocken Books, 1962

——, *Pirke Aboth, The Ethics of the Talmud, Sayings of the Fathers*, New York, Schocken Books, 1962

Hertzberg, Arthur, *The Zionist Idea, A Historical Analysis and Reader*, New York, Meridian Books, 1959

Heschel, Abraham Joshua, *The Earth Is the Lord's and The Sabbath*, New York, Meridian Books, 1963

Holy Scriptures According to the Masoretic Text, The, Philadelphia, Jewish Publication Society of America, 1966

Hoyle, Fred, *Of Men and Galaxies*, Seattle, University of Washington Press, 1964

Huxley, Julian, *Essays of a Humanist*, New York, Harper & Row, 1964

Jaspers, Karl, *Way to Wisdom: An Introduction to Philosophy*, New Haven, Conn., Yale University Press, 1951

Jochsberger, Tziporah, *Havah N'halela: A Method for the Recorder Based on Israel Folk Tunes*, New York, Department of Education and Culture of the Jewish Agency, 1952

Kaplan, Mordecai M., *Judaism As a Civilization*, New York, Schocken Books, 1967

——, *The Meaning of God in Modern Jewish Religion*, New York, Reconstructionist Press, 1962

——, *A New Zionism*, New York, Herzl Press and Jewish Reconstructionist Press, 1959

——, *Not So Random Thoughts*, New York, Reconstructionist Press, 1966

——, *Questions Jews Ask: Reconstructionist Answers*, New York, Reconstructionist Press, 1956

——, Williams, J. Paul, and Kohn, Eugene, eds., *The Faith of America: Prayers, Readings and Songs for the Celebration of American Holidays*, New York, Reconstructionist Press, 1963

——, Eisenstein, Ira, and Kohn, Eugene, eds., *The New Haggadah*, New York, Behrman House, 1942

Kazin, Alfred, Introduction to *Selected Stories of Sholem Aleichem*, New York, Modern Library, 1956

Kohn, Eugene, *Religious Humanism*, New York, Reconstructionist Press, 1953

Lamm, Norman, and Wurzburger, Walter S., eds., *A Treasury of Tradition*, New York, Hebrew Publishing, 1967

Langer, Suzanne K., *Philosophy in a New Key*, New York, New American Library, 1957

Lapson, Dvora, *Dances of the Jewish People*, New York, Jewish Education Committee, 1954

Lauterbach, J. Z., *Rabbinic Essays*, Cincinnati, Hebrew Union College Press, 1951

Levin, Nora, *The Holocaust: The Destruction of European Jewry 1933–1945*, New York, Crowell, 1968

Liptzin, Sol, *The Flowering of Yiddish Literature*, New York, Thomas Yoseloff, 1963

Lorenz, Konrad Z., *King Solomon's Ring*, New York, Crowell, 1961

——, *On Aggression*, New York, Harcourt, Brace & World, 1966

Marcus, Jacob R., *The Jew in the Medieval World*, New York, Meridian Books, 1961

Maslow, Abraham H., *Toward a Psychology of Being*, Princeton, N.J., Van Nostrand, 1962

Maybaum, Ignaz, *Jewish Existence*, London, Vallentine Mitchell, 1960

Metzger, Bruce M., ed., *The Oxford Annotated Apocrypha*, New York, Oxford University Press, 1965

Millgram, Abraham E., ed., *Great Jewish Ideas*, New York, B'nai B'rith, 1964

——, *Sabbath the Day of Delight*, Philadelphia, Jewish Publication Society of America, 1959

Montefiore, C. G., and Loewe, H., *A Rabbinic Anthology*, New York, Harper & Row, 1965

Moore, George Foot, *Judaism*, Cambridge, Harvard University Press, 3 vols., 1954

Nathanson, Moshe, *Manginot Shirenu*, New York, Hebrew Publishing, 1939

Newman, Louis I., and Spitz, Samuel, eds., *The Hasidic Anthology*, New York, Schocken Books, 1963

Noveck, Simon, ed., *Contemporary Jewish Thought: A Reader*, New York, B'nai B'rith, 1963

——, *Great Jewish Personalities in Ancient and Medieval Times*, New York, B'nai B'rith, 1964

——, *Great Jewish Personalities in Modern Times*, New York, B'nai B'rith, 1964

——, *Great Jewish Thinkers of the Twentieth Century*, New York, B'nai B'rith, 1963

Pfeiffer, Robert H., *Introduction to the Old Testament*, New York, Harper & Row, 1948

Plaut, Gunther, *The Rise of Reform Judaism*, New York, World Union for Progressive Judaism, 1963

Portmann, Adolf, *Animals as Social Beings*, New York, Viking Press, 1961

Roth, Cecil, *History of the Jews*, New York, Schocken Books, 1961

Rubenstein, Richard L., *After Auschwitz*, Indianapolis, Bobbs-Merrill, 1966

Sachar, Howard M., *The Course of Modern Jewish History*, New York, Dell Publishing, 1963

Samuel, Maurice, *Prince of the Ghetto*, Philadelphia, Jewish Publication Society of America, 1961

Schauss, Hayyim, *Guide to Jewish Holy Days*, New York, Schocken Books, 1962

——, *The Lifetime of a Jew Throughout the Ages of Jewish History*, New York, Union of American Hebrew Congregations, 1957

Solis-Cohen, E., Jr., ed., *Hanukkah: The Feast of Lights*, Philadelphia, Jewish Publication Society of America, 1960

Spiegel, Shalom, *Hebrew Reborn*, New York, Meridian Books, 1962

Steiner, George, *Language and Silence*, New York, Atheneum Press, 1967

Torah, The, Philadelphia, Jewish Publication Society of America, 1962

Werblowsky, R. J. Z., and Wigoder, Geoffrey, eds., *The Encyclopedia of the Jewish Religion*, New York, Holt, Rinehart and Winston, 1965

Wieman, Henry Nelson, *Intellectual Foundation of Faith*, New York, Philosophical Library, 1961

Zborowski, Mark, and Herzog, Elizabeth, *Life Is with People*, New York, Schocken Books, 1962

CHILDREN'S BOOKS

Abramson, Lillian S., *Jeremy and Judy's Hanukah*, New York, Behrman House, 1956

Cedarbaum, Sophia N., *Chanuko: The Festival of Lights*, New York, Union of American Hebrew Congregations, 1962

——, *Purim: A Joyous Holiday*, New York, Union of American Hebrew Congregations, 1960

Chanover, Hyman, and Chanover, Alice, *Happy Hanukah Everybody*, New York, United Synagogue of America, 1954

——, *Pesah Is Coming!* New York, United Synagogue of America, 1956

Edelman, Lily, *The Sukkah and the Big Wind*, New York, United Synagogue of America, 1956

Klaperman, Libby M., *The Dreidel Who Wouldn't Spin*, New York, Behrman House, 1950

——, *Jeremy and Judy Say the Sh'ma*, New York, Behrman House, 1956

——, *Jeremy's ABC Book*, New York, Behrman House, 1957

Kolatch, Mollie, *What's a Mitzvah?* New York, Behrman House, 1957

Pessin, Deborah, *Aleph-Bet Story Book*, Philadelphia, Jewish Publication Society of America, 1961

Simon, Norma, *Every Friday Night*, New York, United Synagogue of America, 1961

——, *Hanukah in My House*, New York, United Synagogue of America, 1960

——, *Happy Purim Night*, New York, United Synagogue of America, 1959

——, *My Family Seder*, New York, United Synagogue of America, 1961

——, *Our First Sukkah*, New York, United Synagogue of America, 1959

——, *The Purim Party*, New York, United Synagogue of America, 1959

——, *Rosh Hashanah*, New York, United Synagogue of America, 1959

——, *Tu B'Shvat*, New York, United Synagogue of America, 1961

——, *Yom Kippur*, New York, United Synagogue of America, 1959

Weilerstein, Sadie Rose, *Jewish Heroes I*, New York, United Synagogue of America, 1953

——, *Jewish Heroes II*, New York, United Synagogue of America, 1956

——, *The Adventures of K'tonton*, New York, League Press, 1937

——, *What the Moon Brought*, Philadelphia, Jewish Publication Society of America, 1959

MILLER. ALAN W

MILLER, ALAN W

AUTHOR
GOD OF DANIEL S.

TITLE

DATE DUE	BORROWER'S NAME

MARATHON JEWISH
COMM. CENTER
LIBRARY